PENANCE AND ABSOLUTION

IS VOLUME

51

OF THE

Twentieth Century Encyclopedia of Catholicism

UNDER SECTION

V

THE LIFE OF FAITH

IT IS ALSO THE

63RD

VOLUME IN ORDER OF PUBLICATION

Edited by HENRI DANIEL-ROPS of the Académie Française

PENANCE AND ABSOLUTION

By *JOHN M. T. BARTON*

HAWTHORN BOOKS · PUBLISHERS · *New York*

First Edition, April, 1961

NIHIL OBSTAT

Daniel Duivesteijn, S.T.D.

Censor Deputatus

IMPRIMATUR

E. Morrogh Bernard

Vicarius Generalis

Westmonasterii, die IX FEBRUARIS MCMLXI

The Nihil obstat and Imprimatur are a declaration that a book or pamphlet is considered to be free from doctrinal or moral error. It is not implied that those who have granted the Nihil obstat and Imprimatur agree with the contents, opinions or statements expressed.

CONTENTS

INTRODUCTION

The treatise on the sacrament of penance, as it is traditionally taught in the Catholic theological schools, is one that can be studied at considerable length or dealt with summarily, so as to present the main theses with a minimum of elaboration. The present volume in this series is somewhere near the half-way line, in the matter of length, between very full works such as those of the late Abbé A. Tanquerey of Saint-Sulpice and Fr Dominic Prümmer, O.P., of Fribourg (Switzerland) and such "excellent pemmican" as the treatise by Mgr G. Van Noort, and the luminous essay by my late class-fellow and friend, Fr Henry Harrington, in the work entitled *The Teaching of the Catholic Church*.

The larger treatises are made up in varying degrees of dogmatic theology, moral theology, canon law and history, with some good measure of Holy Scripture. In this volume history has to be content with a small share, found mainly in the chapters on the power of the keys in tradition, on confession and on indulgences. Even so, more than one of the longer treatises contains less history in proportion to its length.

The plan of the book has been, as in some larger works, to proceed by way of Scripture and tradition to the matter and form of the sacrament, and then to study in turn the effects of the sacrament, its necessity, its minister and its subject. This is more satisfactory than the attempt made in one or two works to deal in chronological order with all these elements at once.

Indulgences have been treated with reasonable fullness, since they tend to be given rather short measure, at times, in such works. I have seen no advantage in using the expression "pardons", which is somewhat ambiguous, and, even in the

sense required, puts one in mind of Chaucer's "gentil par-
doner" whose

> Walet lay beforn hym in his lappe,
> Bretful of pardoun, comen from Rome al hoot. . . ."

I have had an advantage denied to former writers in English
on this subject of being able to refer to the second volume of
Sources of Christian Theology, edited by Fr Paul F. Palmer,
S.J., and published as recently as the present year of grace.
While I have learnt much from Fr Palmer's sourcebook, as
also from the Anglican writer Mr O. D. Watkins' *A History
of Penance*, I have preferred normally to supply my own
versions of the extracts quoted in these pages.

I acknowledge help received from a large selection of
works, some of which have already been mentioned. My old
masters of Roman days, Fr Réginald Garrigou-Lagrange,
O.P., and the late Fr Édouard Hugon, O.P., have been of
special service. The abbreviation *Sources* . . . refers, of course,
to Fr Palmer's *vade-mecum*, while *Denz.* stands for Denzinger's famous *Enchiridion Symbolorum* in the 28th edition,
published in Barcelona in 1952.

I should wish to dedicate this small work to the memory
of my first teacher of moral theology at St Edmund's College,
Ware, the late Canon John Arendzen, D.D., Ph.D., M.A. He
was in truth a man of deep piety, charming simplicity and
profound learning. I shall always remember the pains he took
to give us an interest in the treatise on penance, and in the
documents that help to register its long history. *Lux perpetua
luceat ei.*

JOHN M. T. BARTON

*Feast of our Lady's Immaculate Conception,
    December 8th, 1960*

CHAPTER I

THE VIRTUE OF PENANCE

INTRODUCTION

St Ambrose in his *Apology for the prophet David*, in which
he is commenting upon the events related in 2 Kings 12. 1–16,
wherein is told the story of Nathan's visit to the king after the
latter's sin with Bethsabee and the planned murder of her
husband, Urias the Hittite, stresses both the vileness of David's
sin, and the sincerity of his repentance. He writes: "David
sinned, a thing not rare among kings; but he did penance, he
wept, he groaned, as kings are not wont to do. He confessed
his fault, he sought for pardon. Prostrate on the ground, he
wept bitterly over his misery, he fasted, he prayed and, pub-
lishing abroad his grief, he left a witness of his confession to
all posterity" (*Apol.* 1, c. 4). So, nearly a thousand years
before Christ's coming, David is an example of the virtue of
penance in action, and points to the truth announced by St
John, the beloved disciple, in his first epistle (1. 8–9): "Sin is
with us; if we deny that, we are cheating ourselves; it means
that truth does not dwell in us. No, it is when we confess our
sins that he forgives our sins, ever true to his word, ever deal-
ing right with us, and all our wrong-doing is purged away."

MEANING OF PENANCE

The word "penance" translates the Latin *paenitentia*, which
is itself of uncertain etymology, but is rendered by Professor
A. Souter in his *Glossary of Later Latin* "regret for sin". The
corresponding Greek word is *metanoia*, translated in Liddell

and Scott's lexicon as "change of mind or heart, repentance, regret". In its theological use *paenitentia* refers to three closely allied conceptions. The first is the virtue of penance; the second is the sacrament of penance; and the third is that part of the same sacrament that is also called satisfaction, and that is well illustrated in the words regularly used by confessors: "Will you say for your holy penance . . .?" and by their penitents in the phrase: "I received absolution after my last confession, and said my penance."

THE VIRTUE OF PENANCE

Before adding anything further about the sacrament of penance, a few ideas about penance as a virtue may be briefly presented. Following St Thomas Aquinas, the virtue of penance is commonly defined as "a supernatural habit, whereby man is made ready to be sorry for the sin he has committed in so far as it is an offence against God, with the intention of emending his life". This moral *habit* is, in the first place, *supernatural*, since no ordinary natural sorrow would be sufficient for the forgiveness of sins. The Council of Trent in its third canon on justification (Denz. 813) condemned the heresy that a man could sorrow for sin in such a way as to deserve the grace of justification, unless he has first received the help and inspiration of the Holy Spirit of God. Further, the Council declared (Denz. 798) that five supernatural impulses are required for true penitence, namely, acts of divine mercy, faith, holy fear, hope and, at least in some initial degree, love. Again, this virtue must be of such a kind as *to make a man ready to be sorry for sin he has committed, in so far as it is an offence against God*. No ordinary sorrow would be adequate; it must be a sorrow that clearly recognizes the loathsomeness of sin because it is an offence against God. Finally, this sorrow must be accompanied by *the intention of emending his life*, since true sorrow includes not only regret for the past, but a firm intention of never committing the sin any more. So it is taught that three dispositions are required for any true act of penitence, i.e. sorrow, detestation of sin and an intention of not relapsing into the sin again.

NECESSITY OF PENANCE

There are many interesting questions about the virtue of penance that are discussed in St Thomas's 85th question of the third part of his *Summa Theologica.* Is penance a special virtue? With which of the cardinal virtues is it associated? (The answer here is: with the virtue of commutative justice.) What is the relation between the virtue of penance and the fear of the Lord, which is, as Scripture tells us, the quintessence of wisdom? Here it may be sufficient to refer in some detail to the topic of the *necessity* of penance, and one must distinguish, as theologians are accustomed to do, between the necessity attaching to a means indispensable for salvation, and a necessity that is founded upon a precept to be observed. According to received teaching, penance is necessary in both these senses. Many passages in Scripture point to the paramount need of this virtue. Thus Ezechiel, speaking in God's name, exhorts his hearers: "Repent and turn from all your transgressions, lest iniquity be your ruin" (18. 30. Revised Standard Version). And the words of our Lord himself, when he is speaking of the Galileans who had come to Jerusalem with sacrificial offerings, and "whose blood Pilate had shed in the midst of their sacrifices," are quite formal: "Do you suppose, because this befell them, that these men were worse sinners than all else in Galilee? I tell you it is not so; you will all perish as they did, if you do not repent" (Luke 13, 2–3). St Thomas gives the theological reason for this when he writes: "For the forgiveness of an offence against God it is required that man's will should be changed and converted to God, with detestation of his sin, and a purpose of amendment" (*Summa Theol.,* III, qu. 86, art. 2, on the 3rd objection).

It is no less clear that both the natural law and the Christian

revelation call for penitence on the part of those who have
sinned. For the law of nature sin is an offence against justice,
a violation of the honour due to God. And penance is again
and again commanded with divine authority in the pages of
the New Testament. St Peter, after the healing of the lame
man at the Beautiful Gate of the temple, calls upon his
audience to "Repent, then, and turn back to him to have your
sins effaced" (Acts 3. 10). Again, he adjures Simon the sor-
cerer, who had tried to buy the gift of the Holy Ghost for
cash: "Repent of this baseness of thine, and pray to God, in
the hope of finding pardon for the thought which thy heart
had conceived" (Acts 8. 22). This is, indeed, the theme of our
Lord's preaching from the very beginning of his public
ministry. St Matthew tells us that, from the time of his arrival
at Capharnaum, "Jesus began to preach; Repent, he said, for
the kingdom of heaven is at hand" (Matt. 4. 17).

WHEN IS IT NECESSARY?

Theological writers are not entirely agreed about the obligation of doing penance at some particular time. Evidently
there is a duty to be really sorry if some precept or obligation
is to be carried out for which repentance is necessary. Thus a
priest in a state of mortal sin must be at least truly penitent,
even if confession is for some reason impossible, before he
ventures to administer any sacrament. Similarly, the obligation of penance is incumbent upon a man in the hour of death
or when there is grave danger to life. It is not so clear that
there is a strict obligation to be penitent immediately after the
commission of a mortal sin, although a notable delay in doing
penance may itself be a grave sin, even if there is no complete
agreement among the authors as to what constitutes a notable
delay. The Church's demand for annual confession would
seem to prove that a delay of more than a year would be a
serious one, but even here there is weighty authority for not
blaming too severely sinners who put off their repentance until

the time of the Easter duties, in circumstances where this
would involve rather more than a year's delay.

FALSE VIEWS OF PENANCE

Apropos of the necessity of penance one may refer to the
tendency shown by the Protestant reformers to restrict
penance to what is known as resipiscence, which stands for
recognition of errors committed in the past, and a return to
a better state of mind or opinion. A man acting on these lines
might say to himself: "I have thought things over, and I admit
that I have been foolish. I shall try to be more sensible in the
future." This imperfect and incomplete idea of penance is
specially associated with Martin Luther, and it was against
Luther's teaching that the Council of Trent declared that contrition for sin implies "sorrow and detestation in regard to sin
committed, with a purpose of not sinning again" (Denz. 897).
The Council further defines, as against the Lutheran heresy
that no satisfaction is required for the temporal punishment
due to sin, that it *is* needed, in order that Christ's satisfaction
may be applied to us, and that we may share in the work of
our salvation, in accordance with St John the Baptist's command: "Come, then, yield the acceptable fruit of repentance"
(Matt. 3. 8).

RELATION BETWEEN THE VIRTUE OF PENANCE AND THE SACRAMENT

This relation is made clearer by St Thomas (*Summa Theol.*,
III, qu. 65, art. 1) where he discusses the problem whether
there should be seven sacraments of the new law. In his reply
he states that the sacraments were instituted for two reasons
—to perfect man in the things that pertain to divine worship,
and as a remedy against sin. So spiritual rebirth is brought
about by baptism; growth and strengthening by confirmation;
and the nourishing of the spiritual life by the Eucharist. The
place of penance is thus described: "Since man from time to

time contracts both bodily and spiritual infirmity (the latter
being sin), a cure for his infirmities is needed, and this is twofold. The first healing is that which restores health, and its
place in the spiritual life is taken by penance. The other cure
takes away the remains of sin", and this cure is extreme
unction.

It seems unnecessary to delay here over the arguments that
point to the antecedent probability of there being an external,
judicial, effective rite to bring about absolution from sin.

PENANCE BEFORE CHRIST

There is, however, one aspect of penance as a virtue that is
not always studied at length in the textbooks. This is the
subject of confession and forgiveness of sins before the coming
of Christ. Fr Galtier, S.J., in the third volume of his trilogy
on penance[1] has devoted a chapter to this topic, in which he
produces evidence from the literature of the nations that never
had any relations with Israel, the literature of the nations
surrounding Israel, and the Jewish literature itself. In the last-
named group he studies in turn the Jewish law and expiation
for sin; the sense of sin in the psalter; sacrifices for sin and
confession; the sense of sin after the captivity, with special
reference to the psalms of Solomon; the persistence of the
sacrificial ritual in New Testament times; excommunication
as practised by the Jews; and the preoccupation with sin and
its consequences and with the idea of salvation on the eve of
Christ's coming. Among many other passages he quotes the
high priest's prayer on the solemn day of atonement, as it is
recorded in the Mishnah, when as representative of the nation,
he spreads out his hands over the bullock that was to be
offered in sacrifice, and prays:

O God, I have committed iniquity, transgressed and sinned
before thee, I and my house. O God, forgive the iniquities
and transgressions and sins which I have committed, and

[1] *Aux Origines du Sacrement de Pénitence* (Rome, 1951), pp. 1–32.

sinned and transgressed before thee, I and my house, as it is written in the law of thy servant Moses (Lev. 16. 30): *It is a day of atonement on your behalf, to cleanse you from all fault and make you clean in the Lord's sight* (*Yoma,* 3. 8).

In his classic work on Palestinian Judaism in the time of Christ the late Fr J. Bonsirven, S.J., writes: "With the approach of the Christian era confession of sins on the day of expiation had probably become already far more wide-spread. Individuals were invited to confess at least those sins that they had committed since the last feast."[2] The same author tells us that the people were expected to confess all sins that had done injury to their neighbours, and that this confession of faults formed part of the sacrificial rite. Criminals awaiting execution were pledged to confess their sins before enduring the torment, so that by this means they might ensure their salvation. Confession of this kind was intended to be sincere, and to include always a purpose of not sinning again. It was recognized that confession, or any other act of penitence, that did not include a purpose of amendment was a deliberate deception, and could not obtain God's forgiveness.

To be genuine, confession had to be made for its own sake, and not from any human motive; it was expected to be the outcome of love, not of fear. To those who confessed fully and sincerely, God's pardon was assured, as we read in the so-called Psalms of Solomon: "He cleanses from sin a soul when it makes confession, when it makes acknowledgement" (9. 12).[3]

The rabbinical authorities insist upon the need for being reconciled with one's neighbour, and of repairing any injustice done to him. On these conditions, they say, pardon will be granted by God. The theme of the efficacy of repentance is a favourite one in the Jewish extra-biblical literature. It is often

[2] *Le Judaisme palestinien au temps de Jésus Christ* (Paris, 1935), II, pp. 99 ff.
[3] Cf. also Josephus, *Wars of the Jews,* V, 9. 4 (Whiston's translation): "God is easily reconciled to those who confess their faults and repent of them."

recalled that God welcomes penitents, shows mercy to them, pardons them. The sins they have committed are completely wiped away. The words used show that offences are considered to be forgotten, taken away, suppressed, pardoned and purged. Sinners are interiorly renewed, as by some new act of creation —an expression that recalls G. K. Chesterton's famous passage on the effects of a good confession, in his *Autobiography*.

Thus the voice of the Jewish doctors before and after the tragedy of A.D. 70 calls for confession, as a means to gain pardon and peace of soul.

CHAPTER II

THE POWER OF THE KEYS
IN HOLY SCRIPTURE

THE CHURCH'S DOCTRINE

A great Anglican teacher, the late Professor H. B. Swete (1835–1916) of Cambridge, has written: "The Church was sent forth from the Upper Room at Jerusalem to preach the Forgiveness of Sins, and provided with the power of imparting it."[1] This power was shown to the world of that day, when in Newman's words "It first came forth from its divine author", in the bestowal of Christian baptism on the many thousands who flocked to receive the rite from the day of Pentecost onwards. For those who were guilty of sins committed after baptism the same divine power of forgiveness was manifested in the administration of the sacrament of penance.

The Catholic Church has solemnly declared that Christ gave his apostles and their successors, the bishops of the Church, the power of forgiving or retaining all sins that might be committed, whether before or after baptism, and that this was to be brought about, for those already baptized, by a judicial act, and by a rite distinct from baptism. Among its numerous canons on penance enacted in the Council's fourteenth session (November 25th, 1551) the following deserve special mention here. It was defined by Trent:

(1) That penance is a sacrament truly and properly so called for the forgiveness of post-baptismal sins (Denz. 911).

[1] Art. "Penitential Discipline in the First Three Centuries", in *Journal of Theological Studies*, iv, p. 321.

(2) that anyone who claims that our Saviour's words in instituting this sacrament are *not* to be understood of the remitting and retaining of sins "as the Church has always understood from the beginning", and interprets these powers as referring only to preaching the gospel of repentance, lies under the anathema of a general council (Denz. 913).

(9) that anyone who says that sacramental absolution is *not* a judicial act, but a mere ministry for declaring sins to be forgiven, provided that the penitent believes that his sins have been pardoned; or who insists that a priest may absolve merely in jest; or that confession of sins is not required for absolution, lies under the same ban (Denz. 919).

Here are serious and precise statements about the will and intention of Christ our Lord. What proof can be offered from Holy Scripture that Christ did in fact institute a rite of this kind? When we examine the New Testament evidence for a penitential rite it is well to remind ourselves that the words in the passages to be cited are the authentically recorded utterances of Christ himself, and that they have been interpreted from the beginning by the Christian Church, which has ever claimed to have the mind of Christ.

CHRIST FORGAVE SINS

We need not delay too long over the clearly emphasized truth that our Lord himself claimed to forgive sins. A reading of St Mark's Gospel (2. 1–12) that narrates the cure of the paralytic at Capharnaum (an event also recorded in Matt. 9. 2–8 and Luke 5. 17–26) proves that the miracle was wrought "to convince you that the Son of Man has authority to forgive sins while he is on earth" (v. 10), in which Christ "uses [the phrase] *bar nasha* [Aramaic for Son of Man] in a sense which was Messianic to himself, but non-Messianic, yet a challenge to reflection, in the hearing of his opponents."[2]

[2] Dr V. Taylor, *The Gospel according to St Mark* (London, 1952), p. 200.

A later incident in our Lord's public ministry is recorded by St Luke alone (7. 36–50), when a woman who had been a sinner anointed Jesus' feet in the house of a pharisee named Simon. In the final verses of the story Simon, the host, is rebuked and the woman is praised for the love she has shown for our Lord. Christ declares that, just because she has loved him much, her sins, however terrible, have all been pardoned. "Then he said to her: Thy sins are forgiven. And his fellow guests thereupon thought to themselves, Who is this that he even forgives sins? But he told the woman, Thy faith hath saved thee: go in peace" (7. 48–50).[3]

It has been maintained by some scholars in the past that the first of these stories means no more than that man, as such, had power to forgive sins. But as the writer just quoted, Dr Vincent Taylor, reminds us: "Apart from the philological objections, this explanation is not probable in itself. It is exposed to the fatal objection that it is alien to the mind of Judaism and of early Christianity" (*op. cit.*, p. 199).

THE POWER PROMISED

In two passages in the Gospels our Lord promises to confer upon his apostles a share in the divine power of forgiveness. Both of these are well known, the first in particular, since it forms part of St Matthew's account (16. 13–20) of St Peter's confession of faith, and of Christ's promise of the supreme jurisdiction in the Church to him and to his successors. After St Peter had answered our Lord's question: "Who do *you* say that I am?" with the words: "Thou art the Christ, the Son of the living God!"

> Jesus answered him, Blessed art thou, Simon son of Jona; it is not flesh and blood, it is my Father in heaven that has

[3] In the Old Syriac (Curetonian) version the words in v. 50 are: "Thy faith hath saved thee alive." Professor F. C. Burkitt in his *Church and Gnosis* has commented upon the tendency of the Old Syriac to translate the Greek words *soteria* and *sozein* (salvation, and to save) by "life" and "to cause to live".

revealed this to thee. And I tell thee this in my turn, that thou art Peter, and it is upon this rock that I will build my Church; and the gates of hell shall not prevail against it; and I will give to thee the keys of the kingdom of heaven; and whatever thou shalt bind on earth shall be bound in heaven; and whatever thou shalt loose on earth shall be loosed in heaven.

Of the four metaphors used in this context the first two (of the rock on which the Church is to be built, and of the gates of hell) are not our immediate concern here. But the power of the keys implies authority over the whole house, of which Christ remains the master, while delegating a share of his power to his representative. The phrase recalls God's guarantee to Eliacim the son of Helcias, as it is found in Isaias 22. 22–24: "I will give him the key of David's house to bear upon his shoulders; none may shut when he opens, none open when he shuts . . . all the honour of his father's house will rest upon him . . .", a passage which is applied in Apoc. 3. 7 to Jesus himself. Our Lord promises that Peter will enjoy a share in his authority, and that he himself will ratify in heaven the decisions taken by Peter on earth. These decisions are envisaged in the twin metaphors of binding and loosing. In the language employed by the Jewish rabbis, in our Lord's time and later, the two verbs *asar* to bind, and *shera* to loose, occur in the sense "to declare something forbidden" or "to declare something to be permitted" respectively. The power seems here to belong primarily to the dogmatic and disciplinary spheres, yet this does not exhaust the meaning of the words, which imply a genuine power of rule or jurisdiction of a kind befitting one who has the keys of God's kingdom. It is not merely a question of giving rulings on speculative problems that may arise. Christ offers the practical authority needed for casting out of the kingdom or for reinstating therein.

It has been argued that there is a possible connection with our Lord's words in Luke 13. 16, uttered after his healing of the paralytic woman, whose illness was, it seems, attributed to some malign influence. In answer to the ruler of the synagogue, who had protested against a healing on the sabbath, our Lord demands: "And here is this daughter of Abraham, whom Satan had kept bound these eighteen years past; was it wrong that she should be delivered on the sabbath day from bonds like these?" Yet, though there is mention of binding, and the same verb is used as in Matt. 16. 19, it is not certain that St Luke's narrative refers to loosing from any bond of *sin*.

In any event, the promise made to St Peter was followed at a later date by one made to the apostles as a body, though the two are not identical, and the second promise does not bestow the primacy. In Matt. 18. 15–20 Christ speaks first of fraternal correction, and then of judgement pronounced by the rulers of the Church.

> If thy brother does [thee] wrong, go at once and tax him with it, as a private matter between thee and him; and so, if he will listen to thee, thou hast won thy brother. If he will not listen to thee, take with thee one or two more, that the whole matter may be certified by the voice of two or three witnesses. If he will not listen to thee, then speak of it to the church; and if he will not even listen to the church, count him all one with the heathen and the publican. I promise you, all that you bind on earth shall be bound in heaven, and all that you loose on earth shall be loosed in heaven.

Christ is here establishing rules for the future when his bodily presence will no longer be with his apostles. In accordance with the law of Deut. 19. 15 where it is a matter of an offence or crime (as we should say, of a criminal charge) "every question must be settled by the voice of two witnesses or more". The final decision here rests with the Church. If the sinner will not listen to the Church, then he is to be regarded, at any rate temporarily, as cut off from the Christian body, as if by the sort of excommunication that was perfectly familiar to the Jews, and that could be inflicted only by those with special authority.

The last verse of the passage (18) is one in which the

argument passes by a natural sequence from authority as exercised in the Church to the power of binding and loosing already conferred upon St Peter. The Council of Trent decided that this power was not granted to all the members of the Church, and according to the text it is reasonable to conclude that the immediate recipients were those to whom Christ was speaking, that is to the apostles, who had already received singular powers over the Christian family, and who were now being granted some, but not all, of the privileges already assigned to Peter.

It is important to notice that in both the passages in which the power of binding and loosing is promised, *there is no hint of any restrictions placed upon the exercise of this power.* In both passages, though the Greek varies slightly, it is guaranteed that "*whatever* you (*or* thou) shall bind upon earth, shall be bound in heaven".

THE POWER CONFERRED

As regards the gift of the Eucharist it is well known that the promise is found in St John's sixth chapter alone, whereas the fulfilment is related in all three Synoptic accounts of the Last Supper, as well as in St Paul (1 Cor. 11. 23 ff.). Conversely, the power of the keys is promised in two passages of St Matthew's Gospel (16. 19 and 18. 18), whereas the fulfilment is related only by St John (20. 19–23), even though another account of the same appearance of the risen Master occurs in St Luke (24. 36–49). In St John's narrative we read, earlier in the same chapter, of Mary Magdalen's visit to the tomb, of the later arrival of Peter and John, and of Mary's second visit, during which our Lord appears to her in the garden. Thereupon she seeks out the disciples and tells them that she has seen the Lord and that he has spoken to her. St John's account continues:

And now it was evening on the same day, the first day of the week [that is, the first Easter Sunday]; for fear of the

Jews the disciples had locked the doors of the room in which they had assembled; and Jesus came and stood in the midst; Peace be upon you, he said. And with that, he shewed them his hands and his side. Thus the disciples saw the Lord and were glad. Once more Jesus said to them, Peace be upon you! I came upon an errand from my Father, and now I am sending you out in my turn. With that he breathed on them and said to them, Receive the Holy Spirit; when you forgive men's sins, they are forgiven; when you hold them bound, they are held bound.

Mgr Knox's rendering of the final verse in this pericope is not quite satisfactory. It has been pointed out that the words of the Greek may be rendered with equal accuracy *Whose soever sins you forgive* (as in the Revised Version) or *If you remit the sins of any* (as in Moffatt's translation). Either rendering brings out the sense of unrestricted power, of power without limitation to any particular class or category of sin.

We have no complete certainty that the apostles alone were present at the time when the commission to absolve was received from Christ. It is, however, the more natural sense of the language used by St John that the gift was conferred on them, and on no others. It is in this sense that the passage is interpreted by early writers such as St Justin Martyr, Origen and St Cyprian. The last-named Father writes: "The power of remitting sins was given to the apostles, and to the Churches which they set up as sent by Christ, and to the bishops who succeeded them by vicarious ordination" (*Epistle* 75. 16).

Again, the gift bestowed includes not merely the preaching of forgiveness to all nations, but the power of forgiving sins according to the example of Christ when he was on earth. A bishop of the Protestant Church of Ireland, Dr J. H. Bernard, writes on this point: "It was in the power of this Spirit of God that they were authorized not only to proclaim universally the message of God's forgiveness (Acts 10. 43), but to say in individual cases 'thy sins are forgiven'."[4]

[4] *The Gospel according to St John* (Edinburgh, 1928), II, p. 679.

It may be further argued from Christ's words that the power was to be exercised in the Church by a judicial process, which involved instructing a cause and pronouncing sentence. The power of binding and loosing called for a full understanding of the sins committed, and this could not be estimated, by any but the divine founder of Christianity himself, except by personal interrogation of the penitent. Only in this way could the apostles and their successors decide whether to loose from sin those who were properly disposed for absolution or to bind (or retain) the sins of those who might be judged to be unfit to receive the grace of divine forgiveness.

ST PAUL AND THE CORINTHIANS

We find a striking exercise of the power to bind and to loose in St Paul's First Epistle to the Corinthians (5. 1–5), apropos of the incestuous Corinthian. Here the apostle censures the members of the Church for not casting out the evil-doer from their midst. In default of such action by the Church of Corinth, St Paul, though absent in body, writes:

I have already passed sentence on the man who has acted thus. Call an assembly at which I will be present in spirit, with all the power of our Lord Jesus Christ, and so, in the name of our Lord Jesus Christ, hand over the person named to Satan, for the overthrow of his corrupt nature, so that his spirit may find salvation in the day of our Lord Jesus Christ (5. 3–5).

This interesting chapter raises many problems, but one thing at least is certain—that the handing over to Satan has the effect of what would now be styled excommunication, or expulsion from the Christian community. It is possible that further pains and penalties were to be foreseen as a result of Satan's attacks, and that these might include severe illness, or even death. However this may be, the whole process is to be regarded as medicinal in character—the chastisement of the man's body is carried out in order that "his spirit may find salvation in the day of our Lord Jesus Christ". We are not told explicitly, but we may infer that, if the sinner were to be moved to true repentance, he would be received back into the Church that had temporarily cast him out.

Another example confronts us in the First Epistle to Timothy, 1. 19–20. St Paul has spoken of the duty of serving God with faith and a good conscience. He continues: "Some, through refusing this duty, have made shipwreck of the faith; among them Hymenaeus and Alexander, whom I have made over to Satan, till they are cured of their blasphemy."[5] Fr C. Spicq, O.P., in his commentary on the pastoral epistles remarks: "This temporary or definitive excommunication was a penal measure already in use among the Jews of Palestine and of the diaspora for all sorts of religious and even civil offences, which excluded the culprit from all relations with his fellow countrymen and co-religionists."[6]

OBJECTIONS CONSIDERED

Throughout the course of this chapter attention has been drawn to the entire lack of any hint that the power of forgiving sins was limited by Christ our Lord to any particular class of sin. There are, however, several passages in the New Testament that might at first sight suggest some exceptions to the universal nature of divine forgiveness, and that might be interpreted as teaching that there is a class of sin which, when committed after baptism, admits of no forgiveness. Readers of Sir Edmund Gosse's *Father and Son* (ch. XI) will recall his story of an acquaintance of his youth, a retired nonconformist minister who was wholly persuaded that he had committed the sin against the Holy Ghost, and even at the present day there may well be people who indulge in the same fancy about themselves or their neighbours.

[5] Mr J. B. Phillips in his version *The New Testament in Modern English*, p. 437, paraphrases the last words: "I had to expel them from the Church to teach them not to blaspheme."

[6] *Les Epîtres pastorales* (Paris, 1947), p. 51.

The chief passages in question include the Epistle to the Hebrews (6. 4–8) in which the author declares that "those who have received once for all their enlightenment ... and have then fallen away, cannot attain repentance through a second renewal". Again, in Matt. 12. 32 Christ himself teaches that blasphemy against the Son of Man may be forgiven, "but for him who blasphemes against the Holy Spirit there is no forgiveness, either in this world or in the world to come". Lastly, St John in his First Epistle (5. 16) speaks of "a sin that kills" (also rendered "a sin unto death") for the perpetrator of which it is profitless to pray. As against these passages there are other pericopes such as that verse of the same epistle of St John, already quoted in chapter I, which in the Westminster Version reads: "If we confess our sins, he is faithful and just, so as to forgive us our sins, and to cleanse us from all iniquity."

Some non-Catholic writers on penance do not make any intensive effort to reconcile the two sets of passages. On the verses from the Epistle to the Hebrews, Mr Oscar D. Watkins in *A History of Penance* (I, p. 16) writes: "It is best understood as favouring the sterner attitude, at least as regards apostates." Actually, examination of the passages that seem to refer to an irremissible sin suggests that the emphasis is not on any particular class of grave fault, but upon the obduracy and hardheartedness of the sinner, who is unwilling to seek pardon and reconciliation with God.

In his admirable commentary on the Epistle to the Hebrews Fr Spicq, O.P., has carefully analysed the teaching of ch. 6. 4–8, and is able to claim that there is no question here of impossibility in the strict sense. The adjective *adunatos* is used frequently in the Greek Old Testament, and it is only in regard to God that it stands for something that admits of no exception (as in Wis. 16. 15, where it is written of God: "Thine is a power there is no escaping"). Elsewhere the references are to something that, while difficult, is not wholly impossible. Fr Spicq in his long *excursus* on this topic concludes that the sinner cannot *of himself* renew his first fervour, cannot *of himself* return to that dawn of the spiritual life when, through baptism, he became "a new creature in Christ" (1 Cor. 5. 17) and was "clothed in the new self, which is created in God's image, justified and sanctified through the truth" (Ephes. 4. 24). Short of some intervention of the divine mercy, which remains always possible, "it is rigorously exact to say that the apostate cannot renew himself".[7]

A similar interpretation may be applied to "the sin against the Holy Ghost" in Matt. 12. 12, and "the sin unto death" in John 5. 16. In both instances it is not the sin itself that is beyond pardon; rather the state of mind of the sinner makes it exceedingly hard for him to ask for pardon, and to be again converted to God.

As we shall note later, although these texts can and should be explained in a manner that excludes any truly irremissible sin, they have, as might be expected, been construed in a narrow and rigoristic sense at various times in the Church's long history.

[7] *L'Epître aux Hébreux* (Paris, 1933), II, p. 171.

CHAPTER III

THE POWER OF THE KEYS

IN TRADITION

THE ARGUMENT FROM TRADITION

Whereas the teaching of Holy Scripture on penance is relatively straightforward and is within the control of almost
anyone who possesses a copy of the New Testament, the
history of this sacrament in the Christian Church is complex,
much debated and difficult to summarize within the narrow
limits of a few pages. Mr Watkins, the Anglican author of
A History of Penance, now just forty years old, has told the
story in a two-volume work of nearly eight hundred pages.
Even so, his book is far from being complete, has never been
supplemented or brought up to date, and takes the narrative
no further than the year 1215, the date of the Fourth Lateran
Council. The present, very short treatment of a vast subject
can do no more than provide some facts and conclusions in
regard to the period from the age of the apostolic Fathers
down to the first of the General Councils, held at Nicaea in
A.D. 325.

Among the numerous difficulties that beset a study of this
kind there is one of special importance, namely, the problem
arising from the lack of adequate documentation for the
earliest period. Many years ago, when a popular magazine
invited its readers to name some historical character who
might be recalled from a distant past, Mr Hilaire Belloc
selected the figure of St Ignatius of Antioch (*c*. 35–*c*. 107)

because, as he explained, the saint could tell us many things
we still need to know about the organization and practice of
the very early Church.

Sundry reasons have been given to explain this scarcity of
documents, of which two are outstanding. First, there can be
no doubt that many works which we should be glad to possess
perished in the times when Christians were being actively
persecuted for their faith, while others wore out in use and
were not replaced, or were destroyed by storage under un-
suitable conditions. Again, it has rightly been said, the attention of many writers in the early centuries was concentrated
upon the most vital beliefs—the unity of God, the trinity of
divine persons, and the divinity of the Word Incarnate and of
the religion founded by him.

SOME PRELIMINARY EVIDENCE

Fortunately there is sufficient evidence to be found in the
New Testament alone to rebut the theory that a penitential
rite was not required in the early Church, inasmuch as the
first communities of Christians were made up of men and
women who passed their lives in a state of closest union with
God. Of this theory the New Testament itself supplies a direct
refutation. To many this may seem fairly obvious, but it is a
fact that the great German Protestant scholar, Adolf von
Harnack, did his best to popularize the view that the primitive groups of Churches were composed wholly of saints, so
that sinners would have been entirely excluded. We have
already seen the texts on the decisive action taken by St Paul
against the incestuous Corinthian and, though it has been
maintained that the Church of Corinth was set in surround-
ings that did not encourage sanctity, we have no reason to
think that the Corinthian Christians were worse than many
of their neighbours.

In his second epistle to Corinth St Paul writes that "on this
new visit God has humiliation in store for me when we meet;

I shall have tears to shed over many of you, sinners of old, and still unrepentant, with a tale of impure, adulterous and wanton living" (2 Cor. 12. 21). But the Apostle is equally scathing towards the end of his letter to the Galatians, and presents them with a long list of sins, ranging from adultery to murder and drunkenness, in regard to which he writes: "I warn you, as I have warned you before, that those who live in such a way will not inherit God's kingdom" (Gal. 5. 15–21). A few verses later (6. 1) he adds that those who are spiritually minded "ought to show a spirit of gentleness in correcting" a sinner, from which one may judge that the possibility of sin was always present to St Paul's mind, as was also the need and value of chastisement.

Even in the letter to Philippi, which in general is full of the spirit of joy and thankfulness, St Paul declares that "there are many [presumably in the Philippian Church] whose lives make them the enemy of Christ's cross" (3. 18). In his first letter to Thessalonika his fatherly heart is moved to remind his converts of the "warnings we have handed on to you by the command of the Lord Jesus" (4. 2) and to implore them not to despise the Christian life of holiness (4. 8).

The Apocalypse of St John contains, as many people are aware, a frightening message to the Church of Laodicea on the score of its lukewarmness, for which, says the divine judge, "Thou wilt make me vomit thee out of my mouth" (3. 16). These and other passages that might be adduced are sufficient proof that sin committed after baptism was, even in the lifetime of the apostles themselves, not merely a possibility, but a frequently recurring and most disturbing reality.

THE APOSTOLIC FATHERS

We may now turn from such evidence as there is in the New Testament documents to that available in the years immediately following the New Testament period, that is, to the age of the apostolic Fathers. These are the Christian writers who, while not themselves apostles, may be reckoned to have known one or more members of the apostolic body or, at any rate, to have been in touch with its immediate disciples. The writings themselves are usually limited to those composed between the last years of the first century and the first half of the second century.

The Didache

Among these writings one of the most celebrated was discovered as recently as 1873 and published in 1883. It is of unknown authorship, and is known as the *Didache* or Instructions of the Apostles. From the time of its first finding by Bryennios, an Orthodox metropolitan, its date has been much in dispute. The latest, very full study by Fr J. P. Audet, O.P., entitled *La Didachè: Instruction des Apôtres* (Paris, 1958), presents arguments for a very early date, at some time when the first generation of Christians was still, in some part, surviving, between A.D. 50 and 70.

The book is extremely short, occupying no more than thirteen pages of Greek text in the *Loeb Classical Library* (edited by Professor Kirsopp Lake in 1912) and is made up of sixteen chapters. Of these 1–6 contain a catechism of moral teaching; 7–10 are concerned with liturgical matters, such as baptism, prayer and fasting, and the Eucharist; and there are disciplinary rulings in 11–15. The final chapter (16) is an instruction on the second coming of Christ.

In chapter 4 there is a reference to individual confession of sins in the assembly ("In the congregation thou shalt confess thy transgressions, and thou shalt not occupy thyself in prayer with an evil conscience"). In chapter 14 the confession of sins appears to take on a more official character, since we read: "On the Lord's day assemble for the breaking of bread and the Eucharist, after having first confessed your sins that your sacrifice may be spotless. But let not him that has a quarrel with his neighbour join in your assembly until reconciliation has taken place, in order that your sacrifice may not be contaminated." No details are supplied about the time or place of this confession; it is not clear whether it is to be made in general or specific terms, or whether it is to be addressed to the congregation as a whole or to the rulers of the local Church. It can be noted, however, that it is certainly made for the forgiveness of sins, and with a view to a worthy reception of the eucharistic gifts.

St Clement of Rome

St Clement's epistle was written about the year 96, and has as its object the abolition of schisms and dissensions in the Church of Corinth. It contains much moral teaching and information about the hierarchy of the Church. In chapter 56 the saint stresses the value of prayer for those who have transgressed, and the purpose of correction leading to improvement of life. "You see, beloved," he writes, "how great is the protection granted to those who are chastened by the Master. For, being a good Father, he corrects us in order that we may obtain mercy through his holy chastisement." He continues (chapter 57): "You therefore, who were responsible for beginning the dissension, submit yourselves unto the presbyters, bowing the knees of your hearts." It may be reasonably concluded that the desire for pardon carries with it the duty of submission to the rulers of the Church, and that *even so great a sin as schism may be forgiven in this way.* There is no indication here of any formal rite or set form of words, but some type of discipline or correction is to be inflicted on the authors of the schisms by those who hold office in the assembly.

"Second Clement"

This ancient homily, which is neither by St Clement of Rome nor an epistle, is usually dated to the middle of the second century (i.e. *c.* 150) and contains several passages on repentance. In chapter 18 the writer suggests the need of being sorry for sin while we are still in this life; there is no vestige of a hint that any class of sin is beyond forgiveness: "For after we have departed out of this life, we can no more make confession or again repent."

St Ignatius of Antioch

St Ignatius, the martyr bishop of Antioch, who traditionally suffered in the Flavian ampitheatre about 107, writing to the Philadelphians stresses as usual in his epistles the need for avoiding schism and of being united with the bishop. Those, he writes, who are followers of a schismatic will not inherit the kingdom of God (chapter 3). Later, he writes: "Where there is division and anger, God does not make his abode. To those, however, who repent, the Lord gives pardon, provided that their penitence leads them to the unity of God and to the bishop's council" (chapter 8). It may well be inferred that the approach to the bishop's council involves communion with the bishop and submission to his authority. Hence the phrase recalls St Clement's "Submit yourselves to the presbyters, bowing the knees of your hearts".

St Polycarp of Smyrna

Another glorious martyr bishop, St Polycarp, was a disciple of St John the Evangelist, and suffered death at the age of eighty-six on Saturday, February 22nd, 156. When writing to the Philippians (about the year 110) he recalls the duty of the presbyters to be "compassionate, merciful to all men, bringing back those that have gone astray" (chapter 6).

With the exception of the *Didache*, all these writers set out clearly the fact that sin will be pardoned, however great it may be, and this pre-eminently through the presbyters of the Church. The Didache has, it is true, a reference to the sin against the Holy Ghost (chapter 11. 7), but simply as an argument against testing or examining any prophet who claims to speak with divine authority.

The Shepherd of Hermas

This, the last document in this group to be examined, is a
curious and singular one, best described by Mgr Duchesne's
phrase: "A vast examination of conscience on the part of the
Roman Church." Unlike most of the documents belonging to
this group it is quite a lengthy treatise, which in the Loeb
edition takes up one hundred and fifty pages of Greek text.
The author is identified by the famous Muratorian fragment
with a certain Hermas, brother of Pius I (140–50), who wrote
his book during the pontificate of Pius. He has divided his
work into three parts, comprising five visions, twelve precepts
(or mandates) and ten parables or similitudes. Of these the
most important vision for our purpose is that of the tower
(vision 3) built upon the waters, and constructed of many
glistening square stones. Of the various stones prepared for
the tower some are fixed into the building, some are thrown
away and some are broken in pieces and left lying. The lady
who acts as guide to Hermas claims that the tower is herself,
the Church of Christ. As regards the stones that make up the
building the square white ones are "the apostles and bishops
and teachers and deacons, who have lived holy lives in
God (Vis. 3. 5. 1). . . . . Those which were cast away . . . are
those who have sinned and wish to do penance. And therefore
they are not cast far outside the tower, for if they do penance,
they will be useful in building" (Vis. 3. 5. 5). All the stones,
she declares, will have an opportunity to do penance, but not
until they "have undergone torments and fulfilled the days of
their sins" (Vis. 3. 7. 6).

An even more celebrated passage occurs in the fourth
mandate (3. 1 ff.). After mentioning some teachers who, taking
a rigoristic line, declared that there could be no penance after
baptism, Hermas announces that there is indeed a second
chance given through penance, but it is available only once.
On the other hand, it is applicable to all sins, as even those
authors who argue for the existence of three reserved sins in
the early Church are constrained to admit. The only exception

to this rule is in regard to those who are unwilling to repent. Hermas gives three separate enumerations of the sinners who may be forgiven as a result of penance, and only those who are too hardened to repent are refused forgiveness. So in this work there is no question of any irremissible sin, though there are two classes of men who, in practice, are not pardoned. The first is that of the neophytes who sin very soon after baptism, and so manifest their lack of sincere purpose. The second class is made up of those who have once been pardoned after baptism. They cannot be again pardoned, because the remedy is available only once.

As in other writings of the group no clue is provided about the exact means of forgiveness, except that, in the main, it is given through the Church, and by way of the Church. A great authority on all this literature, the late Fr Adhémar d'Alès, S.J., wrote on this point:

> We are of the opinion that neither the symbolism of the tower, nor the parallelism of the double repentance, before and after baptism, nor yet the whole of the work can have any acceptable meaning if they are held to represent anything other than repentance directed and controlled by the Church, and if inclusion in the building of the tower is not taken in the sense of reconciliation with the Church.[1]

So, in the writings of the apostolic Fathers there is a strong emphasis on *the mercy of Almighty God towards sinners*, and there is considerable evidence that the Church is the source of that forgiveness. The quotations from St Clement of Rome and St Ignatius of Antioch tend to show that there was, at least in an incipient stage, some sort of penitential system in the hands of the Church's rulers. The regulation about the non-repetition of public penance, as it is announced by Hermas, is, as Fr d'Alès has insisted (p. 134), the only known law of this kind that has no justification in Holy Scripture, when account is taken of the virtual irrelevance of Heb. 6. 4–8

[1] *L'Edit de Calliste* (Paris, 1913), p. 112.

in this context. It also remains true that two classes of penitents are not, in practice, pardoned, because they lack a
sincere will to repent.

Clement of Alexandria

In so rapid a survey we must pass over some testimonies
from the close of the second century, which, on the whole, do
nothing to alter the impression that, in spite of a severe
discipline, the Church was willing and anxious to show mercy
to those who were truly penitent. A striking illustration of
this tendency occurs in the writings of Clement of Alexandria
(c. 150–c. 215) in the treatise *Who is the rich man that is
saved?*[2] The story of a former protégé of St John the Evangelist and his conversion from his life as a robber-chief is a
moving one. St John had sought out the robber, and when
they finally met, the chief embraced the apostle, confessed his
faults and was baptized anew, as it were, in his own tears.
St John then assured his former friend that "he had found
pardon for him from the Saviour, and knelt and kissed his
right hand, as now cleansed by his penitence, and led him
back to the Church" (p. 363). The story well exemplifies the
attitude of the Church towards a man who had committed
many crimes, including a number of murders.

Tertullian

At about the time usually associated with the writing of
the Shepherd of Hermas, Tertullian, the first of the grand line
of African Christian writers, was born in Carthage (where he
later in adult life practised as a lawyer). He became a Christian about 195, and it is generally accepted that he was
ordained priest c. 200. Among his thirty-one works three are
concerned either with Christian initiation (*On Baptism*) or
with penance (*On Penitence* and *On Purity*). Of these the
first two were composed in his Catholic period between 200

[2] Cf. *Clement of Alexandria* (Loeb Classical Library), tr. by G. W.
Butterworth (London, 1919), pp. 356–65.

and 206, whereas the last was the final product of his Montanist period, and is dated to 217–22.

The work *On Penitence* is a small treatise of only twelve chapters. The first six deal with the penance that should come before baptism; the last six with penance for sins committed after baptism which, as he says, is also the last. Tertullian mentions this second penance with reluctance, since he fears that, by referring to it, he may seem to allow opportunity for sinning again (chapter 7). In chapter 9 he gives a valuable description of the rite of *exomologesis*, the penitentual process "by which we confess our sins to the Lord". It includes the wearing of a sordid garment (such as sackcloth and ashes), very plain food "not for the belly's, but for the soul's sake", fasting, lamentation, prostration before the presbyters (compare St Clement of Rome's words about submission to the presbyters "bowing the knees of your heart") and kneeling before the faithful. The purpose of this rite is that "it may act in place of God's wrath, and that by means of corporeal affliction it may, I will not say prevent eternal torments, but discharge them".[3]

Mr Watkins in *A History of Penance* (I, 116) says that it is not easy to satisfy oneself whether the confession of sins was made openly or privately. Fr J. A. Jungmann, S.J., in his recently translated book on *The Early Liturgy* gives the answer: "It may be noted that, though the penance was public, there is no indication (except in isolated instances, which were condemned as abuses) that a public confession of individual sins was ever exacted" (p. 242). The reconciliation effected in this way was made directly and immediately to the Church, but indirectly and mediately to God.

Tertullian, writing his treatise *On Penitence*, in his Catholic period, makes use of many passages from Scripture to prove that a *penitentia secunda*, a second, post-baptismal penance, exists. But, at some date after his writing of his treatise, about

[3] Cf. W. P. Le Saint, S.J., *Tertullian: Treatises on Penance*, "Ancient Christian Writers" (London, 1959), p. 32.

207, he became a Montanist, a member of a Phrygian sect
founded by a would-be prophet named Montanus, which
accepted a third and final revelation (of the Paraclete) and
announced the imminence of Christ's second coming. The
moral teaching of Montanism was excessively harsh. It for-
bade second marriages, increased the number of fasts and
would not forgive sins committed after baptism. It was after
his "conversion" to Montanism that Tertullian attacked the
Catholic Church on the various points which separated Montanism from Catholicism. His final and most violent attack
was also the last of his extant works, the treatise *On Purity*
which was written some fifteen to twenty years after his earlier
work *On Penitence*. In the treatise *On Purity* he puts forward
the thesis of remissible and irremissible sins, of which the
former can be pardoned by the Church, the latter only by
God. In a sense that contradicts his former teaching he uses
the parables of divine mercy recorded by St Luke (chapter 15)
—the lost sheep, the lost coin and the prodigal son. He was,
as might be expected, unable to find any argument from
tradition to support his contention. He is especially severe in
his judgement on a certain bishop, at one time regularly
identified with Pope St Callistus (218–22), who had issued an
edict clearly affirming his right to absolve sinners from the
guilt of adultery, provided that the sinner had duly taken his
place in the rite of public penance. It is admitted by most
students of this and the earlier treatise that Tertullian's meaning is often hard to seize. He may, however, be regarded with
good reason as an unwilling witness in favour of the Catholic
Church's reaction against undue rigorism, her confidence in
her power to absolve and her rejection of the severe Montanist
teaching, which cast out from the community not only adul-
terers and fornicators, but even those who had embarked upon
second marriages.

His principal charge against the Church he had abandoned
was that, in the issue of the edict normally known as the edict
of Callistus, she showed herself to be inconsistent, since she
professed to absolve an adulterer, and denied pardon to

murderers and idolators. Was he sincere in claiming that murder and idolatry were regarded by the Church as irremissible sins? It is surely a fact worth recalling that such a claim was a contradiction of his former teaching in the treatise *On Penitence*. Fr G. H. Joyce, S.J., in his article "Private Penance in the Early Church"[4] puts the issue clearly. "The suggestion that Tertullian was perfectly aware [when writing *On Penitence*] that no pardon was accorded for adultery, murder or apostacy, but omits to mention the fact, needs no refutation. A view which calls for such a supposition stands self-condemned." We must conclude that Tertullian was speaking here as an advocate, who like many of his kind, before and since, overstated his case.

We do not know the date of Tertullian's death; he may have arrived at extreme old age. There is no ground for thinking that he was ever reconciled to the Church.

Hippolytus

Whether or no Callistus was the bishop against whom Tertullian inveighs so bitterly in the treatise *On Purity*, it is certain that this same pope was attacked by Hippolytus, a priest of the Roman church (born *c.* 170–5), who suffered martyrdom under Maximinus the Thracian about 235. His complaint is the same as Tertullian's—that Callistus had shown undue leniency in reconciling those guilty of fleshly sin, even if the emphasis is rather upon scandalous reforms in discipline. Yet Hippolytus himself had preserved in his well-known work *The Apostolic Tradition* a prayer for the consecration of a bishop which asks on behalf of the elect that "by the high priestly Spirit he may have authority to *forgive sins* according to thy command . . . to *loose every bond* according to the authority thou gavest to the apostles . . .".[5]

[4] *Journal of Theological Studies*, xlii, p. 22.

[5] Cf. Hippolyte de Rome: *La Tradition Apostolique*, ed. B. Botte, O.S.B. (Paris, 1946), p. 29.

DECIAN PERSECUTION AND NOVATIAN

Some years later came the Decian persecution of 250, which resulted in many martyrdoms, and a large number of apostates from the faith. At that time there was a priest in the Roman local church named Novatian, who had been ordained by St Fabian, pope from 236 to 251 and himself the first martyr of the Decian reign of terror. During the vacancy of the Roman see Novatian became well known as the writer of one or more letters to St Cyprian, bishop of Carthage from 249 until his death by beheading on September 14th, 258. Cyprian had taken a certain line regarding those who had lapsed during the persecution; he had decided to reconcile those apostates who were ill or dying, but to postpone judgement on the others until a council had been convened to determine the matter. This course was approved by the Roman clergy, of whom Novatian was then the leading spirit.

In March, 251, the clergy and laity of Rome met to choose a new bishop, and their choice fell upon Cornelius. Novatian, as an unsuccessful candidate for the bishopric, managed to obtain episcopal consecration from three bishops who are described by Cornelius as "too simple to meet the artifices and ruses of these wicked men".[6] He then proclaimed himself to be the true bishop of Rome, and, in order to justify his schism, adopted a policy of extreme severity towards the lapsed. As in the affair of Tertullian this conduct served to emphasize the relative leniency of the Church's attitude. Unfortunately Novatian and his followers succeeded in creating a schism, the first of its kind to lure away members of the Church, and this schism lasted for two centuries. Its characteristic note was the stress laid upon the uselessness of penance, since pardon was alleged to be in many cases impossible. Even at the time of the schism it was asked: What exactly was the nature of Novatian's error? There seems to be no doubt that, apart from some trinitarian inexactitudes,

[6] Cf. Eusebius, *Ecclesiastical History,* VI, 43. 7.

the extreme rigorism he taught did, in effect, deny the Church's right to absolve from the sin of apostasy, even in the hour of death, whereas he was prepared to reconcile those guilty of sins of the flesh when suitable penance had been performed. This refusal to reconcile apostates was extended even to the class known as the *libellatici*, who had not actually sacrificed to the pagan deities, but had obtained certificates testifying to their having sacrificed.[7]

END OF RIGORISM

Rigorism, of which, in its extreme form, Novatian was the representative, was virtually at an end by 252, except in the churches administered by the Novatianist schismatics (often as a result of expulsion of the lawfully established hierarchy) and in a limited degree, in Spain. A slightly later landmark in the history of penance is the so-called Canonical Epistle of St Gregory the Wonderworker (*Thaumaturgus*) (213–70). Its eleventh canon sets out the various degrees or grades for those admitted to penance in eastern christendom. First came the *mourner*, who was not permitted to enter the church. He stood outside the church door, and begged the prayers of those who entered. The second grade (that of *hearer*) stood inside the church door, in the narthex, until the moment when the catechumens left the building after the reading of the scriptures and the instructions, but *before* the beginning of the Mass of the Faithful. The third grade (that of *fallers* or *kneelers*) remained on their knees in the nave until the catechumens departed. The fourth and last grade (that of *bystanders*) took their place with the faithful and did not follow the catechumens out, but were not permitted to make the offering or to receive the Blessed Sacrament.

Council of Elvira

Early in the fourth century (*c.* 305) the Spanish council of Elvira established fifty canons of great severity, of which the

[7] On this question cf. E. Amann, art. "Novatien et Novatienisme", in *Dict. de théol. cath.* (Paris, 1931), XI, columns 837–41.

first gives an adequate sample of the legislation. It enacts that any adult who, after baptism, goes to a pagan temple to take part in the idolatrous worship may not be admitted to communion even at the close of life, since he has committed the greatest of all crimes (*quod est crimen principale*).[8] Yet a reading of the canons makes it evident that the nineteen bishops who met at Elvira were in no sense Novatianists, inasmuch as they did not deny the Church's power to forgive these serious offences, but decided, as they were entitled to do, that in practice and in the circumstances of the time, the Church *would* not forgive such crimes, even in the hour of death.

Council of Arles

A later council, that of Arles in Gaul (314), in which, it is estimated, six hundred delegates may have taken part, gave more general reference to the legislation prepared at Carthage and Rome in mid-third century. It ruled that: "In regard to those who apostatize and never present themselves before the Church, or seek in any way to do penance, and who afterwards when seized upon by sickness demand communion, it was decided that communion should not be given to them, apart from the case of their recovering and bringing forth fruits worthy of penance."[9]

This, the twenty-second canon, is not excessively severe. It is taken for granted that those who *did* present themselves before the Church in time of good health would be reconciled, after a period of penance, and likewise that those who brought forth worthy fruits after recovery would receive the same grace.

St Peter of Alexandria

An example of benignity and mildness is shown in the Canonical Epistle of St Peter of Alexandria (martyred 311),

[8] Text in Watkins, *A History of Penance*, I, p. 261. Translation in the same (I, p. 277) and in Palmer, *Sources* . . ., p. 66.

[9] Text in Watkins, I, pp. 267–8, translation, pp. 282–3.

written about 306, concerning those who had lapsed through human frailty when under torture. He decides that, since some are now bewailing their lapse for a third year, it will be sufficient for them to do penance, from the time of their approach, for a further forty days. Those who were merely prisoners and were not tortured must do penance for a year. Those who had lapsed without enduring either torture or imprisonment must undergo penance for a period variously estimated at three or four years.[10]

Council of Nicaea, 325

Finally, we arrive at the date of the first General Council, that of Nicaea in 325. For our purpose the most important canon is the thirteenth, which rules that, in the hour of death, viaticum is not to be refused to the dying. In the event of recovery the penitent, if he has been reconciled, is "to take his place with those who have the fellowship of the prayer only". Whenever a request is made for viaticum, the bishop is to grant this, after due inquiry.

This brief outline of a complicated history must come to an end here. It leaves many questions unanswered, and some sixteen centuries of penitential practice uncharted. A later chapter will discuss the matter of private penance, and its establishment in the Church. Meanwhile, the Church had decided, some three centuries after the birthday of the Christian *ecclesia*, that she was willing to remit all sins in the hour of death, and this was promulgated by the infallible voice of a General Council.

[10] Text in Watkins, I, pp. 264–5, translation, pp. 280–1.

CHAPTER IV

PENANCE IS A SACRAMENTAL RITE DISTINCT FROM BAPTISM

In the two preceding chapters evidence has been accumulated to show that the Church possesses, as a gift from Christ her Lord, the power of the keys for binding and loosing the sins committed by those who have already received God's grace in baptism. We have seen that the Council of Trent defined explicitly that the rite of penance was a true sacrament of the New Law, and was instituted by Christ. It is further declared that "If anyone, by some confounding of the two sacraments, shall say that baptism is itself the sacrament of penance, as though these sacraments were not distinct, and that, in consequence, penance is not rightly called *a second plank after the shipwreck*, let him be anathema" (Denz. 912).

THE SECOND PLANK

The phrase "a second plank after the shipwreck", which is found in some part in classical writers such as Seneca and Cicero, was, as Fr Le Saint explains in his edition of Tertullian's two treatises on penance, to some extent Christianized by the most illustrious of all converts to Montanism "to describe the salvation of man through the means of grace given him by God". Seneca has the phrase *dare tabulam naufrago* ("to give a plank to a shipwrecked man") and Cicero speaks of "snatching a plank from a shipwrecked man" (*tabulam de naufrago arripere*). Tertullian's own words (*De Paenitentia*, ch. 4) is "as one who is shipwrecked holds to a plank of salvation". He never uses the precise phrase about the *second* plank, as it is quoted by the Council. "As far as can be ascertained," writes Fr Le Saint, "this was first done by St Jerome" (*Epist.* 130. 9). It is more usually explained as meaning that baptism is the first plank to be thrown to the sinner, and penance the second. It seems that Tertullian is thinking of penance in general, without distinguishing between the two planks.[1]

PENANCE A SACRAMENT

To prove that penance is a sacrament of the New Law it must be shown to be a "sensible" sign (i.e. one perceptible by the senses) that produces grace and was permanently instituted by Christ. Now the rite of penance is, quite certainly, one perceptible by the senses, since it is exercised by a judicial process that calls for the audible manifestation of guilt (prescinding from exceptions made for the dumb, who may use signs), and an externally manifested sentence or declaration on the part of the judge. Further, it is a sign that produces grace, being appointed for the forgiveness of mortal sin in particular, which can be effected only by the inpouring of divine grace. "Moreover," writes Fr L. Billot, S.J., "the ministers of the Church most certainly cannot forgive sins except by sacramental means, since they have power to confer grace (as St Paul decides in 1 Cor. 4) only in so far as they are dispensers of the mysteries, that is, of the sacraments of God."[2] That the rite was founded by Christ has been already proved in chapter II.

---

[1] Cf. W. Le Saint, S.J., *Tertullian: Treatises on Penance*, pp. 149–50, n. 54.

[2] *De Sacramentis Ecclesiae*, 8th ed. (Rome, 1947), II, p. 23.

A striking testimony to this sacramental power is that of St Pacian, bishop of Barcelona from 343 until 391. He is writing to Sempronianus, a Novatianist, who had sent him a treatise embodying the teaching of the sect. Pacian maintains that God would not utter threats against the impenitent, if he were not ready and willing to pardon the penitent, and continues:

> You say: God alone could do this, and this is, indeed, true. But what he does through his priests is done by his own power. For what is it that he said to his apostles: *Whatsoever you shall bind on earth shall be bound in heaven; and whatsoever you shall loose on earth shall be loosed also in heaven*? Why this, if it were not permitted to men to bind and to loose? Or is this permitted to the apostles alone? Then also to them only is it permitted to baptize, to them alone to bestow the Holy Spirit, to them alone to purge the sins of the nations—because all this is commanded to none other than the apostles.[3]

This passage helps to elucidate the Church's faith about the bestowal of the gift, which was instituted by Christ for all time, upon the apostles and their successors, since the power of forgiving sins is as necessary now as it was in the first days of Christianity.

PENANCE DISTINCT FROM BAPTISM

The distinction between baptism and penance is indicated by a comparison of the two rites, which differ widely. In particular, it is to be remarked, there is no trace in baptism of *judicial authority* on the part of the baptizer, who may well be a layman or even an unbeliever, provided he is willing to use the correct matter and form, and to have the intention of doing what the Church does. Moreover, the subject of baptism, the catechumen, is not, antecedently to his baptism,

[3] Watkins, I, pp. 394 (text) and 454 (translation). Palmer, *Sources*, p. 94.

a member of the Church or subject to her tribunals. Lastly, there is, beyond all question, no power of *retaining* exercised in baptism, which is designed primarily for the remission of original sin and of offences committed by adults before they receive the rite. Undoubtedly the Church has the right to refuse baptism to one who gives proof of lack of sincerity or faith, but that is something very different from *retaining* in the sense used regarding the sacrament of penance.[4]

The whole of the Church's doctrine on this matter is summarized in Can. 870 of the Code of Canon Law: "In the sacrament of penance sins committed after baptism are forgiven, in respect of a member of the faithful properly disposed for it, by judicial absolution conferred by a lawful minister."

[4] The question of retaining might arise exceptionally in regard to an adult who was not truly penitent at the time of baptism. For liceity (*not* for validity, see below, p. 135) faith and attrition are required in an adult. It is conceivable that one who had lacked attrition might make some pre-baptismal sin the matter of his first confession after baptism and might even be refused absolution, if his dispositions remained insufficient.

CHAPTER V

THE MATTER OF THE SACRAMENT: CONTRITION

THE MATTER AND FORM OF PENANCE

We are accustomed to refer to the matter and form of the sacraments and, in this use of the words, "matter" stands for the material thing used (water in baptism, oil in confirmation and extreme unction, bread and wine in the Eucharist) and "form" for the words that determine the purpose for which the matter is being employed. Sometimes the same matter is used for various purposes. One example of this might be the laying-on or imposition of hands, which is used in baptism, confirmation, the ordination of bishops, priests and deacons, the blessing of abbots and abbesses, and other rites of blessing, such as the blessing of the sick. In all these uses of the same matter it is the form of words accompanying the imposition that determines the precise purpose.

In two of the sacraments (penance and matrimony) the terms "matter" and "form" are employed with a difference, since there is no "matter" in the ordinary sense, as there is in the other five sacraments. There is, however, an undetermined element, and also an element that determines the signification. In matrimony, which is in this respect in a class by itself, the matter and form of the sacramental rite are, alike, the consent given by the two parties, usually in some form of words, though a nod or some other sign may be sufficient. *In the sacrament of penance* the matter is ordinarily taken to be the

three acts of the penitent (contrition, confession and satisfaction) and the form is the words of the priest administering
the sacrament, when he pronounces the absolution.

It is true that theologians also distinguish what is styled
the *remote* matter (also called "the matter with which the
sacrament is concerned") and this remote matter is all the
sins of the penitent that he has committed since his baptism.
Since the existence of some matter to be confessed is essential
for the bestowal of absolution (one cannot absolve sins that
have never existed) we can see the relevance of this distinction.

It is equally true that there has been a good deal of controversy about the *proximate* matter of penance, as it is styled
by contrast with the remote matter (the penitent's sins). Some
medieval theologians (e.g. Alexander of Hales) thought that
a laying-on of hands, which occurred three times in the
ancient penitential rite, was the proximate matter of the
sacrament. This imposition of hands was not, however, a
necessary part of the rite, and therefore cannot be considered
to be the essential matter. A more influential school, that of
the Scotists, who followed in the footsteps of the great John
Duns Scotus (*c.* 1264–1308), also known as "the subtle
doctor", judged that the words said by the confessor in absolution were both the matter and the form, whereas the penitent's three acts were no more than dispositions, or necessary
conditions, for validity. This view has certainly not prevailed,
and the ordinary teaching of most theologians today is that
the matter consists in the three acts already mentioned.

This, the more usual interpretation, finds support in the
decrees of both the Council of Florence (Denz. 699) and the
Tridentine Council (Denz. 896, 914), which speak of the
penitent's acts as the "quasi-matter" of penance, in which
expression they are following St Thomas, who writes suc-
cinctly: "The fourth sacrament is penance, of which the acts
of the penitent are the quasi-matter."[1] The Catechism of the
Council of Trent, which enjoys great authority, and whose

[1] *Opusculum de articulis fidei et Ecclesiae sacramentis.*

authors knew well the mind of the Council, says that: "These acts are called by the Council the quasi-matter, not because they have not the nature of true matter, but because they are not matter of the same kind as that which is used externally, such as water in baptism."

Nonetheless, the Scotist hypothesis is by no means improbable, and may find some confirmation in the undoubted truth that, in case of extreme necessity, a penitent may be given conditional absolution, even when externally manifested signs of contrition are lacking.

MEANING OF CONTRITION

The first of the penitent's acts, and in many respects the most important, is contrition, which is defined by the *Shorter Oxford Dictionary* as (1) in a long-obsolete, literal sense "the action of rubbing together; grinding, pounding or bruising so as to pulverize", and (2) in a still flourishing, *figurative* sense: "The condition of being bruised in heart; affliction of mind for some fault or injury done, and especially, penitence for sin." The word *contritio* occurs only nine times in the *Imitation of Christ* (five times as a noun, and four times in some verbal form of *conterere*), whereas the word *compunctio* is found seventeen times in all (thirteen times as a noun, and four times in a verbal form of *compungere*). "Compunction" is defined by the *Oxford Dictionary* as meaning "Pricking or sting of the conscience or heart; uneasiness of mind consequent upon wrong doing; remorse; contrition". It is curious that, as the dictionary notes, it is now ordinarily used of *slight* discomfort of mind, whereas among theologians it is sometimes employed in the sense of abiding sorrow for sin.

In the first chapter of this book St Thomas's definition of the virtue of penance was given, and it may be seen to be closely equated with the Council of Trent's classic formula: "Sorrow of mind and detestation of sin committed, with the resolution not to sin again" (Denz. 897). The Tridentine formula is one that might have reference to both the Old and the New Testament dispensations, and does not, at this point, distinguish between perfect and imperfect contrition.

Taking each clause of the definition separately one may remark:

(1) Contrition is, first and foremost, *sorrow*, in so far as any sinner who sincerely wishes to return to God, after deserting him by mortal sin, must grieve for the offences that have led to his turning away from his creator and last end. This sorrow is pre-eminently sorrow of mind and will, and should not be confused with emotional outbursts that may be simply the result of frustration or disappointment.

(2) Contrition is also *detestation* or hatred of sin, arising from a due appreciation of its malice. This hatred of sin is coupled with a desire to undo what has been done, if that were possible, so that a sinner can say in all sincerity: If this sin had not been already committed, I should wish to refrain from committing it.

(3) The sorrow and hatred are concerned with *the sin itself*, and not, at any rate primarily, with the punishments due to sin.

(4) The last clause is: *With the resolution not to sin again*, since nobody can genuinely detest a sin, or, at any rate, a mortal sin, without having the will, here and now, not to commit the offence again.

It is noticeable that the Council of Trent wished to define contrition *as it has been available in every age*, long before the institution of the sacrament of penance. This is evident in the explanation that follows hard on the definition just given:

> Now this working of contrition has been necessary at all times to obtain pardon of sins, and, in regard to one who has fallen into sin after baptism, it prepares him at length for the forgiveness of sins, if it is joined with trust in the divine mercy, and with the intention of procuring all that is required for the valid reception of this sacrament (Denz. 897).

TWO KINDS OF CONTRITION

The distinction is between contrition properly so called or *perfect* contrition, and contrition less correctly so called, which is *imperfect* contrition or attrition. It is important not to consider these two sorts of contrition as differing merely in degree or, as it were, quantitatively, as though, for example, everything depended upon the amount of time spent in working up the contrition, so that no contrition could be perfect unless it required, let us say, ten minutes to produce. The distinction is a specific one, and the two kinds of contrition differ both in regard to their motives and in their efficacy.

Contrition properly so styled is motivated by charity. The love of God (that is, our love for him) is *either* the love of desire (also called the love of concupiscence) whereby God is loved for the sake of the gifts he gives to men, *or* the love of benevolence, by which God is loved for his own sake, as being infinitely good, perfect and lovable. This love of benevolence, where it exists in an exalted degree, is styled the love of friendship, which consists in the mutual love existing between God and man, so that man loves God as he is in himself, not only as the highest good, but as his friend.

MEANING OF ATTRITION

Attrition is well defined by the *Oxford Dictionary* as "an imperfect sorrow for sin, not amounting to contrition or utter crushing, and having its motive not in love of God, but in fear of punishment". It has, as the motive that inspires it, a supernatural motive, but not the love of charity. Such a motive might be the ugliness of sin or the punishment inflicted, whether eternally or temporally, by God on account of sin. Yet these motives must be *supernatural* ones, deriving from the light of faith and from actual grace. It is not sufficient, for example, to regard adultery as merely ugly and sordid, or for a murderer to be sorry for his sin merely because he has become liable to a capital sentence.

EFFICACY OF PERFECT CONTRITION

Regarding the efficacy of *perfect* contrition (as contrasted with attrition) it is Catholic doctrine that perfect contrition brings about *forgiveness of all sins*, whether mortal or venial, provided there is also an intention of receiving the sacrament of penance. Various passages in Holy Scripture can be quoted as lending support to the first part of the proposition, e.g. Deut. 4. 29: "If thou wilt have recourse to the Lord thy God, if thou wilt but have recourse to him with all thy heart, in the bitterness of thy tribulation, thou wilt find him again." In St John 14. 23, perhaps the loveliest chapter in the whole of his Gospel, we read: "If a man has any love for me he will be true to my word; and then he will win my Father's love, and we will come to him, and make our continual abode with him." So in Holy Scripture there is a clear and firm promise that God's friendship may be won by a genuine act of love, which necessarily contains within itself an act of perfect contrition. Among the decisions and definitions that the Church has made in the course of many centuries one may quote St Pius V's condemnation of Baius (Michel du Bay, of Louvain) when the latter wrote: "A crime is not forgiven through contrition, even when this is coupled with perfect charity, and the purpose of receiving the sacrament, except in case of necessity or of martyrdom, *unless the sacrament has been actually received*" (Denz. 1071).

The purpose or intention of receiving the sacrament need not be explicit; an implicit intention of doing all within one's power to save one's soul is entirely adequate.

VALUE OF ATTRITION

Catholic teaching on imperfect contrition is summed up in two sentences. First, that attrition is insufficient to justify a man, where there is merely the *intention* of receiving the sacrament. Secondly, that genuine attrition is sufficient for obtaining justification in and with the help of the sacrament of penance.

Regarding the first statement (on the insufficiency of attrition by itself) one may recall the *Oxford Dictionary*'s definition with its emphasis on the fact that attrition has its motive "not in love of God, but in fear of punishment". The motive is, therefore, not enough to constitute perfect contrition, which alone is capable of taking away mortal sin without the help of the sacrament, even though the intention must be present of receiving it. This is not, as has been already stated, merely a question of degree. Hence St Thomas and other theologians deny that attrition can ever become contrition, and one of the later Thomists writes: "From what has been said you may infer (as against Cajetan) that attrition can never formally become contrition, since it differs from contrition essentially ... one cannot become the other by the addition of some new stage or anything of that sort, because there is need of an essential change, and this is impossible."[2]

Yet, though attrition itself can never become contrition, one who is attrite can become contrite by means of the sacrament. He will receive through absolution sanctifying grace and, at the same time, the infused virtue of charity, which engenders contrition.

The second proposition (that attrition with the sacrament is sufficient for justification) was not universally accepted by theologians before Trent, and Peter Lombard and St Bonaventure are reckoned among those who required perfect contrition as essential for the reception of the sacrament. It is not, however, true to say that, before the thirteenth century, it was generally held that contrition properly so called was necessary. The older theologians, like some of their successors, often use "contrition" to include imperfect contrition. Since the Council's ruling on the subject it is commonly held that the opinion rejecting the sufficiency of attrition in con-

[2] J. B. Gonet, O.P. (c. 1633–81), *De Paenitentia*, dist. vii, art. 2, n. 20.

junction with the sacrament must rank as temerarious. Long before Trent, St Thomas himself had ruled: "When a man comes to confession who is *attrite, but not fully contrite,* grace and forgiveness of sins is given to him through confession and absolution, provided that he sets no obstacle to it."[3]

The Council of Trent (Session xiv, of November 25th, 1551, chapter 4, Denz. 898) follows St Thomas's teaching when it declares: "Even though attrition without the sacrament of penance cannot of itself bring a sinner to justification, it can dispose him to obtain God's grace in the sacrament of penance (*ad Dei gratiam in sacramento poenitentiae impetrandam disponit*)." It may be concluded from this chapter of Trent that perfect contrition proceeds from charity, and justifies a sinner who has the firm purpose of receiving the sacrament, *even before he has actually received it.* Imperfect contrition or attrition does not proceed from a motive of charity, and does not of itself justify, but it does dispose a sinner to receive grace through the sacrament, in so far as it is a good impulse, and a free and salutary act of the will, proceeding from the influence of the Holy Spirit who moves the sinner by actual grace, even though he is not yet present in the soul by sanctifying grace.

THE CHURCH'S PRACTICE

An argument in favour of this effect of attrition may be found in the Church's general practice of giving conditional absolution to those who are both in danger of death and insensible, provided there is ground for presuming the sick man's desire to be properly disposed for receiving the sacrament. This practice would assuredly not be countenanced if attrition with the sacrament were not sufficient for valid absolution. For, in the absence of perfect contrition, the absolution would then be invalid; whereas, if perfect contrition

[3] *Commentary on the Sentences,* dist. 22, 1. 2, a. 1, sol. 3.

could be presumed, the absolution would be unnecessary, since the sinner would have already been forgiven without the help of the sacrament.

IS FEAR SUFFICIENT?

The question must now be faced whether attrition motivated simply by the fear of what we style in our act of contrition "God's dreadful punishments", is or is not a good thing. The ordinary Catholic teaching has, at one time or another, been heavily attacked by Luther, the Jansenists and some other writers, on the ground that a man who is attrite acts simply under coercion from fear and that this makes him a hypocrite and a still greater sinner. Here one must distinguish between two kinds of fear. It is possible, no doubt, to be afraid of God's punishments in such a way that the sin is avoided simply because of the penalties attaching to it, so that the sinner remains with all the will and the desire to sin, if only he could escape from the consequences. This, as most people would admit, is a wholly unworthy state of mind, and is not the sort of fear that the Council would accept as sufficient for true sorrow. Here is Trent's own statement of the conditions exacted for genuine attrition:

> The Synod declares that imperfect contrition, which is styled attrition, since normally it is conceived *either* from a consideration of the foulness of sin *or* from fear of hell and its punishments, provided that the will to sin is excluded by it, and it is accompanied by a hope of pardon, *not only does not make a man a hypocrite and a greater sinner, but is also a gift of God,* and an impulse of the Holy Spirit, who indeed does not yet dwell in the sinner, but merely moves him, so that, helped in this manner, he may prepare a way for justification (Denz. 898).

The same doctrine has been formulated in a canon (no. 8) to this effect: "If anyone shall say that the fear of hell, by which we have recourse to God's mercy while bewailing our sins, or abstain from sinning, is a sin, or that it makes men worse sinners, let him be anathema" (Denz. 818).

The following argument from reason helps to explain the propriety of attrition as understood in the sense required by the Council. There are in attrition three elements: (1) The motive directing it, which is the fear of hell and the will to avoid so frightful a punishment. This is unquestionably a good purpose for a man to have, and our Lord himself has commended it to us: "Fear ye not them that kill the body . . . but rather fear him that can destroy both soul and body in hell" (Matt. 10. 28, Douay Version). (2) The means of avoidance of hell, and this is sorrow which, even though it is imperfect, is a good thing. (3) It is good that this means should be directed towards the end to be attained, and that such sorrow should lead us to avoid hell.

IS LOVE REQUIRED?

A further point that may be briefly mentioned is this: Is it enough, in order to obtain absolution, to have attrition motivated solely by the fear of hell, without any degree of love, even in an initial stage? This was a problem which, from the sixteenth century onwards, led to a great deal of discussion between the so-called "Contritionists", who required some element of love as a necessary part of attrition, and their opponents, the "Attritionists", who denied the necessity of love, even in an incipient stage. The dispute became so violent that finally Alexander VII issued a decree, on May 5th, 1667, which denied the right of either party to call the other side by injurious terms, or to attach any censure to one or other opinion. It is interesting to remark that the pope speaks of the opinion denying the need of any love as the one more common in the Catholic schools of his day.[4]

It has since been argued, probably with success, that the

[4] Text and French translation in A. Beugnet's article "Attrition" in *Dict. de théol. cath.*, I, columns 2260–2.

whole controversy is a somewhat unreal one. Both parties would presumably admit that love in its initial stage would not be charity, since this would imply contrition, not attrition. Therefore the love in question would be that of benevolence or of concupiscence. Now one who is truly attrite is bound to detest sin and, so far as may be, to put away any affection for sin, and this certainly involves a serious effort to keep the commandments. Among these, in the very first place, is the commandment calling for the love of God above all else; there would also be, in one with even the slightest instruction in the faith, some desire to attain everlasting happiness in heaven, and to enjoy the closest of friendships with God. Hence, it might well be judged that true attrition would be impossible without including *some* love of God, at least in an initial stage. Otherwise it would be difficult to distinguish this attrition-wholly-without-love from the type of fear that merely wishes to avoid God's punishments, and that has no real intention of abandoning sin and the affection for sin.

It is not, therefore, astonishing that nowadays most theologians call for some *initial* degree of love in attrition, so that the larger numbers are no longer on the side of the "Attritionists", as they were in the time of Alexander VII.

CHARACTERISTICS OF CONTRITION

It is generally held by theologians that there are four characteristics or qualities of all contrition, whether this is perfect or imperfect.

(1) It must be *sincere, interior* contrition. It is not sufficient to recite a form of words without any corresponding inward sorrow and hatred of sin. Nor is it enough to have merely what is reputed to be contrition by the penitent himself. He must take pains to be as sure as possible that he is really sorry. Yet, as has already been said earlier, it is not necessary to show signs of emotion, such as sobs and tears. Contrition is, first and foremost, an act of the will, and may be quite

genuine even though it is not manifested violently. It is far more important to *be* sorry than to *feel* sorry.

(2) It must be a *supernatural* sorrow, as one elicited with the help of divine grace, and as deriving from a supernatural motive that relates in some degree to God. A merely natural motive is insufficient, and Innocent XI condemned the proposition that "It is probable that natural attrition is sufficient, so long as it is morally correct".[5] Natural motives would be, for example, the fear of imprisonment, inflicted for moral faults, or the misfortunes consequent upon such a penalty. Among supernatural motives might be mentioned fear of punishments to be inflicted *by God*, the supernatural turpitude of mortal sin and the loss of any hope of an eternal reward.

(3) The sorrow must be *supreme* in so far as the penitent should persuade himself that sin is the greatest of all evils, and be willing to bear anything rather than offend God. It is not required that the motives proposed should necessarily excite the most intense and vehement sorrow which surpasses in intensity all other sorrows. St Thomas explains: "However small the sorrow may be, provided it suffices for contrition (i.e. sin is detested above all other evils) it cancels all guilt."[6] But it must be supreme, because, as the Council of Trent says: "The will to sin is excluded by it," and that cannot be effectively brought about, unless sin is truly regarded as the worst of all evils. This is far more important than any visible signs of emotion. It is always possible that one who is not easily given to tears or sighs may grieve more deeply and interiorly than a more emotional type of sinner.

(4) Finally, sorrow must be *universal*, that is, it must extend to all mortal sins, whether remembered or forgotten, so long as they remain unforgiven. It is not strictly required, though it may be useful at times, that the sinner should go over in his mind separately all the mortal sins he may have committed,

[5] Decree of Holy Office of March 4th, 1679 (Denz. 1207).
[6] *Supplement* to the *Summa*, qu. 5, art. 3.

but he must have a universal sorrow that excludes no sin or category of sin from its range.

In regard to *venial* sins, it is not absolutely necessary that contrition should extend to all venial sins. The reason for this is that venial sins do not destroy friendship with God, and there is no strict obligation to confess them. Nonetheless, if the penitent has nothing but venial sins to confess, he must have true sorrow for one, at least, of them, or else for some sin of his past life already confessed; otherwise absolution would be given in vain, in default of any proximate matter for absolution.

THE PURPOSE OF AMENDMENT

The purpose of amendment is neither a mere wish without any relation to practice nor a strict promise or vow to avoid all sins. There are times, no doubt, when a confessor might demand a promise, if he were uncertain of the penitent's sincerity in regard to his intention not to sin again or to avoid an occasion of sin. There are two sorts of "purpose" in this sense. One is explicit and formal, and is a special act distinct from the act of contrition. The other is implicit and virtual, and is contained in any serious act of contrition, which has reference not to the past alone, but to the avoidance of temptations in the future. In this country we end our usual act of contrition with the words: "And I firmly resolve with the help of thy grace never to offend thee again, and carefully to avoid the occasions of sin."

At least an implicit purpose of amendment is required as part of any valid confession. It is as necessary as contrition itself for the absolution of mortal sins. So it has been held that contrition has two offices to fulfil—it must detest and be sorry for past sins, and it must guard in advance against any future sins. The fact that a man is sincerely sorry for the sins he has already committed implies that he will do his best to guard against any repetition of them in the future.

Just as an implicit purpose is necessary, so it is now morally certain that it is sufficient. In practice most penitents who are genuinely sorry will, at some time or other during their preparation for receiving the sacrament, have firmly decided to avoid sin from that time onwards.

The qualities of a good purpose of amendment are three in number; it must be firm, efficacious and universal. Its firmness has regard, in the first place, to the present. It may still be firm, even though it has not been fully tested as regards the future. What is needed is a firm resolution, *here and now*, to sin no more. It is not required that the penitent should be fully persuaded that, in fact, he will never sin any more. The absence of such a conviction does not prove that the penitent is in any sort of despair about leading a good life. It only proves that he has had experience of his own weakness in the past.

Secondly, the purpose of amendment must be *efficacious*, defined as "that which produces, or is intended to produce, the desired effect". In order to achieve this result the penitent must, in the first place, be ready to take the means necessary for avoiding sin in the future, such as prayer, watchfulness and mistrust of self. Secondly, he must be prepared to avoid any occasions of sin that might lead him to fall a second time. Lastly, he must be able and willing to make good the harm that may have resulted from his sin. So, for example, a thief must be ready to give back the goods that he has stolen. The efficaciousness of the purpose of amendment is related to the present time; the penitent should have here and now the intention of avoiding not only sin but all that may lead him into sin.

Thirdly, the purpose of amendment must be *universal*, for it must cover *all* mortal sins without exception. If it so happens that the penitent has only venial sins to confess, he must, nonetheless, have a purpose of amendment in their regard, since this, like true sorrow, is required for the validity of the rite. He may decide (a) to avoid all mortal sins (and this is, of course, obligatory, where mortal sins have been confessed); or (b) to avoid at least one venial sin; or (c) to shun some particular kind of sin; or (d) all deliberate venial sins; or (e) to reduce the number of venial sins committed.

Confessors of repute have suggested that it is possible for a penitent to spend overmuch time in confessing his venial sins in great detail, and yet to be less anxious about the need for avoiding sin in the future. Even as regards venial sins, the sinner should be prepared to take the necessary means to avoid them. The fact that, in the future, he may relapse into these sins does not imply that, here and now, his intention to sin no more has been anything less than fervent and sincere.

It is not uncommon for good and conscientious people to ask for advice when, as they think, they have formed no explicit purpose of amendment. In such cases it is usual to advise them not to repeat their confessions, since it is extremely probable (to say the least) that they have in reality made some resolution of the kind, even though they have not adverted to the fact at the time, or no longer remember it. As has been said already, it is far from certain that an explicit purpose is required, however useful and salutary it may be.

CHAPTER VI

THE MATTER OF THE SACRAMENT: CONFESSION

WHAT IS CONFESSION?

By confession we mean "the accusation that a man makes of his own sins to a priest, with a view to receiving absolution". There are some distinctions to be established such, for example, as that between confession made to a priest in private (sometimes also called *auricular* confession, since it is "told privately in the ear"), and public confession, at which, it is conceivable, people other than the priest and the penitent might be within earshot. There is also a distinction to be made between a *generic* confession (not to be confused with a *general* confession, which is a term far better understood), in which sins might be mentioned in a way that avoided the particular, and a *specific* confession, in which sins are mentioned according to their number and species. Again, a specific confession may be either integral or non-integral. In an integral confession all mortal sins are manifested that have been committed since baptism and that have not yet been forgiven through the power of the keys. They are, moreover, mentioned according to their number and species, at least in so far as this is reasonably possible.

OBLIGATION TO CONFESS

This will be treated more fully in a later chapter, apropos of the necessity of confession. Meanwhile, it may be said briefly that, according to Catholic teaching, it is divinely ordained that all mortal sins must be confessed according to their number and various kinds. There are exceptional circumstances, as in danger of death, when for good reason sins may be confessed only in part, or even confessed generically, not specifically.

Two canons of the Council of Trent have special importance here. These are the sixth and seventh:

> If anyone shall deny either that sacramental confession was instituted or that it is required for salvation by divine right; or shall say that the method of confessing privately to the priest alone, which the Catholic Church has always observed from the beginning, and [still] observes, is inconsistent with Christ's institution and command, and that it is a human invention, let him be anathema.

> If anyone shall say that for the forgiveness of sins in the sacrament of penance it is not necessary by divine command to confess each and every mortal sin . . . along with the circumstances which change the species of the sin . . . let him be anathema (Denz. 916, 917).

The chief argument from Scripture is based on the words: "Whose sins you shall forgive...." If, as we believe, the sacrament of penance is mediated to men by a judicial process, and forgiveness is normally conferred under certain conditions, it should be clear that the minister of the sacrament is obliged to know accurately what mortal sins have been committed, and how far the sinner is really sorry for them. Otherwise, no sure judgement can be passed on the penitent's state of mind and soul. It is not enough to know the penitent and his *general* dispositions; it is essential that there should be a full disclosure, at least of all previously unconfessed mortal sins, according to their number and kind.

TRADITION AND CONFESSION

The Church's tradition is represented, in the first place, by the Council of Trent's declaration in the fifth chapter on penance that: "The Church universal has always understood that Christ, when he instituted the sacrament of penance ... instituted as well an integral confession of sins, and that such confession is necessary, of divine right, for all who have fallen after baptism" (Denz. 899).

We have studied in an earlier chapter quotations from the *Didache*, St Clement of Rome and other early writers, indicating that some form of confession of sins was required. More detail is provided in Tertullian's two treatises already mentioned, and in the works of the great Alexandrian doctor, Origen (*c*. 185–*c*. 254), who refers many times in his writings to the institution of penance. Thus in his second homily on Leviticus (No. 4) he writes: "There is a seventh way of finding forgiveness, albeit a hard and laborious one—the remission of sins through penance, when the sinner ... does not blush to indicate his sin to the priest, and to ask for a cure."

In another passage (taken from his commentary on Ps. 37, Hom. II, p. 6), in which he urges the sinner to choose a confessor with care before deciding to let the sin become known to the Christian community as a whole, the important clause is: "Follow his advice if he foresees that your malady is one that ought to be made known and healed in the assembly of the whole Church ... this calls for much deliberation and very prudent judgement on the part of that physician."

This is important for its recognition that, even in the third century, the confessor's task was regarded as one calling for experience and skill.

St Cyprian, bishop of Carthage, in his treatise *On the Lapsed*, pleads with his readers to make their confessions while there is still time. "Let each one confess his sin, while he who has sinned is still in this world, while his confession can still be heard, while satisfaction and forgiveness conceded through the priests are still acceptable to God."[1] The Catholic Church, as is well known, has continued to emphasize the

[1] Cf. Fr M. Bévenot, S.J., "Ancient Christian Writers", xxv. *St Cyprian, The Lapsed* (London, 1957), ch. 29, p. 36.

importance of internal sins, even where these have not been manifested in word or action, and St Cyprian refers expressly to these sins of thought in a slightly earlier passage in the same treatise. He has in mind those who have not lapsed, either as sacrificers to idols or even as *libellatici*, but who have contemplated apostasy, at least as something that could happen to them, and presumably with full consent to the thought. He implores them, because they have even contemplated such a crime, to make a full and sincere confession, cast off the load upon their minds, and seek out a salutary medicine for their wounds (Bévenot, *op. cit.*, ch. 28, pp. 35–6).

Lactantius, the celebrated author of the *Divinae Institutiones* (Bk. 4, c. 30), writes: "But because each individual assembly of heretics thinks that its members are Christians, and that it is the Catholic Church, it should be known that the true [Church] is that in which there is confession, and penance, and which healthfully cures sins and wounds."

Aphraates (Afrahat), the oldest Syrian Father of the Church, who flourished in the first half of the fourth century, declares: "Let him who is assailed by Satan not be ashamed to confess his fault, to abandon it, and to beg for penance as a remedy. He who is ashamed to show his wound, will be attacked by gangrene . . . but he who does not blush to exhibit his wound, will be healed." (From *Demonstratio VII de Paenitentia*, No. 3.)

St Augustine, the greatest of the Latin doctors, in his sermon *On the Usefulness of Penance* (No. 351) exhorts one who has committed grave sin after baptism to "come to the bishops (*antistites*) by whom the keys are ministered to him . . . and to accept the measure of his satisfaction from the stewards (*praepositis*) of the sacraments, so that, if it seems to the bishop to be expedient for the good of the Church, he will not refuse to do penance in such a way that it will be generally known to the community". We may find here a proof that in the west (as in the east, as Origen's second extract shows) private confession would precede the solemn penitential discipline that was administered in public.

These witnesses, and others that could be cited, prove that the early Church insisted upon the need for confession of grave sins, and did not exclude grave sins of thought from the sphere of penance, even though it is uncertain whether the full penitential discipline took cognizance of sins of thought.[2]

The patristic quotations also go to show that the early Church would not have distinguished, as did at least one excellent non-Catholic in recent years, between the mortal sins that the penitent might decide to confess, and those that he might prefer to keep to himself. They would not have agreed that it was helpful, but not wholly necessary, to confess *all* mortal sins. In other words, the Church's teaching about the need for integral confession of mortal sins would have had the fullest support in the early centuries, and the Fathers would, no doubt, have accepted the Tridentine ruling that a penitent is bound to confess the mortal sins that he has not previously confessed and that are to be discovered after a diligent examination of conscience. It is true that, at times, material integrity is impossible, but there must be at least an intention of confessing as fully as may be, and with all necessary details, and of supplying any omissions at some later date.

THE PUBLIC ADMINISTRATION OF PENANCE

Confession, as has already been remarked, can be either public or private. The latter is now the universal rule throughout the Church, and privacy is also the rule for the whole discipline, which includes the absolution and the giving of the penance for the temporal punishment due to sin. It is certain that public penance is not, by divine command, necessary,

[2] On St Cyprian's attitude in the treatise *On the Lapsed* (ch. 28), cf. Palmer, *Sources . . .*, p. 49, n. 2, referring to the Council of Neo-Caesarea (*c.* 320) which waived any public penance for those guilty of impure desires.

but it is also true that the Church could always sanction public penance now as she did in the past, and for certain persons and in particular circumstances might *demand* it.

In the chapter on "Baptism and Penance" in his admirable work *The Early Liturgy to the Time of Gregory the Great*,[3] Fr Joseph Jungmann, S.J., has stressed the proofs that the Church has, from the beginning, always exercised her powers in the sacrament of penance, but he goes on to show that throughout Christian antiquity the sacrament was sparingly administered, and only in the case of grave and public sins, of the kind mentioned by St Paul in Gal. 5. 21, where the apostle comments: "I warn you, as I have warned you before, that those who live in such a way will not inherit God's kingdom." A grave sin calling for public penance carried with it a form of excommunication, an exclusion in part or in whole from the Christian community. It is, as Fr Jungmann notes, a matter of controversy whether, in the fourth or fifth centuries, there was a chance of a less solemn term of penance to be administered for less serious sins and, above all, for secret offences.

In the west there was a form of penance that seems to have been throughout of much the same type. Fr Jungmann distinguishes three phases in the process:

(1) The sinner confessed his sin to the bishop (or priest) in private, and then, if the sin was sufficiently grave, was excommunicated in the course of a public rite. For so grave a sin he was cast out of the community, in the sense that he might not share its full life (but the punishment was medicinal in character, that is, it was designed to bring him to full repentance and forgiveness), and was enrolled among the penitents. We have already referred to the graded discipline in the Churches of Asia Minor (p. 43), but in the west there was, it seems probable, only one degree, that of penitent. It seems too that the period of penance was shorter than in the east, but, by way of compensation, the penitents laboured under

[3] London, 1960, pp. 249 ff.

various disabilities, even after reconciliation with the Church. They were not allowed to undertake military service, on the ground that St Paul writes that: "The soldier on service ... will refuse to be entangled in public affairs" (2 Tim. 2. 4). They were warned to shun all litigation; they could not take part in the public games. They might not engage in trade. One who had been a penitent was not permitted to marry, and if he was already married, might not have marital relations with his wife. No wonder that the index to Watkins' *A History of Penance* gives a reference (under the ambiguous heading of "Disabilities in the after life") to a passage which claims that: "Alike from St Siricius and from St Leo we learn the disabilities which were yet to dog his [the reconciled penitent's] footsteps, and to hamper his action to the grave" (I, p. 429).

(2) The penitents regularly accepted a special blessing from the bishop that was given whenever the latter was present at a function. The time at which the benison was conferred varied. In the east it was given after the lessons, following which the lower grades of penitent had to leave immediately. In North Africa the blessing took place before the Communion in the Mass; in Rome after the Communion, at which the penitents assisted in silence, and were not, of course, allowed to receive the Eucharist. The purpose of this blessing was to assist them to spend their time of penance more fruitfully, and, in the end, to attain to repentance and forgiveness.

(3) The last and most important of the three stages was reconciliation with the Church at the end of the period, when the penitents were brought back into full communion with the *ecclesia* by a rite that was not merely a lifting of the ban, but a sacramental absolution from sin. By declaring that the penitent had been reconciled, the bishop also absolved him.

THE GELASIAN SACRAMENTARY

In Rome the reconciliation took place on Maundy Thursday, and we find an account of the rite in the *Gelasian*

Sacramentary, which contains a series of prayers going back, in some part at least, to the sixth century or earlier.[4]

The *Ordo agentibus publicam poenitentiam* (Order for those doing public penance) begins by stating that on this day there is no singing (i.e. of the introit of the Mass) and that the salutation *Dominus vobiscum* ("The Lord be with you") is not uttered. Another rubric orders:

> *The penitent comes forward from the place where he has performed his penance, and is presented in the bosom of the Church with his whole body prostrate upon the ground. And the deacon makes request in these words* (addressed to the bishop):
>
> Venerable Pontiff, the accepted time is come, the day of divine appeasement, and of human salvation, in which death has been annihilated, and eternal life has received its beginning, when in the vineyard of the Lord of hosts a planting of fresh roots is so to be effected that the care of that which is old may be cleansed. . . . On the one side there is joy in the reception of those who are called; on the other gladness in the absolution of the penitents. . . . As he thus supplicates and with afflicted heart beseeches the mercy of God, restore in him, O apostolic pontiff, whatever is ruined by the cleavage of the devil. . . .
>
> *After this* [says a further rubric] *he is admonished by the bishop, or by some other priest, that what he has washed away by penance he may not call back by a repetition of the offence. After this the priest says these prayers over him.*

There follows a series of seven prayers, some of which may, it seems, be alternatives, though this is not stated. The last of the seven contains all the elements of a form of absolution:

> Holy Lord, Almighty Father, Eternal God, look down upon this thy servant who has been overwhelmed by the hostile tempest of this world, and now with tearful lamentations acknowledges his excesses in such a manner that thou wilt

[4] Cf. H. A. Wilson, *The Gelasian Sacramentary* (Oxford, 1894), pp. 63-8.

mercifully accept his prayers and groans, and bring him back from darkness to light, and grant to him who confesses a remedy, to the penitent salvation, and to the wounded a healing antidote. Let not the enemy have power over his soul any more, but, freely accepting his confession, restore him purified to thy Church, and bring him back to thy altar, so that, admitted to the sacrament of reconciliation he may deserve to give thanks with us to thy holy name. Through our Lord Jesus Christ. Amen.

This concludes the rite of reconciliation as it is found in the *Gelasian Sacramentary*, but some prayers follow which are to be used for reconciling a penitent in the hour of death. The editor of the sacramentary suggests that these prayers, together with one that is intended for use after reconciliation or after the penitent has communicated, may have been joined to the form for use on Maundy Thursday "on the principle of bringing material of the same kind together" (*op. cit.*, p. 68, n. 1). The first of these additional prayers, which begins in the Latin with the words *Deus misericors, Deus clemens . . .* , occurs in the present "Order for the recommendation of a departing soul" immediately after the prayer *Proficiscere, anima christiana* ("Go forth, Christian soul"), which itself follows the short litany for the dying. There are one or two quite unimportant variants, but the prayer is all but identical in the *Sacramentary* and in the modern *Roman Ritual*. Here is the translation of *Deus misericors*, as it is found in the appendix to the 1915 *Ordo administrandi sacramenta*:

O merciful and gracious God, O God, who according to the multitude of thy mercies blottest out the sins of such as repent, and graciously remittest the guilt of their past offences, mercifully regard this thy servant N., and grant him a full discharge from all his sins, who with a contrite heart most earnestly begs it of thee. Renew, O merciful Father, whatever has been vitiated in him by human frailty, or by the frauds and deceits of the enemy; and associate him as a member of redemption to the unity of the body of the Church. Have compassion, O Lord, on his sighs, have compassion on his tears; and admit him, who has no hope but thy mercy, to the sacrament of thy reconciliation.

None of the few short rubrics that accompany the Gelasian rite of penance mentions any imposition of hands by the bishop or priest who carries out the office. Hence Watkins (*A History of Penance*, I, p. 429) goes so far as to claim that: "There is no direct evidence that the laying on of hands was employed in the great annual solemnity for ordinary penitents." Yet, two centuries or so before the *Gelasian Sacramentary* makes its first appearance, St Innocent I (402–17) had ordained that converts from Arianism should be received after the manner of penance "by means of the sanctification of the Spirit through the imposition of the hand".[5] A generation or so later St Leo the Great (440–61) supposes the existence of such a rite when he decides that priests or deacons who have fallen into grave sin are "not to receive an imposition of the hand as the remedy of penance for some crime of theirs".[6] It is, to say the least, unlikely that a practice so firmly established should have been omitted in later centuries. It is more likely that the laying on of hands was so familiar a rite as to call for no rubric on the subject. It survives in an attenuated form at the present day, when the confessor is instructed by the rubric "to raise his right hand towards the penitent" while he pronounces the words of absolution.[7]

PRIVATE PENANCE

"Historians are generally agreed", writes Fr Palmer, "that the practice of private and recurrent penance as the normal discipline for all classes of sinners is to be traced to the Irish Church of the sixth century."[8] If this position were accepted

[5] Cf. Palmer, *Sources* . . ., p. 113.

[6] *Epistle* 167 (to Rusticus). Palmer, *Sources* . . ., p. 118.

[7] *Rituale Romanum*, Tit. III, cap. 2: *Deinde dextera versus poenitentem elevata, dicit.* . . .

[8] *Sources* . . ., pp. 139–40: "The Celtic and English discipline."

by all writers on penance it would put an end to a controversy that has never been one of supreme importance, and has tended to generate more heat than light. The earlier pages of this chapter have emphasized the general rule of only one penance for grave sin committed after baptism and, allowing for the privacy of the confession, this discipline was administered in both east and west by the type of expulsion from the community described, which was followed, when expiation had been made, by a reconciliation with the Church. The rite given in the *Gelasian Sacramentary* is a notable example of this discipline. It must again be insisted that, so far as the evidence goes, there was only one penitential discipline, at any rate in all but exceptional circumstances, and it could never be said that the penitent had, at any rate normally, a "soft option" in the form of a relatively mild alternative discipline that took place entirely in private. Yet Fr Joyce, S.J., in an article already cited on "Private Penance in the Early Church" has claimed that, if public penance had been "imposed for every serious fall", we should be "forced to suppose that a very large proportion of the faithful were living under sentence of excommunication" (p. 29).

One of the available rejoinders to an argument of this kind is that, in fact, the penitential discipline was, in general, extremely severe, and that one result of this was a widespread tendency to postpone the rite, despite all the obvious dangers of delay, until the time of death. We have noticed already the prayers for "the reconciliation of a penitent at the hour of death" that have somehow become attached to the normal rite in the *Gelasian Sacramentary*. The prayer *Deus misericors*, now used in the Roman rite as part of the commendation of a departing soul, has clear reference to the "sacrament of thy reconciliation" which suggests that the formula may have been the deathbed equivalent of the normal penitential rite. Fr Jungmann rightly explains that, in the period from the fourth to the sixth century, there may have been *for cases of occult sin* a private or semi-private administration of penance. This, however, is a controversial issue. What is certain is that "the faithful themselves suffered from this difficulty [of having no facile alternative to public penance] and tried to escape its consequences" (*op. cit.*, p. 248).

A widely accepted alternative to penance in the fourth century was the postponement of *baptism*, and many members of Christian families remained in the condition of catechumens until the end of life. We are all aware that Constantine the Great was not baptized until he was on his deathbed, and some of the Fathers of the Church remained in the state of catechumens until they had long outgrown their youth. St Augustine was brought up as a Christian, was marked with the sign of the cross and enrolled among the catechumens. When he fell sick in his youth he asked for baptism. "However," writes Fr E. Portalié, S.J., "since the danger quickly disappeared, it was put off, in keeping with the deplorable custom of that time."[9] He was thirty-three before he received Christian initiation. Among the eastern Fathers St John Chrysostom did not receive baptism until he was twenty-five, St Basil until he was twenty-six and St Gregory of Nazianzus until he was twenty-eight.

These two arguments (from the frequent postponement of penance and baptism) may be said to be decisive against the existence of any *readily available alternative* to the severe penitential rite.[10]

[9] Cf. *A Guide to the Thought of Saint Augustine* (London, 1960), p. 6.

[10] The effect of extreme severity may be studied in a note to Mgr F. Vincent's *S. François de Sales, directeur d'âmes* (Paris, 1923), p. 281, n. 1. The author quotes from a book by Mgr d'Hulst, *La France chrétienne devant l'Histoire* (Paris, 1896), p. 671: "Cardinal Guibert (1802–86) when he was a young priest of the Oblates of Mary was entrusted, together with one of his colleagues, with the duty of preaching a mission in the suburbs of Barcelonnette [Basses-Alpes], but the jurisdiction he received for confessions from the bishop (Mgr Miollis) was accompanied by numerous reservations,

It should be added, in all fairness, that the champions of a late development of private penance (as distinguished from private confession, which was the general practice) have grossly overworked the argument from silence. The nearest modern equivalent to the old penitential system is an occasional mass-reception of converts. If this took place on a large scale it is more than likely that our Catholic papers would give some prominence to the event, whereas the ordinary quiet work of the parochial confessors in their respective confessionals would pass quite unnoticed. It is always possible that, in the early Church, there was, at least in certain localities, some form of private penance which has escaped adequate mention in the contemporary documents. In an age such as the present, in which so many long-buried records of the past have come to the surface, it would be idle to deny that, at some future date, more light may be thrown upon a subject which, at the time of writing, is still decidedly in the dark.

As regards secrecy about the actual sins confessed one may conjecture that, though the confession itself was private, the faults of those who were subjected to public penance must, in the smaller communities at least, have been fairly well known, the more so if many of these faults were of a public and scandalous nature. Perhaps the severity of the penance imposed may not have been the only reason why so many of the faithful shrank from undergoing the penitential routine.

What was the attitude of the Church of the first centuries

applicable, among other cases, to the following: the sin of drunkenness, *all forms of dancing,* lending money at interest and, in general, habitual relapse into former mortal sins. All penitents who found themselves in one of these categories were obliged to seek absolution from the bishop in person, and for this purpose they had to traverse a mountainous *département.* Can one be astonished, after this, that religious practice was soon everywhere on the decline?" Mgr Vincent comments: "So, in full nineteenth century, a bishop affected by Jansenism classed dancing not merely as a mortal sin, but also as a reserved sin."

towards recidivists (which is the technical term for those who relapsed, who had been through the canonical rite once and had then fallen again into their former sins)? In the "Summary and Appraisal" at the end of his fine collection of *Sources of Christian Theology* (Vol. II), Fr Palmer has considered various solutions that have been offered, and himself decides in favour of the theory that a recidivist was denied any further opportunity of public penance, so that he remained unreconciled throughout the remainder of his active life, but that he was reconciled privately (assuming, no doubt, that his dispositions were wholly adequate) when death seemed to be approaching. Fr Palmer admits that there is no direct documentary evidence for this, but concludes that "after Nicaea, the attitude of the Church towards the dying, as reflected in the writings of Innocent I, Celestine I and Leo the Great, was such that only the most rigorist of bishops would actually refuse to reconcile a dying recidivist who showed signs of true repentance" (p. 381).

THE CHANGE FROM PUBLIC TO PRIVATE PENANCE

What picture should we have in our minds of the gradual change from public to private penance, which began in and after the sixth century? It is generally allowed that this change was initiated by the work of Irish monks, who preached and gave the sacraments in various churches on the continent of Europe. Owing partly to the isolation of the Celtic churches the faithful had never been accustomed to a public, official penance of the kind so widely prevalent in the mainland churches of east and west. The Celtic type of penance was distinguished from the more normal type by being simpler, somewhat less rigorous and, above all, private; it could also (a great concession) be received more than once in a lifetime. Confession to a priest was sufficient, and the intervention of the whole community was not required. Yet the penitential works imposed by the confessors were substantially the same as those in other churches, and did not err on the side of leniency. Two interesting features of the system were that the penance was, at times, commuted into some other good work, and that occasionally it was also "redeemed" by the payment of a sum of money to be devoted to charitable purposes. The second feature, as might have been foreseen, led to numerous abuses, and the richer sort of penitent was in a position of advantage, when it came to availing himself of "redemption" in this rather special sense.

The development of the system of private penance on the continent, which in its origin was available side by side with the older, public system, was, as might have been expected, less well received in some churches than in others. In Spain, which, as the decrees of the Elvira council prove, was a stronghold of rigorism for half a century or more after the other continental churches had become more lenient, there was resistance to the more recent practice. In France, on the other hand, the system of private penance gained ground fairly rapidly.

One of the features of private penance that only gradually established itself was connected with the moment when reconciliation to God and the Church was granted. At first, the standard practice, as in the public rite, was to defer reconciliation until the whole of the penance had been carried out. Later, in some churches, exceptions were made for invalids or the dying, and a provisional reconciliation was granted after confession, with the condition attached that the penance must be carried out in the event of recovery, and that this would be followed by a further reconciliation ceremony. It was not until the eleventh century that it became customary to grant absolution *immediately after* the confession, which, as in our modern practice, allowed the penance to be performed later.[11]

[11] Cf. P. Anciaux, *Le Sacrement de la Pénitence,* 2nd ed. (Louvain, 1960), pp. 80–93.

CHAPTER VII

THE MATTER
OF THE SACRAMENT:
SATISFACTION

MEANING OF SATISFACTION

Satisfaction, the third element in the matter of penance, is defined by the *Oxford Dictionary* as "the performance by a penitent of the penance enjoined by his confessor, as payment for the temporal punishment due to sin". Its more general meaning is some sort of compensation which, if it is concerned with material things, such as the giving back of goods that have been stolen or damaged, is known as *restitution*, whereas if there is question of compensation for an offence or an injury done to another, it is satisfaction properly so called. Since sin is the greatest injury that man can offer to God, satisfaction is designed to compensate for an injury done to the divine majesty. And since man of himself cannot hope to offer any adequate satisfaction to God for sin, a vicarious satisfaction needs to be offered by one who is capable of such an offering. In the treatise on the Incarnation the question is answered: Was the coming of the Incarnate Lord really necessary? The answer is that it was necessary in the hypothesis that God demanded a full and adequate reparation for sin, and that Christ our Lord could and did offer to the Father a reparation that was not merely abundant, but superabundant.

The fullest definition is that which can be assembled from

the data provided by the Council of Trent. Satisfaction is *the voluntary acceptance or endurance of the penance imposed by a confessor, in order to compensate for the injury offered to God, and for the remission of the temporal punishment that may still remain, even after the guilt of the sin has been pardoned.* In so far as it forms a part of the sacrament of penance it is styled sacramental satisfaction, and should be determined by the confessor as part of the rite. Moreover, for the remission of the temporal punishment, it is fitting that the penance given should be both good, and also, in some degree, painful or laborious.

Numerous errors have been formulated regarding satisfaction. Whoever affirms that the *whole* of the temporal punishment is *always* remitted at the same time as the guilt, must necessarily deny the value of satisfaction. So we find that, on August 9th, 1479, Sixtus IV condemned the proposition of Peter of Osma :"Mortal sins, as regards both the guilt and the punishment in the next world, are blotted out by contrition of heart alone, without confession" (Denz. 725). The chief opponents of the doctrine of satisfaction were the reformers, notably Luther and Calvin, who contended that no punishment remained after the forgiveness of sins, or justification, whereby Christ's own justice was imputed to men.

THE CHURCH'S TEACHING

The Church in her definitions on the subject first of all attacked the basis of the reformers' teaching by ruling that the *whole* of the temporal punishment is *not* invariably remitted when the guilt of the sin is forgiven. Further, she maintains that satisfaction is a true part of penance, and is indeed one factor in the sacrament's quasi-matter. Again, the minister of absolution is not entitled to waive the sacramental penance for his penitents or to follow his own inclination in this respect; he should impose a salutary and fitting penance, according to the nature of the sins confessed and the dispositions of the penitent (Denz. 905). Lastly, it is the Church's teaching that, in addition to the penance assigned by the priest in confession, and such voluntary good works as we may undertake, we should patiently endure any temporal afflictions sent to us by God, and thus obtain satisfaction for our sins (Denz. 906).

The chief teaching on satisfaction in the pronouncements of the Council of Trent occurs in chapter 8 of the "Doctrine on the sacrament of penance", entitled: *Satisfaction; its necessity and value* (Denz. 904–905), in which it is decreed that "In the matter of satisfaction the holy Synod declares that it is wholly false and inconsistent with the word of God [to maintain] that the guilt of sin is never forgiven by the Lord without his condoning the entire punishment as well" (Denz. 904. Cf. also 922, 925). The Council points to "clear and manifest examples" in Holy Scripture that disprove this error. Such is the teaching of Gen. 3. 16 ff., according to which Adam and Eve, though later restored to grace, are made subject to death and other afflictions on account of their sin. In Num. 12. 14 ff., it is taught that Moses' sister, Miriam, gained forgiveness for her offence, but was shut out of the camp for seven days. Num. 20. 11 ff. proves that Moses is punished for his lack of trust by being excluded from the land of promise. One could add to this 2 Kings 12. 7 ff., where we are informed that David's sin with Bethsabee is forgiven, but that he is to suffer misfortunes, and the child of his sin is to die. These and other passages go to show that Christ has not suffered for us in such a way as to relieve us of all the obligations of suffering in our own persons, so that St Paul insists upon our privilege of suffering with our Lord, that so we may "help to pay off the debt which the afflictions of Christ still leave to be paid, for the sake of his body, the Church" (Col. 1. 24). An alternative rendering, that of the Westminster Version, reads: "Now I rejoice in my sufferings on your behalf, and make up in my flesh what is lacking in the sufferings of Christ, on behalf of his body, which is the Church."

The authorities are divided about the exact interpretation of these "sufferings of Christ" in regard to which St Paul strives to make up in his flesh "what is lacking". Some think that the expression refers to the sufferings Christ endured during his mortal life, in order to found the kingdom of God. Under this aspect Christ's sufferings are of infinite value, and nothing can be added to them by any one of his followers. It is, however, the work of all in union with Christ to help to apply those sufferings, and the merits resulting from them, to human beings in every age. Other writers prefer to interpret them in terms of the afflictions which Christ continues to undergo in the members of his mystical body. St Augustine speaks of "that total passion of Christ, who has suffered in so far as he is our head, and who suffers still in his members, that is to say in us".[1] It is in this sense that we may interpret Pascal's well-known phrase: "Jesus will be in agony until the end of the world." The late Fr Léonce de Grandmaison, S.J., has expressed this teaching in his commentary on this Pauline text: "This is the basis of it all—to sacrifice oneself, as did Jesus, in order that Jesus' sacrifice may be of profit to many. To sacrifice oneself with Jesus, in order that his love may triumph in many; to have that very great love which lies in giving one's life for one's friends, without any other reward or joy than the eternal love of Jesus, Son of God, the first Love made man."[2]

The witness of the Fathers supports this doctrine. Tertullian, St Cyprian, St Ambrose and St Augustine are cited on its behalf. Hence Trent has rightly defined that this is a truth contained in the deposit of revealed teaching. The proofs from Holy Scripture and tradition are confirmed by the Church's doctrine of purgatory. In addition to the purgation of unforgiven venial sins, and what theologians call the "remains of sin", i.e. the weakness and ineptitude left in us as a result of sin, the purgatorial fires cleanse the temporal

[1] On Psalm 61 (Migne, *P.L.*, 36, 731).
[2] *Ecrits spirituels* (Paris, 1933), I, p. 159.

punishment due to sins, whether mortal or venial, that have been forgiven.

A further confirmation of this dogma of satisfaction is the Church's practice of giving a penance *even when the sins confessed have already been directly forgiven*. This supposes that not all the temporal punishment due to sin is always remitted with the guilt. Hence Trent rules that works of penance are imposed "not for the eternal punishment, which is remitted with the guilt of the sin, either in the sacrament or with the intention of receiving the sacrament, but for the temporal punishment which, as Holy Scripture teaches, is not always wholly discharged" (Denz. 807; Session VI, ch. 14, on Justification).

WORKS OF PENANCE

In its fourteenth canon on penance (Denz. 924) the Council anathematizes the aberration that "satisfactions, whereby sinners redeem their sins through Jesus Christ, are not the worship of God, but human traditions, which obscure the doctrine of grace, and the true worship of God, and the very benefit of Christ's death". Given that there sometimes remains a temporal punishment to be suffered, should this penalty be expiated by suffering, in purgatory or in this life, or can it also be cancelled by voluntary satisfaction? It would not be unthinkable that God might refuse to accept such voluntary satisfaction; actually he does, at times, arrange that some afflictions should be undergone *in*voluntarily in this life. We can, however, make expiation in the present life for the temporal punishments that may remain to be undergone in purgatory. There are texts of Scripture that encourage this belief that works of mercy, almsgiving and the like have the effect of cleansing, redeeming and purifying from sin, even though the distinction between the guilt of sin and its temporal punishment is not always underlined. So the prophet Daniel consoles Nabuchodonosor of Babylon with the words: "Deign, my lord king, to be advised by me; with almsgiving, with mercy to the poor, for fault and wrongdoing of thine make amends; it may be that he will condone thy guilt" (Dan. 4. 24). Joel writes: "Yet, even now, saith the Lord, turn ye unto me with all your heart, and with fasting, and with weeping, and with mourning" (2. 12, Revised Version). And St John the Baptist bids his hearers: "Bring forth, therefore, fruits worthy of penance" (Luke 3. 8, Douay Version).

God would assuredly not command these works of penance if they were without purpose or effect and, since the temporal punishment is part of the liabilities of sin, we may expect that works of penance will help towards the removal of this incubus.

All that has already been said about the severe penitential discipline in the first centuries goes to prove that it was sincerely believed, then as now, that the discipline did, indeed, make reparation for sin, and for the pains and penalties attaching to sin.

BENEFITS OF SATISFACTION

The eighth chapter of the Council's "doctrine on penance" enumerates four fruits or benefits of satisfaction (Denz. 904).

(1) Satisfaction brings home most efficaciously to the penitent that sin is the greatest of evils, and worthy of tremendous penalties.

(2) It renders the sinner more cautious and vigilant, so that he is less likely to fall again into sin.

(3) It is a remedy for the "remains of sin" and helps to eradicate bad habits of sin that have been acquired; it is not primarily vindictive in its effects; it is medicinal.

(4) It makes us like to Christ who is the "atonement made for our sins" (1 John 2. 1), since we have a most sure pledge that: "If we suffer with him ... with him we may also be glorified" (Rom. 8. 17, Westminster Version).

One may add that, whereas satisfaction that is unconnected with the sacrament of penance produces its effect only *ex opere operantis* (or according to the dispositions of the repentant sinner), satisfaction that is part of the penitential order has its effect *ex opere operato* i.e. from the very fact that the sacrament has been validly administered.

THE CONFESSOR'S DUTY

The guiding principle here is that the confessor certainly may, and normally should, oblige the penitent to carry out some penitential work. Not only has he the power of binding as well as that of loosing; as God's minister he should act in conformity with the ways of divine providence which inflicts temporal punishment after the guilt has been forgiven. By omitting to assign a penance he may deprive his penitent of some of the great benefits that sacramental absolution brings with it.

It is generally agreed that there is a grave obligation to impose a penance if mortal sin, not already directly forgiven, has been confessed. As regards a now moribund dispute about the corresponding duty where venial sin or mortal sin already remitted has been confessed, all the authors agree that works of satisfaction should normally be required of any penitent who is capable of carrying them out.

The normal *time* for allocating a penance is before the absolution has been pronounced, since the penitent should accept the penance imposed upon him as one sign among many that he is worthy to receive God's forgiveness through the sacrament.

The *amount* of the penance is to be estimated according to the number and gravity of the sins confessed. In the early Church, as we have already noted, the penances imposed were usually severe and of long duration. Nowadays the tendency is, as it has been for a considerable time past, to give far lighter penances. The rule of thumb is that a penance may be reckoned a grave one, if it would oblige under mortal sin in the event of its being commanded by the Church on some other count. Thus a grave penance would be to hear Mass, to- fast for a day, or to recite the five decades of the rosary or the litany of the saints with the accompanying prayers.

On his side the penitent is obliged to accept the penance, and, having accepted it, to carry it out. Indeed, the intention of accepting the penance is linked up with the validity of the sacrament, since satisfaction is a part of the quasi-matter of penance. The actual fulfilment of the penance need not take place before absolution, and the opinion that the fulfilment should precede absolution has been rejected by the Church, apropos of Peter of Osma's dictum "If the penance has not been fulfilled, the penitents ought not to be absolved" (Denz. 728).

CHAPTER VIII

THE FORM OF THE SACRAMENT

THE WORDS OF THE FORM

By the form of the sacrament we mean the words used by the priest in absolution that complete the whole sign by specifying, as clearly as possible, the minister's intention to confer the sacrament and forgive sin. It is not at all uncommon for non-Catholics to consult a Catholic priest and to make what, so far as concerns the matter, is a confession of sins, which is usually accompanied by genuine sorrow, and by the will to carry out any obligations that a confessor might impose. Yet in many instances a "confession" of this kind cannot be completed on the confessor's side by the grace of absolution. A non-Catholic, however well disposed towards the Church of Christ, is not, in normal circumstances, a subject for sacramental forgiveness. A number of Catholics also, though they may make what has all the appearance of a confession of sin, are not, for one reason or other, able to receive absolution. Again, there are Catholics who make full disclosures to a priest without asking for absolution. They come to the priest for advice and guidance, but it is always possible that this desire is in regard to sins that have already been directly forgiven in some previous confession.

By way of contrast, the giving of absolution in the form sanctioned by the Church implies that the priest is acting not merely as a spiritual father and a director, but as a judge. He is saying in effect: "I have heard your story. I am satisfied that you are really sorry and that you wish to make a complete and sincere avowal of your sins, and to carry out any penance that may be suggested to you. Now, having reached this point, I am able to give you absolution, and so to make you a sharer in the Church's commission to forgive sins."

In the Roman rite the complete form of absolution is as follows:

May Almighty God have mercy upon thee, and, having forgiven thy sins, may he lead thee to eternal life. Amen.

May the almighty and merciful God grant to thee pardon, absolution and remission of thy sins. Amen.

May our Lord Jesus Christ absolve thee; and I by his authority absolve thee from every bond of excommunication [of suspension] and of interdict, as far as I can, and you have need of it. *Therefore, I absolve thee from thy sins, in the name of the Father, and of the Son, and of the Holy Ghost. Amen.*

May the Passion of our Lord Jesus Christ, and the merits of the Blessed Virgin Mary and of all saints, whatever good thou hast done and whatever evil thou hast borne, avail thee for the remission of sins, the increase of grace and the reward of eternal life. Amen.

This somewhat lengthy form contains a few words that are essential, and many others that are so far from being essential that they may be omitted for good reasons. Thus it is agreed that the only part of the form that may not in any normal circumstances be left out is the third prayer beginning: *May our Lord Jesus Christ absolve thee....*

WHAT IS ESSENTIAL?

The Councils of Florence (Denz. 699) and Trent (Denz. 896) have defined that the form of the sacrament consists essentially in the words *Ego te absolvo,* etc. ("I absolve thee"). All writers are agreed that a sufficient form of words is *Ego te absolvo a peccatis tuis* ("I absolve thee from thy sins"), which adequately expresses the minister's action (*I absolve*), the subject in the word *thee* and the matter in *from thy sins.* It is, in fact, probable that the forms "I absolve" or "I absolve thee" are valid forms, but there can never be any real excuse for using them, since one may not employ in conferring a sacrament a form that is only probably valid.

In cases of necessity, such as occurred in both world wars, when large numbers of troops were about to go into action, and there was no time to hear many, if any, individual confessions, a priest may validly and lawfully give a general absolution in the words: "I absolve *you* from *your* sins, in the name of the Father, and of the Son, and of the Holy Ghost." Some older readers may recall a striking painting entitled "The Last Absolution of the Munsters" which portrayed the regimental chaplain seated on horseback, his purple stole upon his neck, at the moment when he was conferring absolution on great masses of men in full battle-kit, who were about to take part in some combined assault, from which many did not return alive.

In case of extreme necessity for the individual it is permissible to use the short form: "I absolve thee from all thy censures and sins, in the name of the Father," etc.

It has already been stated that in the Roman rite the priest is instructed to raise his right hand in the direction of the penitent from the beginning of the second prayer ("May the almighty and merciful God grant thee pardon . . .") until the sign of the cross has been made at the end of the third prayer. This is not a rubric binding under sin, but it is recommended as a suitable reminder of the former imposition of hands that was employed in the ancient penitential rite. For its fuller significance it is better that the palm of the hand, and not merely the little finger, should be turned towards the penitent.

MANNER OF ABSOLVING

Four points are here to be emphasized, not all of them of equal importance.

(1) The absolution must be given orally, and not in writing, or by the use of signs. Hence a priest who is entirely dumb cannot validly absolve. The will of Christ, as interpreted by the Church, is that the form of the sacrament should be expressed *in words*. This is one of several ways in which the sacraments of penance and matrimony differ radically, since the form of the latter may be validly expressed by signs.

(2) Absolution can only be given to one who is morally present, and this means, according to the teaching of St Alphonsus Liguori, that he must not be more than twenty paces distant from the confessor. In case of extreme necessity (such as that of a man who is falling from a roof at a considerable distance away) this moral presence may be interpreted broadly. This question of distance is one that sometimes arises in the ordinary life of an average parish where it is not uncommon for a penitent to leave the confessional before the priest has had time to give him absolution. On such occasions it is often possible to recall a penitent to the confessional, or, failing this, to absolve him, as he moves away from the confessional, while he is still within the prescribed distance. It is not essential that the confessor should be able to see or hear him.

Pope Clement VIII by a decree of June 20th, 1602 (Denz. 1088), condemned the proposition that a confession might be made in writing or through an intermediary in the absence of the penitent, and that absolution might be given in such circumstances (i.e. with the penitent still absent). This ruling does not prevent a penitent from sending a written statement to the confessor in advance, and from later accusing himself in a general way in the presence of the confessor, who already knows the details from the letter. This is an altogether different situation from that condemned by Clement VIII. It does not involve a confession made by a penitent who is absent, or absolution given to him while he is still absent.

Except in case of extreme necessity it is forbidden to give absolution by telephone or by means of a speaking tube, but it is not clear that absolution given in this way would be certainly invalid. Everything depends here upon what it meant by being morally present, and it has been plausibly argued that, if the penitent and his confessor can be said to converse audibly, they may fulfil the condition of being present one to the other.

Is it necessary to add that a certain popular novelist, whose works have been translated into English, is in error if he really believes that a priest can transmit sacramental absolution by telegram?

(3) Except for grave reasons to the contrary, the form of absolution should be used *absolutely*, and not conditionally. Conditions have regard to the past, the present or the future. Apart from one special and rare instance in regard to matrimony, it is never lawful, when administering a sacrament, to make any condition regarding the future. In regard to the past or the present, it is sometimes permissible to give absolution conditionally. The point here is that cases arise where to give absolution *un*conditionally might expose the sacrament to the danger of invalidity, whereas to withhold forgiveness altogether would be to put the penitent in danger of grave spiritual harm. Nearly all theologians are agreed that there are times when conditional absolution could and should be given, since the confessor cannot be morally certain that the penitent is in a condition to receive the sacrament fruitfully. In such cases the ultimate decision must be left to God, and the confessor must do his best to safeguard both the reverence due to the sacrament and the spiritual good of the penitent. It has been argued, at any rate in the past, that the three sacraments that give a character to the soul (baptism, confirmation and holy orders) are always conferred subject to the implicit condition that they have not been previously received. Penance does not resemble these three sacraments in being unrepeatable, but here too one may detect an implicit condition—that the penitent is in a state validly to receive absolution. It is not essential that the condition should be expressed in words, but

it is permissible to use before the essential words of the form some such phrase as *Si capax es*, "If thou art capable" (of receiving the sacrament).

The issue of conditional absolution may arise in a variety of ways. It may, for example, be uncertain whether a penitent is alive or dead, or whether a child or a mental defective has sufficient use of reason. Sometimes, after all due inquiry has been made, a doubt persists about a penitent's sorrow for sin and firm resolution to amend his life.

(4) A problem that has now lost most of its actuality, at any rate in practice, is whether the form used should be (as in the present Roman rite) indicative, so that the priest says "*I* absolve thee", or in the form of a prayer ("May our Lord Jesus Christ absolve thee ..."). It is frequently argued in the west that the personal or indicative form is more appropriate to a judicial process, where a judge should speak in his own name. This point about the judge's use of the first person is not invariably true, at least in England. No judge in our English criminal courts says (unless absentmindedly) "I sentence you ...". The form is always: "The sentence of the Court is ...", and the Court consists of not less than two persons, normally the judge himself and the clerk of assize.

It is admitted that for the first ten centuries there is no trace of an independent indicative form; all the forms that have survived are deprecative. We have already seen some instances of this in the *Gelasian Sacramentary's* rite of public penance. The Roman Pontifical in its long form of reconciliation, borrowed in part from the Gelasian and earlier rites, has an *absolutio* in which the bishop prays:

> May he [our Lord Jesus Christ] by my ministry absolve you through the intercession of his precious blood, poured forth for the remission of sins, from all your sins, whatever you have done negligently in thought, word or deed, and may he be pleased to lead you, absolved from the bond of sin, to the kingdom of heaven.

In the eighth and ninth centuries we meet with formulas that are imperative joined to the deprecative, as in the penitential of Egbert, Archbishop of York (*c*. 732): "Mayest thou be absolved by God, Father, Son, and Holy Spirit, from all thy sins," which is a command rather than a simple prayer.

From the eleventh century there is, in the Roman rite, a transition from the deprecative form to the indicative form, as in a certain penitential that adds to the deprecative form the following: "We, by the authority committed to us by God, unworthy as we are, absolve you from every bond of your offences."[1] There is, it would seem, no proof that the indicative form, unaccompanied by the deprecative, was in use in the west before the eleventh century.

In the eastern Churches the more common form, even at the present day, is the deprecative. Thus in the *Euchologion* published by the Congregation of Propaganda in Rome for use by the Melkite Greeks, the first of the formulas provided runs: "Trusting in the words of the Saviour *Whose sins you shall remit* . . . , I presume to say: All that thou hast confessed to my very poor littleness, and all that thou hast not been able to say, whether through ignorance or through forgetfulness, God pardons thee in this world and in the next."

After this there follows a prayer in two parts. In the first part the priest, without making any allusion to his own absolving power, recalls the pardon granted to St Peter, to the woman who had been a sinner and to the publican. In the second part he speaks of the pardon conceded to these three sinners, and also to David and the prodigal son. He proceeds: "May God likewise pardon thee through me, both in this world and in the other; may he cause thee to appear free from condemnation before his terrible judgement-seat. Be not anxious about the sins thou hast confessed. Go in peace!"

No proof is forthcoming that the Church has ever sought to *impose* other formulas of an indicative type upon eastern Christians, though Goar in the *Euchologion* mentions a form

[1] *Magna Bibliotheca Patrum* (Köln, 1618), t. viii, pp. 423 f.

of this kind that was designed for the Italo-Greeks of Sicily, Calabria and Apulia.

By contrast, the archpriest Alexis von Maltzew, the translator into German of the Russian liturgical books, supplies a personal or indicative form of absolution, which, like the form in use in the Roman rite, is combined with a deprecative form.

> May our Lord and Saviour Jesus Christ absolve thee by the merciful grace of his love from all thy sins, my son N. And I, his unworthy priest, by virtue of the authority given to me also absolve thee, and declare thee to be delivered from all thy sins. In the name of the Father . . .

A comparison of this form with the third, and essential, prayer in the Roman Ritual shows, or seems to show, a distinct family likeness between them.[2]

One may summarize the position by saying that, unless it could be argued that many, if not all, of the absolutions given before the eleventh century were invalid, it must be admitted that the deprecative form was a valid one for many centuries, and remains a valid one in most of the eastern Churches, whether Catholic or dissident. Some theologians express a doubt whether the same form would be valid (it would certainly be *illicit*) if used in the Roman rite, but arguments in support of such a distinction may be judged to be precarious. Fr Galtier is in favour of validity.[3]

---

[2] A. von Maltzew, *Die Sakramente der orthodox-kathol. Kirche* (Berlin, 1898), p. 219. Cf. S. Salaville, *Introduction to the Study of Eastern Liturgies* (London, 1938), p. 67.

[3] *De Paenitentia,* p. 458.

CHAPTER IX

THE EFFECTS OF THE SACRAMENT OF PENANCE

RECONCILIATION WITH GOD

The most cheering and glorious effect wrought by the sacrament of penance is reconciliation with our creator and last end. This is made perspicuously clear in the third chapter of the Council of Trent's "Doctrine on the sacrament of penance", determined in its fourteenth session (November 25th, 1551) with the sub-title "The parts and effects of penance" (Denz. 896). The whole chapter should be read again and again; it may be called the sinner's Magna Carta. After defining in the first half of the chapter the essential form of the sacrament, and the quasi-matter or parts of penance, the decree continues:

> In regard to the power and efficacy of this sacrament, the reality (*res*) signified and its effect are, quite certainly, reconciliation with God. For pious people who receive this sacrament with devotion there may well follow at times peace and serenity of conscience, joined with ardent spiritual consolation.
>
> While transmitting this doctrine on the parts and effects of this sacrament the holy Synod, at one and the same time, condemns the opinions of those who maintain that the parts of penance are the terrors of an agonized conscience, and faith [i.e. in the reformers' sense of trust in Christ's righteousness, which allegedly is imputed to us].

For those in a state of mortal sin the primary effect of this sacrament is what is called the first grace, or habitual grace, or sanctifying grace, which brings with it remission of sins. This grace has been described, with a view to promoting a better understanding of its purpose, as the grace of *resurrection*, in so far as it results in the raising of the spiritually dead to the life of grace; or of *healing*, because by it, with the sinner's willing cooperation, the wounds of sin are cicatrized and cured; or of *reconciliation*, since, by the action of divine grace, the injury and insult to God's majesty are repaired, and man is restored to the happy state of friendship with the Most High.

To this essential grace of reconciliation there is added the right to actual graces to be received in due season, whereby the penitent may make satisfaction for past sins, and may avoid sin in the future. At one and the same time the eternal punishment due to sin is remitted and the temporal punishment owing to sin is, at least, diminished. Finally, the merit of previous good works that has been lost by sin is now renewed and restored.

For those who have *not* lost sanctifying grace, at any rate since their last confession, the sacrament brings with it an increase of this same grace, together with an increase of actual graces. It makes the remission of venial sins easier and more complete, and it effects at least a partial cancellation of temporal punishment.

PENANCE FORGIVES SIN

We are frequently reminded by Holy Scripture that true repentance will be rewarded by forgiveness. Ezechiel (18, 21–22) has a striking passage which declares: "It may be that the wicked man will repent of all his sinful deeds, and learn to keep my commandments, and live honestly and uprightly; if so he shall live on; life, not death for him. All his transgressions shall be forgotten, and his uprightness shall bring him life." The earlier verses of this chapter in Ezechiel are a protest against the proverb: "The fathers used to eat sour grapes, and the children's teeth are blunted" (the sense of the

Hebrew in Jer. 31. 29). Contrariwise, man *can* change his conduct and reform his way of life. In this sense Origen writes on John 19. 14: "Those who are in ignorance and unbelief and sins can come to a state of incorruption, if they change, and such a change is possible."

Even better known is a verse of Isaias (1. 18, in G. B. Gray's version): "Though your sins were like scarlet [robes], they might become white as snow; though they were red like crimson, they might become like wool." It was to this end that Christ, as we have already explained, bestowed the power of forgiveness without limitation: "*Whose soever sins you shall remit. . . .*" For the forgiveness of mortal sins the sacrament is required at least in desire and intention; as for venial sins, the Council of Trent reminds us that "they can be expiated by many other means" besides the sacrament of penance (Denz. 899).

It is, moreover, of faith that penance, in so far as it is a virtue or an act of virtue, is so necessary that, according to God's ordinary laws for men, no sin, whether mortal or venial, can be forgiven without it. It is not a question here of God's absolute power, but of his will in the present order of things. The reason given by St Thomas (*Summa Theol.*, III, qu. 86, art. 2) is that mortal sin, being an offence against God, is to be forgiven in the same way as other offences are forgiven. But offences demand for their forgiveness some degree of sorrow, and some truly inward change of will, by which the will is turned away from whatever caused the offence. Now it it possible, says St Thomas, for a man to forgive someone who has offended him without demanding any change of will on the part of the offender. This is not possible (according to his ordinary providence) for God, in so far as mortal sin implies a turning away from God and towards some created thing. Hence, the will of man must be changed and turned again towards God; man must detest his former aberration and have a true purpose of amendment.

In so far as the sacrament of penance is concerned, God

can forgive sin without the instrumental action of the priest in absolution, as he forgave the woman taken in adultery and the woman who had been a sinner, though here, too, he did not forgive in the absence of the virtue of penance.

This need of penance applies even to venial sin, which will not be remitted without some degree of sorrow. For this, it is taught, *virtual* penitence will be sufficient, and this may be operative in a variety of ways, such as asking for pardon of sin, practising the virtues that are contrary to the sins committed, or carrying out acts of other virtues with the intention of winning pardon of sin (*Summa Theol.*, III, qu. 87, art. 3).

PENANCE FORGIVES ALL SINS

This thesis has already been underlined when we considered the power of the keys in Holy Scripture and in tradition. The sacrament of penance, when administered to those who are really penitent, can and does take away all sin. So there is no such thing as an irremissible sin, though there may be sinners who are unwilling to repent.

It follows that one mortal sin cannot be forgiven without the simultaneous forgiveness of all other mortal sins that have been committed and that have not, so far, been submitted to the power of the keys. The reason for this is that through the sacrament of penance sanctifying grace is poured into the soul. Now any mortal sin is wholly opposed to sanctifying grace and *cannot coexist with it*. Further, mortal sin cannot be forgiven without true sorrow, and sorrow of this kind must extend *to all sins hitherto unforgiven*, if it is to be in any way genuine or effective. This, almost needless to say, does not prevent a man from being more than ordinarily sorry for some particular sin or type of sin, provided he also has genuine sorrow for all his sins, and not merely for some of them. The older Samuel Butler's couplet (*Hudibras*, I, c. 1, lines 213–14) concerning those who

> Compound for sins they are inclined to
> By damning those they have no mind to,

has no application to the Catholic doctrine of repentance and forgiveness.

The Council of Trent repudiates the reformers' teaching that penance consists merely in preaching the gospel of repentance, and that the priest's absolution does no more than "declare and pronounce" (in the words of the Book of Common Prayer) that sin has been or can be forgiven. The Church teaches that the sacrament of penance, in common with the other six sacraments of the new law, produces its effects *ex opere operato*, from the fact that the rite has been validly performed, and that this effect is produced definitively, so that neither the guilt of the sin, nor the temporal punishment cancelled in part or whole through the sacrament, will be caused to return by any subsequent sin.

THE REVIVAL OF MERITS

Question 135 of our Catechism asks: "Will faith alone save us?" to which the answer is given: "Faith alone will not save us without good works; we must also have hope and charity." Theologians are accustomed to distinguish four classes of works, which are styled respectively living works, dead works, mortiferous (or death-dealing) works and mortified works. *Living* works are those that are performed under the influence of divine grace and the infused virtues in the soul. *Dead* works are those which, though objectively good, are performed by those in a state of mortal sin.[1] *Mortiferous* works is another name for mortal sin, in so far as it works spiritual death in the soul. Finally, *mortified* works are those performed by one in a state of grace, but subsequently deprived of all their meritorious character by a lapse into mortal sin. As regards these four categories it is evident that *living* works do not need any reviving; *dead* works, in the sense here defined, cannot revive, since they have no principle of life in them; *mortiferous* works are not revived by penance, but may be

[1] "Dead works" in this sense are not to be confused with those in Heb. 6. 1 and 9. 14 where they are the equivalent of "sins".

said to be themselves done to death by it; *mortified* works which were originally carried out in a state of grace, even though the merit attaching to them has been impeded by sin, can and do revive or recuperate when the sinner has received the grace of absolution.

This last proposition is not regarded as part of the deposit of faith, but it is entirely certain and is accepted by all theologians. Several passages in Scripture suggest that a restoration will take place after sin has been forgiven, but they do not say anything explicit about the revived merit of good works. In Ezech. 33. 12 it is said: "As for the wickedness of the wicked, he shall not fall thereby in the day that he turneth from his wickedness" (Revised Version), and in Joel 2. 12, 25 the prophet declares: "Yet even now, saith the Lord, turn unto me with all your hearts, and with fasting and with weeping and with mourning . . . and I will restore to you the years that the locust has eaten," where the primary reference is to renewed temporal prosperity, though this may also stand for spiritual abundance and fruitfulness. St Jerome makes use of the latter text against Novatian, when he writes: "What answer will Novatian give, he who denies that penance exists, and that sinners can be transformed into their pristine state, if there be suitable works of penance?" (*Commentary on Joel* 2). It must be confessed that the reference here is, in the first place, to the possibility of repentance after even the gravest sins.

Nothing has been explicitly defined by the Church on this subject, but Trent in its decree on justification (Sixth session, January 13th, 1547, ch. 16; Denz. 809) says: "The words of the Apostle are to be set before men who have been justified, whether they shall have kept without interruption the grace they have received, or shall have recovered that which was lost: *Stand firm, my beloved brethren, . . . since you know that your labour in the Lord's service cannot be spent in vain*" (1 Cor. 15. 58).

The reason given for this revival is that, in accordance with all we know of the divine mercy, works which have once been good, meritorious and acceptable to God should always remain so, unless some serious obstacle should impede them. It is true that mortal sin is an obstacle of this sort, but it is taken away by absolution. Therefore, if the sin has been remitted, the merits that have accrued before the lapse into sin may be recovered.

So much is generally accepted, but the degree in which the merits lost through sin may be recovered is a matter of much debate. Are the merits restored in full, as the great Jesuit theologian, Suarez, contended? Or is the restoration something that depends upon the present dispositions of the penitent, or on what might be styled the existing level of charity and penance to be found in him at the moment when he recovers the grace of God? These are the main positions adopted by the authors, but there are some other views that depend upon rather fine distinctions and cannot be elaborated here. It may be said with confidence that the opinion championed by Suarez is the most kindly one, and the one that gives the widest scope to God's abounding mercy. It appears to find some support in the Tridentine teaching (Denz. 799) that all the good works of a just man merit eternal glory, provided that he dies in a state of grace; therefore, it is argued, the good works that have been "mortified" and then revived, may be said to merit their own proper degree of glory. It is unnecessary, therefore, to enter into any calculations regarding the exact degree of charity and penitence at the moment of rehabilitation.

This deduction from Trent's teaching has some traditional backing in the jubilee Bull promulgated by Pius XI, on May 29th, 1924, which is quoted in very small part in the recent editions of Denzinger's *Enchiridion* under the heading "The revival of merits and gifts".[2] Pius XI teaches that those who fulfil the conditions for gaining the jubilee indulgence, among

[2] Bull *Infinita Dei misericordia*, Denz. 2193. The excerpt is taken from the *Acta Apostolicae Sedis*, 16 (1924), p. 210.

other heavenly gifts, "procure again (*reparant ex integro*) and acquire that abundance of merits and gifts which they have lost by sinning". It is not astonishing that the opinion associated with Suarez is the one more commonly held by theologians at the present day. Yet this is not to say that the many other opinions on this topic may not be freely held and taught in the Catholic schools.

FORGIVENESS OF VENIAL SINS

The Fathers of Trent have already been quoted for the statement that, whereas the forgiveness of mortal sin calls for the sacrament or for perfect contrition with the desire of the sacrament, venial sin "can be expiated by many other means" (Denz. 899). Yet the fact must not be overlooked that venial sin requires a supernatural remedy, and that, as the second Council of Orange (589) declares in its fourteenth canon, by way of a quotation from St Prosper of Aquitaine (*c.* 390–*c.* 463): "No wretched man can be freed from his misery, of whatever size it may be, unless he is forestalled by the mercy of God" (Denz. 187). In other words, even venial sin most assuredly cannot be remitted by man's natural powers. Nor can actual grace alone remit venial sin in one who is not already justified and admitted by habitual grace to supernatural friendship with God. It follows that venial sin which is conjoined with mortal sin in a human soul cannot be remitted by actual grace, but needs habitual grace, the supernatural life of God in the soul.

In one who is already justified venial sin, since it is not a privation of grace, does not demand for its forgiveness any new infusion of sanctifying grace. Since, however, venial sin implies some inordinate affection for creatures, there is required a supernatural impulse of charity or penitence, which is the result of actual grace. This impulse, by which the contrary impulse towards creatures is suppressed, implies a true interior change of heart, under the influence of actual grace. It is clear, then, that no merely natural impulse can take away sin, whether that sin be mortal or venial.

It has already been said that, for the remission of venial sin, a fresh infusion of sanctifying grace is not required; an act proceeding from grace suffices, whereby the penitent detests the venial sin either explicitly, or at least implicitly, by a fervent turning to God. Hence it is maintained that venial sin can be forgiven in three ways. (1) By an inpouring of sanctifying grace; and so not only penance but all the sacraments of the new law remit venial sin. (2) In so far as there is some impulse of detestation of sin. Thus, among various means of forgiveness, one may mention general confession of sin, and the recital of the words *Forgive us our trespasses* . . . in the Lord's prayer. (3) By way of an impulse of reverence towards God and the things of God, which includes virtually an act of sorrow for sin. Under this heading may be included a bishop's blessing, sprinkling with holy water and the use of other sacramentals approved by the Church.

To summarize what has been explained here or elsewhere, it may be said, by way of premiss, that venial sin may be forgiven either extra-sacramentally or by means of the sacrament. *Extra-sacramentally*, the sin is remitted *ex opere operantis* by an act of contrition or of charity. Some kind of sorrow is always required; otherwise the will remains fixed, as it were, in its former attitude towards the sin. It is held that attrition is probably sufficient for the forgiveness of venial sins, in that these sins compared with mortal sin are less serious (though still detestable and to be avoided) and do not require for their pardon the same degree of contrition as is needed for the forgiveness of grave sin.

In the sacrament venial sin is forgiven *ex opere operato* (by the fact that the sacrament has been validly administered), provided there is no obstacle such as complacency in regard to the sin. This is certain in regard to baptism, penance and extreme unction, all of which have the forgiveness of sins as their proper *raison d'être*; it is probable in regard to the remaining four sacraments.

CHAPTER X

THE NECESSITY OF THE SACRAMENT OF PENANCE

BAPTISM AND PENANCE

It is not the purpose of this chapter to consider the necessity of confession as such in isolation. The issue here is the necessity of penance as a whole, first from the point of view of the sacrament as a means of man's salvation, and secondly in relation to the Church's practical rules for man's reception of this sacrament.

The Tridentine "doctrine of the sacrament of penance" condenses all the essential teaching into one short sentence: "This sacrament of penance is as necessary for salvation for those who have fallen [i.e. into mortal sin] after baptism, as is baptism itself for those not regenerate" (Denz. 895). Hence, in the Council's words both sacraments are necessary for salvation in their respective spheres of influence, though the subjects of the two sacraments differ in state. Baptism confers the first grace upon those not hitherto regenerate, whereas penance restores that grace to those who have lost it after baptism. It is determined, then, that both are necessary by the necessity of means of salvation, though this necessity is said by theologians to be a hypothetical or relative one. This means that in either sacrament, where it is impossible for the rite to be actually carried out, the desire or intention of receiving it, if present at least implicitly, may suffice. And as, after the baptism of desire, the obligation of receiving the baptism of water remains, so, even though a man has attained to perfect contrition with the intention of receiving the sacrament of penance, there still remains the obligation of submitting his sins to the exercise of the keys. This submission represents the redemption of the pledge that was offered at the time of his making his act of contrition.

There is a further likeness between the two rites, inasmuch as perfect charity always justifies an unbaptized person, even if he could actually receive water-baptism at that time. Similarly, perfect contrition, with the intention of receiving the sacrament of penance, always justifies a baptized Christian who has fallen into mortal sin, and not only in case of necessity.

The deeper theological meaning of this reconciliation with God is explained by St Thomas in his discussion of the effects of baptism (*Summa Theol.*, qu. 69, art. 1, in reply to the second objection):

> No redemption from sin can take place, except in virtue of the passion of Christ. Hence the apostle says in Heb. 9. 22: *Unless blood is shed, there can be no remission of sins.* So the effort of the human will, as it is found in the penitent, does not suffice for the remission of guilt unless there be present faith in the passion of Christ, and an intention of participating in it, either by receiving baptism or by submitting oneself to the power of the keys. And therefore, when an adult penitent comes to be baptized, he receives remission of all his sins by the intention of being baptized, but this is perfected by the actual reception of baptism.

In the sixth question of the *Supplement* to the *Summa* (art. 2) St Thomas resolves the problem whether confession is necessary by reason of the natural law. His conclusion is that: "Confession which is necessary as a sacrament, [obliges] by reason not of the natural law, but of the divine law." And in his answer to the first objection he distinguishes between confession made to God in acknowledgement of sin, which is imposed by the law of nature, and confession made to a man, in order to receive remission of sins from God, which is made obligatory by divine law.

EARLY TEACHING

This divine law is a positive one, in so far as it is comprised in Christ's will to institute a sacrament for the remission of post-baptismal sin, with the consequent duty of confessing one's guilt to a man acting as God's minister. So the necessity of penance as a sacrament is proved by reference to the terms of its institution by the Incarnate Word.

We have already seen that, from the beginning, in the New Testament writings as in the later tradition, the power of the keys and the need for the exercise of that power were clearly taught. This teaching was confirmed in practice in a variety of ways, such as the regulations made at an early date for the penitential discipline to be applied according to the seriousness of the sins admitted. Likewise many of the Fathers, while insisting upon the severe nature of the penitential rite, called upon the faithful to submit to it, in spite of any natural shrinking from so arduous a task. On their side, the faithful recognized the duty of seeking forgiveness of sins through the Church's ministry though, as we have seen, there was a tendency to postpone the reception of the rite until the hour of death. Both the rulers of the Church and their flocks betrayed great anxiety, lest any of the faithful should die without having received the Church's absolution.

THE SCHOLASTICS

Anything approaching a *speculative* discussion of this problem was postponed for some centuries, and is first apparent in the writers of the early scholastic period. Their teaching has been studied in painstaking detail, with copious extracts from rare and inaccessible works, by M. Paul Anciaux, now president of the major seminary at Malines.[1]

[1] *La Théologie du Sacrement de Pénitence, au XIIe siècle* (Louvain, 1949), p. 645.

M. Anciaux writes in his introduction that, before the rise of scholasticism, "the Church had simply lived on the richness of her sacraments, without attempting to enter deeply into their nature, or to determine their elements and their efficacity" (p. 3). She had always taught in her everyday life and practice that sins committed after baptism could be remitted by means of the discipline of penance. As regards confession itself St Anselm of Canterbury (c. 1033–1109), whose life was for the greater part lived in the eleventh century, speaks of the *sacramentum confessionis* (the sacrament of confession). St Peter Damian (1007–72) comes near to echoing Tertullian's language when he refers to penance as "the first plank after the shipwreck". The author of the work *De Vera et Falsa Poenitentia* (On True and False Penance) insists upon the need for confessing sins to a priest, because God has given to his priests the power of forgiving sins. Yet this last-named work does not claim that confession to a priest is absolutely necessary. In an emergency one may make an avowal of sins to a layman. Even though such a one has not the power of forgiveness, the fact of admitting the sin, together with the desire for absolution from a priest, is sufficient to make the penitent worthy of pardon. The idea of confession to laymen occurs much earlier in St Augustine's work *On Baptism*, and is met with again in some of the twelfth-century writers.

In spite of these exhortations, and the existence of many opportunities for shriving, confession was regrettably infrequent in this early period, and various councils speak of penalties to be inflicted on those who do not confess often enough and call upon the faithful to make their confessions at the beginning of Lent. But the law of obligatory confession within a stated period still awaited promulgation by the Fourth Lateran Council in 1215.

In the early twelfth century there are three names of particular importance among the scholastic writers. These are Peter Abelard (1079–1142), the Victorines (the school of Canons Regular attached to the abbey of St Victor in Paris, which included many famous authors) and Peter Lombard (*c.* 1100–60), the "Master of the Sentences", best known to students of sacramental theology as having been one of the first to maintain that there were seven sacraments, and to distinguish these seven from the sacramentals.

Peter Abelard

Of these, Abelard tends to exaggerate the importance of contrition among the three acts of the penitent that make up the quasi-matter. He considers that, given true penitence, the sin is remitted and the soul is no longer deserving of eternal punishment. From the moment when the sinner is prepared to confess his sin and to carry out the satisfaction allotted by his confessor, he is reconciled with God. True, even though he has attained to reconciliation, he is still bound to confess his sin and work out the satisfaction assigned to him but, in the context, this implies that confession is simply a complementary rite, which derives most of its value from its rôle in the remission of temporal punishment. This last theme is one that recurs frequently in later writers.

Hugh of St Victor

Abelard had many disciples, but his position in regard to penance was vigorously challenged by one of the greatest of the Victorines, Hugh of St Victor (*c.* 1096–1141), whose chief service to learning was that he "rescued the dialectic method from the discredit brought upon it by Abelard".[2] Hugh reacts against the theory that the priest does little more than officially declare that sin has been forgiven by sorrow. On the contrary, he claims, sin cannot be, as it were, shaken off by man's natural powers. Confession is needed, not only because it has been commanded by God and the Church, but because it is necessary as a means of salvation. God could, no doubt, have

[2] *The Oxford Dictionary of the Christian Church* (Oxford, 1958), s.v. "Hugh of St Victor", p. 663.

dispensed with human intermediaries but, in fact, he has chosen men as the ministers of his saving grace. Confession, then, is a proof of God's mercy, and priests are God's vicars and the soul's physicians. Satisfaction, when ordered by them, allows a sinner to escape all punishment in the future life.

Peter Lombard

Peter Lombard, in his turn, considered the questions to be decided under three heads. (1) Whether sin could be remitted without oral confession and exterior satisfaction, simply through the heart's contrition. (2) Is it sufficient, at times, to confess to God alone without any priestly intervention? (3) What, if any, is the value of a confession made to laymen? On the first point, he decides that sin may be forgiven without oral confession and exterior satisfaction, by contrition alone, whereby man is delivered from his sin and from eternal punishment. Most certainly confession must not be brought into contempt. It remains of obligation, and there can be no true penitence without the *will* to confess. Sin has, however, already been forgiven before confession has been made, as soon as the penitent makes up his mind to confess. On the second issue, Peter Lombard is concerned to reject any arguments that might seem to tell against the duty of confession. Once again, he repeats that it is obligatory. On the third question, he discusses St Bede the Venerable's opinion that only grave sins need be confessed to a priest. He holds that a sinner should confess his sins to a layman if no priest is available. Yet it is safer to confess even venial sins to a priest. Confession is a proof of humility, and gives the priest an opportunity for imposing a suitable penance.

It will be seen that Peter Lombard takes over, in some measure, the Abelardian teaching about the efficacy of contrition, but he also insists upon the presence of the will to confess, and for him confession is not the mere complementary rite envisaged in Abelard's minimizing hypothesis.

Alexander of Hales and Bonaventure

All these mighty men died not less than half a century before the Lateran Council of 1215. It is instructive to compare with their teaching that of two of the great Franciscan masters, Alexander of Hales (*c.* 1170–1245), and the seraphic doctor, St Bonaventure (1221–1274), of whom the latter was St Thomas's contemporary. Both of them were firmly committed to the doctrine of attrition as expounded by William of Auvergne (*c.* 1180–1245), who was himself fully convinced that the duty of confession derived from the very essence of the sacrament, in so far as the priest was called upon to pronounce judgement on the sinner, and so must be fully informed about the faults that had been committed.

It cannot be claimed that either Alexander or St Bonaventure held a wholly satisfactory theory about the forgiveness of sins in the sacrament. Like the twelfth-century doctors, but in a less challenging manner, they exaggerated the part played by contrition, which they regard as the cause by which the guilt of the sin and the eternal punishment are remitted. Confession, absolution and satisfaction serve to remit or diminish the temporal punishment. Both of them, nonetheless, insist upon the necessity of confession, for which, according to Alexander of Hales, there are three motives at work. (1) The binding force of Christ's precept in his institution of the sacrament. (2) The appropriateness of the avowal, since by it the sinner is reconciled with the Church. (3) Its usefulness, on account of its many salutary effects. He amplifies the last point when he writes:

> Confession makes known the malice of sin; by reason of the discomfiture it engenders, it makes up part of the satisfaction; it lessens the punishment, by virtue of the power of the keys; it increases the number of those who intercede for us; it contributes towards increase in grace and remission of guilt, because, if a man before confession is not duly contrite, he acquires sorrow in the course of the confession itself.

St Bonaventure does not merely echo the teaching of his master, but agrees with him in the main lines of his doctrine. Confession is exceptionally useful, and is necessary on account of the command given in the New Testament by the apostles and the Church (and in this context he adduces as a proof-passage James 5. 16: "Confess your sins to one another, and pray for one another, for the healing of your souls"). It is also necessary on account of the precept of annual confession established by Pope Innocent III at the Fourth Council of the Lateran. Apropos of the Council, St Bonaventure does not hesitate to rule that any denial of the necessity of confession, if the denial came after the Council's legislation, would clearly be heretical.

St Thomas's teaching on this subject has been already set out in the first pages of this chapter.

John Duns Scotus (c. 1264–1308)

For Scotus, the subtle doctor as he has been styled, who was a child of ten at the time of St Thomas's death in 1274, the duty of confession is, as St Thomas himself taught, imposed not by the natural law but by the positive divine law. It is binding upon all baptized persons who have come to the use of reason. The time at which confession should be made is fixed by the Church's law (which had been in full operation for nearly fifty years at the time of Scotus' birth). Venial sins do not come within the scope of the legislation. It is most useful to confess any circumstances that may aggravate the guilt of the sin. Unlike his predecessors among the scholastics, Scotus, as we noted in chapter VIII, regards the essence of the sacrament as being comprised in the form of absolution; the penitent's acts are integral, but not essential, parts of the sacrament.

THE FOURTH LATERAN COUNCIL (1215)

Having summarized the teaching of some, at least, of the greater scholastics on the necessity of penance, we must now pass to the Lateran decree of 1215. Here is the text of the operative clause, as it was finally settled:

> Let every one of the faithful of either sex, after having attained to the age of discretion, faithfully confess all his sins in secret (*solus*) to his own priest, at least once a year, and take pains diligently to carry out the penance enjoined upon him, receiving with reverence, at least at Easter, the sacrament of the Eucharist, unless perhaps, on the advice of his own priest, he decides that for a good reason he ought to abstain from its reception. Otherwise, let him be prevented from entering the church while he is alive, and be deprived, when death comes, of Christian burial (Denz. 437).

More than three hundred years later, the Council of Trent explained what was, and what was not, in the minds of the pope and the bishops who took part in the council of 1215.

> The Church, at the Council of the Lateran, did not in any way establish the precept of confession for the faithful, since she knew well that by the divine law this was necessary and was already in existence. She merely ordained that all the faithful, and each one in particular, should, on arriving at years of discretion, fulfil this obligation of confession at least once a year (Denz. 901).

This is, in effect, a disciplinary regulation, though it has a dogmatic basis in the necessity of penance and the Eucharist as means of salvation. No doubt this dogmatic substratum to the decree is what St Bonaventure had in mind when he was ready to tax with heresy one who denied the necessity of confession subsequent to the Lateran decree of 1215. As regards the actual limits assigned for the reception of penance and the Blessed Sacrament, it has always been understood that the Church could, at some future time, alter the existing conditions. So Suarez is quoted as writing that there is nothing to prevent the Church from deciding to impose the duty of confession less frequently, for example, at intervals of two or three years. It may be suggested, however, that the tremendous increase in the number of communions received, as a

result of St Pius X's legislation in 1905 on frequent communion, and in 1910 on the age for making the first communion,
together with the more recent rulings on the eucharistic fast,
make any lengthening of the period supremely unlikely.

HOW DOES THE LAW BIND?

The subjects of the law are all who enjoy the use of reason,
and have mortal sins to confess. Hence, the law does not
oblige complete imbeciles, children below the age of reason
and persons not conscious of mortal sin. In regard to the
third class, as they are not strictly bound to confess venial
sins, they cannot be forced to make their confessions before
receiving their Easter communion. It is true that St Thomas
was of the opinion[3] that even a man whose conscience was
free from mortal sin should, once a year, present himself to
the priest, not necessarily to make his confession, but in order
that the priest might be better informed about the spiritual
welfare of his flock. Nowadays, however, the law calling for
confession to the penitent's own priest has been altered, and
it is not strictly required that a man who has no more than
venial sin to acknowledge should appear before his priest
even once in the year. An author of high standing has declared
nonetheless that, if a man were not normally willing to confess
his sins at least once a year, there might well be something
unbecoming or even pernicious about his behaviour. In the
first place, he would undoubtedly deprive himself of many
graces, and more especially of those given in the sacrament
of penance. Again, it would be all too easy for such a man to
deceive himself about the distinction between mortal and
venial sin and, as we should say, to let himself off too easily.
Lastly it appears, to say the least, to be indecorous that one
who is habitually a prey to deliberate venial sin should, time
after time, present himself at the altar rails without having

[3] *Supplement* to the *Summa,* qu. 6, art. 3, in reply to the third
objection, and qu. 8, art. 5, in reply to the fourth.

done his best to free his soul from guilt. Doubtless it is possible, as the Council reminds us, to obtain forgiveness of venial sins in many other ways (Denz. 899). The question remains: Would one who refuses to make his confession even once in the year be likely to cleanse his conscience adequately by these other means?[4]

There is no absolute agreement among the authors about the exact reckoning of the time at which confession should be made from one year to another. Some have thought that the civil year, from January to January, should be the guide. Others reckon from Easter to Easter. Still others say that the year should begin from the moment when the first mortal sin may have been committed. Nowadays there is the all but universal custom of calculating from Easter to Easter, so that the faithful who follow the calendar in this matter do not offend against the law of annual confession, even if rather more than a calendar year elapses between one Easter confession and another, provided that each one falls within the current time for making the Easter duties. This period for Easter duties varies from country to country, according to the regulations laid down by the local hierarchies.

It is quite certain that a sacrilegious confession does not satisfy the law concerning Easter duties, and Alexander VII, on September 24th, 1665, condemned the proposition stating that "One who makes a confession that is deliberately invalid, satisfies the Church's command" (Denz. 1114).

WHEN DOES THE DIVINE PRECEPT BIND?

Apart from the times fixed by the Church's canon law, there are occasions when the divine law makes confession obligatory. The principal occasion for this is, undoubtedly, when death or danger of death threatens. At such a time it would be in itself a grave sin to neglect an opportunity for

[4] Dominicus Prümmer, O.P., *Manuale Theologiae Moralis* (Barcelona, 1946), III, sect. 361.

making one's confession *if* one were conscious of mortal sin not yet directly forgiven. There are some other occasions, such as the coincidence of a state of mortal sin and the will to receive communion, when confession becomes obligatory, because an act of contrition is then insufficient. Yet another occasion may well be a time of serious temptation which cannot readily be overcome without the aid of the sacrament of penance.

CHAPTER XI

THE MINISTER OF THE SACRAMENT

PRIESTS ALONE THE MINISTERS

Among the forty-one propositions from the works of Martin Luther that were condemned in the Bull *Exsurge Domine* of June 15th, 1520, the thirteenth is couched in these terms: "In the sacrament of penance and remission of guilt the pope or a bishop does no more than the least of all priests; moreover, when there is no priest, any Christian would serve as well, even if such a one were a woman or a boy" (Denz. 753). Doubtless the Tridentine legislators had this proposition in mind when they decreed in the tenth canon on penance (Denz. 920):

> If anyone shall say that... priests alone are not the sole ministers of absolution, but that to each and all of Christ's faithful it was said: *All that you bind on earth shall be bound in heaven, and all that you loose on earth shall be loosed in heaven* (Matt. 18. 18) and *When you forgive men's sins they are forgiven; when you hold them bound, they are held bound* (John 20. 23); and that in the power of these words anyone can absolve from sins, i.e. from public sins by correction only, if the one corrected shall acquiesce; but from secret sins by spontaneous confession, let him be anathema.

This canon gives in an abbreviated form the substance of the sixth canon of the fourteenth session, which goes on to condemn the heresies of Wyclif and the Waldensians, in so far as they denied that a priest in mortal sin could validly administer this sacrament. The Code of Canon Law (c. 871) briefly asserts: "The minister of this sacrament is a priest, and a priest alone."

This definition is held to be of faith when it excludes anyone not in sacred orders from being the minister of the sacrament. Fr P. Galtier, S.J., in his work *De Paenitentia*[1] considers it to be arguable that it is less clearly of faith that deacons cannot be ministers of the sacrament, and compares the Protestant error regarding the purely declarative power of the priest in absolution (which is clearly heretical) with the scholastic opinions, already discussed, which are not so obviously condemned, even though no Catholic would defend them at the present day.

BISHOPS NOT THE SOLE MINISTERS

The difficulties arising out of the thesis that priests alone are the ministers are: (1) The evidence that in the early Church, bishops alone seem to have administered this sacrament, and (2) various facts in the early centuries, and especially in the Middle Ages, which indicate that confessions were, at times, made to deacons, and even to laymen.

On the first point, there is no special guidance to be found in the words instituting the sacrament, but there are many clues discoverable in the Church's practice from the first ages. Doubtless, at the beginning, the bishop was ordinarily the minister of penance, as he was ordinarily the minister of baptism and the Eucharist but, from a very early date, there is proof that the *sacerdotes secundi ordinis*, priests who were not in episcopal orders, administered the sacrament of penance at least in times of emergency. We have already studied the first-century witness of St Clement of Rome, who advises the Corinthians: "Submit yourselves unto the presbyters," who, according to the more general opinion, were not

[1] Rome, 1950, pp. 462–3.

bishops. St Cyprian, in the third century, advises his flock during the Decian persecution not to postpone their penance until he himself would be with them; they should make confession of their crimes to any presbyter who may be available.[2] St Denis of Alexandria, who became bishop of that see about 248–9, is quoted in Eusebius' *Ecclesiastical History* (Bk. VI, 44) as writing about a certain Serapion, an old Christian who had defaulted by sacrificing to the pagan gods and wished to be reconciled. To that end he sent for "one of the priests" when he was at the point of death. The priest was unable to come in person, but sent Serapion a portion of the Blessed Sacrament by the hand of a child, and this the old man was able to receive just before his death. It is unnecessary to multiply quotations or references as evidence of the fact that those who are styled by the officiating prelate in our present service for the ordination of priests *cooperatores ministerii nostri* (fellow-workers in our ministry), fulfilled this duty from early times in the administration of penance.

CONFESSION MADE TO DEACONS

In the passage from St Cyprian's eighteenth letter that has just been quoted, he advises confession to a presbyter in circumstances which preclude the bishop's presence. He continues: "If a presbyter cannot be found and death is imminent, [confession should be made] even to a deacon, so that after the hand has been imposed upon them unto penance, they may come to the Lord with the peace which the martyrs, in their letters to us, have desired that we should grant them." Nor does this passage stand alone. In the thirty-second canon of the Council of Elvira (cf. pp. 43–4) provision is made for a deacon to take Communion to the sick if ordered to do so by a priest. It is argued that, in these circumstances, the deacon may have been expected to administer penance before giving the sick man Communion.

[2] Epistle, 18. Palmer, *Sources* . . ., p. 44.

In later centuries, more especially between the ninth and the thirteenth centuries, sundry collections of canons and local councils are quoted as giving leave to deacons, in case of necessity, to hear confessions, assign penances and admit penitents to Communion. Among regulations of this kind one may refer to Can. 56 of the synodal constitution of St Odo of Paris: "It is strictly forbidden for deacons in any way to hear confessions, except in the most extreme necessity (*in arctissima necessitate*); for they have not the (power of the) keys, and cannot absolve."[3]

Many explanations have been offered of these curious anomalies. Certain writers have even argued that deacons in the early centuries received some kind of special, though temporary, commission as regards penance. Others have reckoned the office performed as no more than the act of an intermediary, who could at least bring to a penitent formal reconciliation in the external forum from a bishop or priest who could not come in person.[4] St Denis of Alexandria, in the letter already mentioned above, gives no hint that the priest acted incorrectly in sending Communion to the aged Serapion by the hands of a small child. It would, perhaps, be more exact to say that, in case of necessity, where no priest could be found, a deacon did all that he could and that the Blessed Sacrament was sometimes administered without any absolution preceding the administration. St Thomas himself writes that, in case of necessity, the penitent should make his confession to any Christian who may be available, in the hope that, in the absence of a priest, the high priest, Jesus himself, will supply the defect. He adds that confession made to a

[3] Cf. P. Galtier, S.J., *De Poenitentia*, p. 467, who refers to Mansi, *Concilia*, XXII, p. 676.

[4] It may be recalled that Cardinal Reginald Pole, then in deacon's orders, in his capacity as papal legate absolved the English nation from censures incurred under Henry VIII and Edward VI, on November 24th, 1564. He was not ordained priest until the following March 20th, two days before his episcopal consecration as Archbishop of Canterbury.

layman is in some manner sacramental (*sacramentalis est quodammodo*), though imperfectly so, since the priestly ministry is wanting. (*Supplement* to the *Summa*, qu. 8, art. 2, reply to first objection.)

NECESSITY OF JURISDICTION

It is, then, established that none but a bishop or priest can validly absolve in the sacrament of penance. But for the full and valid performance of his ministry it is not sufficient that a man should be in priest's orders. He needs also the power of jurisdiction (defined as "the exercise of juridical authority"), and this power is not granted simply as a result of priestly ordination. The first part of this last sentence is of faith according to some, or is, at least, Catholic doctrine, not to be denied without error. Trent declares (Denz. 903) that: "The nature and very reason of a judgement demands that sentence should be passed only on those who are subjects." It has "always been the Church's conviction, and the Synod guarantees its entire truth, that an absolution is to be accounted of no value if it is pronounced by a priest over one in respect of whom he has neither ordinary nor delegated jurisdiction". (Ordinary jurisdiction is that which is annexed to a determined office, such as bishop, parish priest and so forth; delegated jurisdiction is that which is given on a personal title.) Later, Pius VI was to refer to Trent's ruling in his condemnation of one of the propositions of the synod of Pistoia (1786), which had attempted to champion the view that jurisdiction was not strictly necessary, but was merely suitable as a means of avoiding confusion between various parishes in a diocese (Denz. 1537, "On authority for absolving").

It is certain that the constant practice of the Church has been to commit the administration of penance into the hands of those who possess jurisdiction—the bishops in their dioceses, and the priests under their authority. A further reason given by Trent is that absolution, being a judicial process, can be exercised only over those who are subject to the judge's jurisdiction.[5]

ORDINATION NOT ENOUGH

That the exercise of the keys is not given simply by the fact of ordination is certain, but the explanations of the finding differ. There appears to be no good ground for holding that in ordination some special sort of jurisdiction is conferred, which is neither ordinary nor delegated, and which does not provide the holder of it with any subjects. More commonly, with St Thomas and St Bonaventure, it is accepted that no jurisdiction as such is transmitted in priestly ordination, and that therefore a priest does not possess the *exercise* or use of the keys before he is authorized by his bishop or his superior to hear confessions. St Bonaventure writes: "Jurisdiction is, as it were, the power that moves the key, i.e. the hand, and where that which moves the key is lacking, even if the key itself is present, it will never open [anything]; and if this jurisdiction is lost, the operation of the key ceases. . . . Therefore I say that, even if its existence (*quantum ad esse*) results from ordination, it follows upon status and jurisdiction in regard to its exercise."[6] The saint's reference to the existence (*esse*) of the power of the keys recalls two truths that must underlie all discussion. First, it would be beyond the power of Christ's vicar himself to confer power to absolve *sacramentally from sin* upon one who had not received priest's orders at some moment before he came to exercise the concession by actually giving absolution from sin. (It should be added that a man can, nonetheless, exercise very effective jurisdiction in

[5] In the Constance Kent murder trial (1860) the question arose how far her confession made to an Anglican clergyman was privileged. The presiding judge was prepared, he said later, to rule that "absolution was a judicial proceeding, and that a judicial authority could not be questioned as to the grounds of his decision" (*A Victorian Vintage* (London, 1930), pp. 105–6).

[6] Quoted by P. Galtier, *De Poenitentia,* p. 470.

a number of ways without having received the corresponding order. A simple priest elected to the papacy, as was Gregory XVI in 1831, has full jurisdiction over the Church from the moment of his acceptance of office, and not from that of his episcopal consecration.) Secondly, a newly ordained priest could in theory, however unlikely this might be in practice, be given jurisdiction by the Holy See to hear confessions throughout the whole world (this being, in fact, the first of the twenty-four privileges granted to all cardinals from the moment of their promotion in consistory, Can. 239, no. 1). All this suggests that the power of forgiving sins is granted *radicaliter* (in its foundation) by the sacrament of holy Orders, but that, as St Bonaventure observes, status and jurisdiction are required for its valid exercise.

WHEN THE CHURCH SUPPLIES JURISDICTION

There is one apparent, but only apparent, exception to this rule, namely, that, according to the code of canon law, any priest, even though he has not been specifically approved for confessions, can, where there is danger of death, validly and licitly absolve all penitents without distinction from any sins or censures, however strictly reserved and notorious. This concession applies even if a priest who is duly approved also happens to be present (Can. 882). The history of this provision is a somewhat complicated one, which has been well summarized by Abbé C. de Clercq in his contribution to M. Raoul Naz's *Traité de Droit Canonique*.[7] We have already seen that under the old penitential discipline a priest could, without the bishop's express intervention, reconcile a dying person to the Church. Later, the Church continued to allow any priest to give absolution when the penitent was in danger of death. Trent, in a chapter (7) briefly concerned with the reservation of cases, accepts without qualification the disappearance of all reservation at the moment of death (*in*

[7] Vol. II "Des Sacrements", 1st ed. (Paris, 1947), p. 154.

articulo mortis: Denz. 903), whereas the Roman Ritual issued in 1614 under the authority of Paul V (1605–21) restricts the concession to occasions when no approved confessor with jurisdiction is procurable.[8] On June 7th, 1864, the Holy Office decided that, when there was peril of death, a man might confess his sins to a schismatical priest, if no Catholic priest were present, provided that no scandal would be given, and that one could probably conclude that the ceremony would be carried out in accordance with the Church's rites. On July 29th, 1891, the Holy Office accepted the conclusion that, even when a confessor with the necessary jurisdiction were present, a priest without faculties for confession could absolve at the moment of death.

Canon 882 of the Code embodied this ruling and went beyond it. The Church supplies jurisdiction not only at the moment of death, but where there is danger of death. This ruling provides many more occasions for the exercise of this type of jurisdiction, since, according to received teaching, danger of death is said to be present where there is a probable fear that it may ensue, even if it should later be established that there was no genuine ground for such fear. This danger is said to exist during a serious illness, or throughout a difficult labour, or when battle is joined. In an answer given on May 29th, 1915, to a query from the bishop of Verdun, the Sacred Penitentiary ruled that every soldier in a state of warlike assembly or mobilization could be considered, by reason of that very fact, to be in danger of death, and could be absolved by any priest he might encounter.[9]

There can be no doubt that these exceptional powers may be used, under certain conditions, to impart a general or collective absolution of the kind mentioned above (p. 90). In the course of the second world war permission was granted

---

[8] Title III, ch. 1, n. 1. This has been altered in more recent editions, and now reads "even if an approved priest were present".

[9] *Acta Apostolicae Sedis*, VII, p. 282. Cf. Bouscaren, *Canon Law Digest* (Milwaukee, 1934), I, pp. 411–12.

to absolve without previous confession being made, if time were lacking for individuals to be heard. Similar leave was conceded for use in air-raids, and has application both to members of the armed forces and to civilians. In an instruction of the Sacred Penitentiary, dated March 25th, 1944, regulations were provided "in order to remove doubts and difficulties" about the extraordinary powers granted in emergencies. Priests, even when they had not been approved for confessions, could absolve combatants collectively when a battle was imminent, or in progress, if individual confessions could not be made. Where it was impossible, or very difficult, to give absolution at such times, it was permitted to absolve the fighting men "as soon as may be judged necessary", a decision which left a wide range of choice to the confessor's discretion. Leave was also accorded for certain cases where imminent danger of death was not involved, as, for example, "if the penitents would otherwise, without any fault on their part, be deprived for a long time of sacramental grace and holy Communion". But, to avoid any abuses of these considerable "grants in aid" the duty of approaching the local Ordinary was stressed "wherever this is possible, so that he might make a decision about the conditions for general absolution".[10]

GRANTING OF JURISDICTION

Apart from the instances just discussed, where for some exceptional reason the Church supplies jurisdiction, it is normally taken for granted (Can. 877) that faculties for confessions will not be conceded, either by diocesan bishops or by religious superiors, unless the candidates have proved their fitness for administering the sacrament by some form of examination. A dispensation from this may be granted where there is question of a priest whose theological acumen has been tested in some other way. If there is any reason for

[10] Cf. Bouscaren, *Canon Law Digest* (Milwaukee, 1954), III, pp. 377-9.

doubting whether a priest who has previously held faculties, still possesses the required knowledge, the bishop or superior may oblige him to submit to a fresh examination. It is worthy of note that, in Rome, all priests below the episcopal dignity, even though they may be consultors of the Roman congregations or professors in the pontifical faculties, are obliged to pass examinations bearing upon the whole of moral theology, if it is desired that they should hear confessions.

LIMIT OF JURISDICTION

Another point that is sometimes overlooked by those who are unfamiliar with these matters is that the Ordinary can, if he so chooses, restrict jurisdiction in one way or other. In regard to the *time* during which the concession lasts, it is customary to give jurisdiction for a limited period, after which the faculties have to be renewed. It sometimes happens also that the powers conferred are limited to a certain type of penitent, as in Rome, where it is not the custom to give written delegation for hearing women's confessions to priests who are not yet thirty years of age, though the permission may sometimes be granted by word of mouth.

The canon law does not insist that all delegation of this kind must be conferred in writing; it may also be given orally, provided that the terms of the issue are made clear. Tacit jurisdiction, which supposed for its exercise that the Ordinary knew that it was being used but did nothing to hinder it, is now suppressed in the Church in the west, though it still has currency in the east.

Priests, whether secular or regular, who have faculties for confessions in a certain area, may validly and licitly absolve not only their own subjects, but various sorts of visitors from other dioceses, as well as members of the eastern Churches (Can. 881, sect. 1).

An important rule, which is sometimes of great service when a bishop or parish priest is travelling on a pilgrimage with diocesans or parishioners, is that he can confess and absolve his own subjects in any part of the world (Can. 881, sect. 2).

THE SEAL OF CONFESSION

Even in the days of the old penitential discipline, when the organization of the public rite could easily arouse suspicions about the kind of sin that was being expiated, there was no obligation to confess openly sins that were by their nature secret. There is a famous passage in a letter addressed to the bishops of Campania by St Leo the Great (440–61) in which he protests against an abuse that has crept into the penitential discipline, i.e. the public reading by a penitent of a list of his sins, written on a chart. "It is sufficient", writes the saint, "that the guilty conscience should be made known to the priests only in secret confession." He praises those who are willing to humble themselves publicly in this manner, but adds: "All sins are not of such a character that a penitent would fearlessly publish them" (*Epistle* 168; Denz. 145). From the east has come Armenian and Syrian conciliar legislation that inflicts deposition from office on any priest who reveals the secrets told to him in confession. The Fourth Council of the Lateran in 1215, in the same chapter in which annual confession as a minimum is made the rule, also warns the confessor:

To take the greatest care not to betray the penitent by word or sign or in any other way whatsoever; but, if he should need more skilled counsel, let him seek it cautiously without in any way revealing the person, since we decree that anyone who ventures to make known a sin disclosed to him in the tribunal of penance must not only be deposed from his priestly office, but must also be incarcerated in an enclosed monastery, to do perpetual penance (Denz. 438).

The code of canon law (Can. 889, sect. 1) takes over the Lateran terminology, adding to the clause "by word ... whatsoever" the phrase "for any cause whatsoever" (*quavis de causa*), thus meeting in advance the suggestion that there might be some loophole in respect of the opening sentence of the canon: *Sacramentale sigillum inviolabile est*, "the sacramental seal is inviolable". Under the present law the penalty for direct violation of the seal (that is, for revealing at one and the same time both the name of the penitent and the sin confessed) no longer includes a withdrawal from the world, but is, nonetheless, one of the most severe of all those inflicted by the Church's law. It involves excommunication incurred *ipso facto* (that is, as a result of the deed itself, knowingly and wilfully committed) which is most specially reserved to the Holy See (Can. 2369, sect. 1). The words used are *qui sigillum sacramentale directe violare praesumpserit* ("he who shall presume to break the sacramental seal directly"). "To presume" is one of the received formulas which, according to Can. 2229, sect. 2, imply that full knowledge and deliberation is required; a confessor talking in his sleep would not incur the censure. In fact, any lessening of the imputability on the part of mind or will would exempt from the penalty's being incurred.

The seal of confession is, according to the simplest definition, that of St Thomas, "nothing more than the duty of the confessor to conceal (what was said to him in confession)". More fully it is defined as "a most strict obligation to keep secret all things said by the penitent with a view to absolution, the disclosure of which would make the sacrament burdensome or vexatious".[11] It is sometimes quite mistakenly believed by the laity that the duty of secrecy is binding upon the clergy alone. In fact, it binds all who, whether accidentally or by design, have overheard anything said in confession, with the one exception of the penitent himself. Not all confessionals are completely sound-proof, and there are times when those waiting for confession kneel nearer to the confessional than is strictly necessary. Such people, in common with interpreters

[11] D. Prümmer, O.P., *Manuale Theologiae Moralis* (Barcelona, 1946), III, p. 315.

(whose occasional presence is provided for in Can. 889, sect. 2) and those who may happen to find a written confession belonging to someone else, are bound to the most entire secrecy. If they deliberately transgress the rule imposed on them by the canon law, they are held to be guilty of sacrilege, and in terms of Can. 2369, sect. 2, they may be punished in a variety of ways that include, in the last resort, excommunication.

The matter, or quasi-matter, covered by the seal of confession includes all mortal sins according to their kinds and degrees, all venial sins, and whatever else may be known through confession which might be detrimental to the penitent if it were disclosed to any third person, apart from the confessor and the penitent himself. The last class would include the circumstances in which the sins were committed, the names of any who might have shared in the penitent's sins and the penitent's own weaknesses and defects, as these are known to himself. On the other hand, the penitent's virtues and good deeds are not strictly caught by the seal, but are usually regarded as natural secrets.

The penitent himself is not bound by the seal as such, but is obliged to keep what is both a natural secret and one committed to him (or entrusted to him), more especially if harm could come to the confessor as a result of a disclosure.

Outside the act of confession the priest is not entitled to speak even to the penitent himself about the sins confessed, unless he has the latter's permission, freely given, to discuss these matters. He may, however, in the confessional speak about sins already confessed.

"The sacramental seal is inviolable" (Can. 889, sect. 1). The authors find that the obligation is most strictly prescribed by the natural law, the divine law and the Church's canon law. Under the *law of nature* itself there is a sort of contract between the confessor and his penitent; implicitly the latter says: "I am revealing these facts only in so far as I am guaranteed absolute secrecy." The *divine law* on this subject is not explicitly promulgated but seems to call for an implicit obligation, arising out of the truth already established that penance is administered by a judicial process, which of its very nature calls for a hearing *in camera*. No doubt there are, in all countries that follow the normal process of law and justice, many judgements given in public, but these are not concerned with the secrets of the heart (of which the law usually takes no cognizance) which are often incapable of legal proof. It is quite easy to imagine what disasters would follow if secrecy were not among the most solemn duties of the confessor. Christ our Lord may, then, be said to have instituted this sacrament with an implicit desire that the sins manifested should be kept secret. The provisions of the *canon law* have already been mentioned.

The obligation of the seal is so strict that no dispensation can be given from it. The penitent alone can permit the revelation of the secrets he has confessed. This is now commonly admitted by all the authors, notwithstanding the opinions of Alexander of Hales, Scotus and a few other scholastics, who denied that even the penitent could authorize disclosure, or effect it. Apart from any *direct* violation of the seal, there are many ways in which the seal might be broken *indirectly*, so that it would be possible for somebody to guess the truth as a result of a confessor's indiscretion. Various penalties can be inflicted by superiors for indirect violation. These include suspension from saying Mass or hearing confessions.

The general rule, which is also the only safe rule, is that the confessor should speak of his penitent's sins only to God, by praying for him, and especially by remembering his needs at Mass.

THE RESERVATION OF SINS

This is an aspect of the sacrament that should be mentioned briefly, though it is probably of less importance at the present day than it was in earlier ages. The reservation of sins implies that the superior who gives jurisdiction to his subjects is entitled to restrict the powers assigned, and may, if he judges it to be necessary, oblige at least the great majority of confessors under his rule to apply to him for leave to absolve from certain sins or classes of sins. So Trent refers to the advantage of keeping the absolution of some sins, especially those that are outstandingly atrocious, in the hands of the pope and the local bishops. "Our holy Fathers decided that it would be greatly for the benefit of discipline among Christian people, if certain crimes of a more serious and horrible kind were to be absolved not by ordinary priests, but by the high priests only" (Denz. 903).

The chief advantage of reservation is held to be that judgement is thereby reserved to those who, in addition to high office in the Church, possess greater knowledge and experience than most, if not all, of their diocesans.[12] The penitents, in their turn, are given a wholesome reminder that their cases have been remitted to a higher tribunal, from which they might normally expect a more severe penance as a condition for absolution. All this remains true, even though it is no longer necessary, as in the days of the penitential discipline, for penitents to go to the bishop in person for the confession of reserved sins. Within the past half-century the Holy Office issued an instruction (July 13th, 1916) calling the local Ordinaries' attention to the need for restricting the reservation of sins to the more heinous offences, and this only after the diocesan synods or the cathedral chapters had been consulted. The gist of this instruction is repeated in the Code of canon law, which was on the eve of publication at the time of the Holy Office's pronouncement. Canon 895 stresses the need for consultation in much the same terms as the 1916 instruction. Canon 897 decides that not more than three, or at most four, cases should be reserved; these should be extremely

[12] There is something analogous to this in the reservation of the most serious crimes to judges of the High Court, so that the jurisdiction of Quarter and Borough Sessions is limited.

grave, external crimes, quite specifically determined. The reservation should not be continued beyond the time needed for extirpating a sin or restoring discipline that has become enfeebled. The reservation affects only those external sins that are both materially and formally mortal sin. Reservation of a venial sin, or an internal sin, or one not specifically determined, would be of no effect.

Apart from the Ordinary himself the canon penitentiary has by virtue of his office (Can. 401, sect. 1) authority to absolve from all sins thus reserved to the Ordinary. A like authority is commonly granted to the vicars-forane of a diocese, with power to subdelegate the confessors who apply to them for authority to absolve from these sins.

Canon 899, sect. 3, declares that parish priests and those of comparable standing may absolve from all episcopally reserved sins during the Easter duties period, as may missioners throughout the duration of a mission. Under certain conditions that cannot be explained here, reservation of this sort becomes inapplicable.[13]

[13] For a full summary, cf. C. de Clercq in *Traité de droit canonique*, II, pp. 170-1.

CHAPTER XII

THE SUBJECT OF THE SACRAMENT

WHO ARE THE SUBJECTS?

The subject of the sacrament of penance is any baptized human being who has been guilty of personal sin after the time of his regeneration or rebirth in the saving waters of baptism. Baptism is the gateway to the other sacraments and, as has sometimes been said, nobody is capable of a resurrection unless he has already been born.

Again, one who has wholly preserved his baptismal innocence and has in no way fallen into sin, even the most trivial and indeliberate venial sin, could not be validly absolved. It should be added that complete freedom from every kind of sin is something that should not be either presumed or expected. It is of faith that even a just man labours under a moral incapacity for avoiding *all* venial sins throughout a lifetime, unless he has received a special privilege, such as was certainly granted to the Blessed Virgin. St James tells us that "We are betrayed, all of us, into many faults" (3. 2), and St John writes: "If we say we have not sin, we deceive ourselves, and the truth is not in us" (1 John 1. 8, Westminster Version). The Council of Milevis (416) condemned the opinion that St John's words are to be interpreted merely as an act of humility, whereas, in fact, they are the truth. And Trent in its sixth session (On Justification), Can. 23, rejects the view that "a man may avoid all sins, even venial sins, throughout his whole life, apart from a special privilege such as the Church holds in respect of the Blessed Virgin" (Denz. 833). This canon does not deny the possibility of avoiding all *deliberate* venial sins, or all sins for a time, or a *particular type* of venial sin. It has reference to *all* sins of whatever kind (deliberate or indeliberate) throughout a whole lifetime.[1] As regards mortal sins it may be safely assumed that the great majority of mankind have committed one or more mortal sins, and so have need either of perfect contrition with the desire of the sacrament, or of attrition with the use of the sacrament, if these sins are to be forgiven.

WHAT INTENTION IS REQUIRED?

For valid reception of this sacrament some degree of intention is needed. As has been explained in the chapters on the quasi-matter of penance, three acts are necessary on the part of the penitent, and these are contrition, confession and satisfaction. For these a *habitual* intention (of the sort that has been elicited at one time, but is no longer operative at the moment when the act is required) is insufficient. There must, at least normally, be a *virtual* intention (that is, an intention that has been elicited, and continues to have a genuine influence upon the act). An example of this would be the state of mind and will of a penitent who had carefully prepared for confession, but did not consciously advert to or intend the act of contrition at the moment of receiving absolution). Nonetheless, if the acts have been duly elicited in advance, a penitent who is, in fact, unconscious at the moment of absolution may be held to have sufficient intention for the forgiveness of his sins, although at that moment his intention is no more than a habitual one.[2]

[1] Cf. E. Hugon, O.P., *Tractatus Dogmatici* (De Gratia), Ed. 5 (Rome, 1927), II, pp. 133–4.

[2] Cf. Mgr G. Van Noort, *Tract. de Sacramentis* (Hilversum, 1926), II, p. 87, n. 1.

NECESSITY FOR FAITH AND PROBITY

How far are faith and probity required in the reception of the sacraments? The general rule, to which there is one exception, is that neither of these is required for the *valid* reception of a sacramental rite. Hence even formal heretics who have received baptism or holy orders from a minister who uses the proper matter and form and has the correct intention of doing what the Church does, would not normally (i.e. in the absence of a serious doubt about the three essentials mentioned) be rebaptized or reordained.[3] The one exception is the sacrament of penance, which calls for true contrition or attrition, and so for some degree of faith and probity.

SINS TO BE CONFESSED

A sincere and uninhibited confession calls for a complete disclosure of all mortal sins committed after baptism that have not already been directly submitted to the power of the keys. The proposition that mortal sins which have been lawfully omitted for some special reason (such as danger of death), or have been forgotten in a confession need not be mentioned in a subsequent confession, was condemned by the Holy Office on September 24th, 1665 (Denz. 1111).

All mortal sins must be confessed as grave, and must be differentiated according to their kind. Hence, in the absence of a reasonable cause (such as danger of death, lack of time to make a detailed confession and so forth) it is not sufficient to say merely: "I have sinned gravely against justice" or some other virtue. The number of sins must be given, so far as this can be ascertained; this number must neither be exaggerated nor diminished, and any notable inaccuracy must be corrected in a later confession. It is, however, generally allowed that a penitent who, *in good faith*, accuses himself of an excessively

[3] In the matter of ordination, it would not follow that, on conversion to the faith, they would be allowed to exercise the orders received.

large number of sins, may be excused from correcting this number later. It is quite otherwise if the exaggeration was wilful, or if he has notably diminished the number.

It is obligatory to mention circumstances that may have changed the category of the sin from venial to mortal, or may have increased the malice of the sin.

The Tridentine chapter on confession (Denz. 899) expressly teaches that *all* mortal sins are to be confessed "even though the sins in question are most secret, and are committed only against the last two commandments of the decalogue" (Exod. 20. 17; Matt. 5. 28), that is, are in the category of evil desires and bad thoughts.

In sundry conditions of sickness or disease (e.g. in regard to dying people, deaf-mutes and others who cannot be understood, or cannot understand, by ordinary means) it is permissible to make use of signs. The rules also allow confession through an interpreter or in writing, but these two methods are exceptional and out of the ordinary, and there is no strict obligation to employ them. The code of canon law (*c*. 903) does no more than *allow* the use of an interpreter, if the penitent calls for one. It can sometimes happen that the interpreter will be of service in asking the penitent questions, and that the latter will reply by signs that can be apprehended by the priest, but not by the interpreter. This is sufficient for the confession's integrity; it is not necessary that the interpreter should have any clue to the penitent's answers.

CHAPTER XIII

THE QUESTION OF INDULGENCES

THE WORD "INDULGENCE"

A great authority on the history of penance, the late Dr Bernhard Poschmann of Münster, wrote in the first line of the fifth chapter of his work on *Penance and Extreme Unction*: "Indulgences, though not a component part of the sacrament of penance, are, nonetheless, closely connected with it."[1] The Latin word *indulgentia*, though not used in its present, technical, sense during the first Christian millennium, occurs from the fourth century onwards with the meaning of *remission of punishment*, and in St Hilary of Poitiers († January 13th, 366) in the sense of *forgiveness* (of sin). In the code of the Emperor Theodosius (401–50) it stands for the amnesty granted to certain criminals by the Christian emperors, more particularly at the time of the paschal festivities. In the code of Justinian (483–565) an "indulgence" remitted the penalty for a crime, without cancelling the infamy resulting from the offence. It seems that, for some centuries, there was no special term in use to designate the remission of *canonical* penalties. From the eighth century onwards, the word *redemptio* or ransom is found; later, as the ransom became less and less formidable, the word *remissio* (= forgiveness *or* pardon) took its place. By 1215, the date of the fourth Lateran Council, *indulgentia* is

[1] *Busse und Letzte Ölung* (Freiburg i/B., 1951), p. 112.

currently employed in the sense it has now borne for over seven centuries. The Bulls granting indulgences have, however, continued to use the older word (in that sense) of *remissio*, side by side with *indulgentia*.

WHAT IS AN INDULGENCE?

The code of canon law gives the following definition of an indulgence in Can. 911: "All men should hold in high honour indulgences, that is to say, the remission before God of the temporal punishment due to sin that has already been forgiven in respect of its guilt. This remission is granted by ecclesiastical authority out of the treasury of the Church, to the living by way of absolution, and to the dead by way of suffrage." This statement contains all that is most essential in the Church's teaching on indulgences. A short commentary on it may help to clarify certain points that are by no means self-explanatory.

One may begin by reminding readers of this book about the Church's doctrine, already set out in some detail above, that, even though the *guilt* of sin has been forgiven, the *temporal punishment due to sin* is not invariably remitted in full. It is for this reason that the confessor is expected to allot a "salutary penance" before he gives absolution to a penitent, yet it is recognized that this penance may not be sufficient for remitting *all* temporal punishment that may have accumulated. Apart from prayer and good works of charity and mortification, such as almsgiving, fasting and vigils, there is a potent remedy for or solvent of the punishment due to sin, and this is made known to us in the doctrine of indulgences.

The code's definition says, in the first place, that an indulgence is *the remission before God of the temporal punishment due to sin.* So it is a calumny to state, as some popular works of Protestant fiction have done in the past, that indulgences are remissive of the *guilt* of sin, even when this is understood of *past* sin. As for indulgences alleged to have been granted for *the future*, they, like absolution given with reference to the future, are unknown outside the works of fiction to which allusion has just been made.[2] It is true that the phrase "indulgence for the remission of sins" sometimes occurs in official documents, but here the word "sin" stands for "penalty due to sin".

The eternal penalty incurred by mortal sin is always remitted when the sin itself is validly absolved. Hence, no indulgence is of any avail in regard to the *guilt* of mortal sin. Any punishment due to original sin is remitted in baptism, so that indulgences are granted for no other purpose than for the remission of the temporal punishment due to *actual* sin. These penalties, it is taught as part of Catholic doctrine, are truly remitted *before God*, and not merely in the eyes of the Church's tribunals. Hence, Leo X condemned Luther's nineteenth proposition (Denz. 759): "Indulgences are not effective, as regards those who truly gain them, for the remission of the punishment due to actual sin in the sight of divine justice." St Thomas rightly emphasizes the truth that, if indulgences availed only to deliver men from ecclesiastical penalties, and not to free them from the punishment to be expiated in purgatory, they would be a gross deception. They would, moreover, be useless to the souls in purgatory, who are no longer subject to canonical penalties.

The further point that the sin or sins covered by the indulgence must have *already been forgiven in respect of its guilt*, has been explained above.

The indulgence is *granted by ecclesiastical authority*. There are broadly four remedies for the punishment due after the guilt of the sin has been forgiven. These are (a) the penance

[2] The late Mr James Britten in his engaging work on *Protestant Fiction* (C.T.S., 1899) cites an example from a novel entitled *The Six Sisters of the Valley*, in which a friar is represented as not only giving absolution to a lady for future sins, but as extending it to all concerned in a particular venture, of whom only the lady herself is present at the time!

allotted by the priest as part of the sacramental rite; (b) works of mortification that are freely undertaken; (c) the patient supporting of the sorrows and afflictions of this life; and (d) indulgences. If none of these remedies can be adequately applied, there remains purgatory, in which any temporal punishment that is still outstanding may be expiated. The Church claims to have the power of granting indulgences, and this claim will shortly be examined.

The grant of indulgences is said to be made *out of the treasury of the Church*. This doctrine supposes another one, that of the communion of saints, as a result of which all the members of Christ's mystical body are closely linked in such a way that they all participate in the spiritual benefits attaching to and arising out of membership. So in this body Christ is the head, and the members are united to him and to one another.

One result of this union is that there is an inexhaustible treasury of the spiritual benefits that derive from the merits and satisfaction of Christ and the saints, and in this all the faithful are permitted to share. Christ's satisfaction, being infinite in value, is superabundant even as regard the redemption of all the sins committed in this world from the beginning of the human race until the end of time. So we read in St John's first epistle (2. 2): "He, in his own person, is the atonement made for our sins, and not only for ours, but for the sins of the whole world." And St Paul (Rom. 5. 20) writes: "As our fault was amplified, grace has been more amply bestowed than before." Hence Clement VI, when writing of Christ's precious blood, recalls the truth that: "It was not a mere drop of his blood that was known to have been shed, though this would have been sufficient for the redemption of the whole human race."[3] In addition to the merits and satisfaction of Christ our Lord, the head of the mystical body, it is the commonly taught doctrine of the Church that far more works of satisfaction were performed by many of the

[3] Bull *Unigenitus Dei Filius*, January 25th, 1343. Denz. 550.

saints during their lifetimes than were needed to satisfy for their own sins. We have only to think of our Blessed Lady herself, of the sufferings of the martyrs, of the virginal lives led by so many men and women and of the countless others who were able to avoid all mortal sin throughout the whole of their lives. Clement VI, in the Bull just quoted, goes on to speak of the treasury of merits, to which all the accumulated satisfactions of Christ and his holy ones have contributed, and still contribute:

> Therefore, lest the compassion that prompted so great an outpouring [of blood] should be rendered useless, or vain, or unnecessary, how great a treasure did the good Father acquire for the Church militant, wishing thereby to enrich his sons, that there might be a *treasure men will find incorruptible, so that those who enjoy it are honoured with God's friendship* (Wis. 7. 13–14).

This treasury of merit, continues the pope, was entrusted to blessed Peter and his successors, his vicars upon earth, that they might dispense it to the faithful, at times for the total, at times for the partial, cancellation of the temporal punishment due to sin, that is, to those who are truly penitent, and have been to confession (Denz. 551).

Indulgences are said to be granted *to the living by way of absolution, and to the dead by way of suffrage.* The second part of this clause is easier to explain than the first. The souls in purgatory are no longer under the pope's jurisdiction, so that indulgences gained on their behalf are offered to God in the hope that he will apply them to the suffering souls. But what is the force of the words *by way of absolution*? On this there are not a few opinions, one of which claims that by an indulgence a living member of the faithful receives something that can be called, in the strict sense, an absolution from the temporal punishment. It is not, of course, an absolution pronounced, as in the confessional, in favour of a particular man or woman. It is in the nature of a *general* declaration made by the Church in advance, as it were, that those who fulfil the conditions attached to the grant will receive the benefit of the indulgence.

Without denying that the Church can pronounce absolution outside the tribunal of penance, it is argued against this opinion that it is contrary to the idea of indulgences that was taught and accepted by the great scholastics. Thus St Thomas (*Supplement,* qu. 25, art. 1, reply to second objection) states clearly that "one who receives an indulgence is not absolved, speaking without qualification, from the debt of the penalty, but rather *is given that wherewith he may pay the debt*". Again it is argued that if the word "absolution" were used in the strict sense, the concession made by the Church in this capacity would be more sure in its action than absolution in the tribunal of penance because, unlike sacramental absolution, it would depend almost uniquely upon the power of the donor, and hardly at all upon the disposition of the recipient.

Fr Billot, S.J., appears to divine the truer sense of the expression "by way of absolution", when he writes: "An indulgence, considered in its primitive *raison d'être,* is nothing else than an indirect absolution from the penances enjoined in this sacrament by a distribution made from the Church's treasury, in order to extinguish the sinful condition for which the penances were instituted."[4] "Sinful condition" here has reference not to the guilt of the sin, but to the temporal punishment that still awaits cancellation. To explain this a reference must be made to the history of indulgences.

BRIEF HISTORY OF INDULGENCES

It is important to realize, as Fr. P. Galtier, S.J., reminds us, that from the fact of its being of faith that the Church from the beginning has had the power to grant indulgences, it does not follow that, from the first, it was always clearly perceived in what precisely this power consisted, and how far it might extend.[5]

[4] *De Sacramentis Ecclesiae* (Rome, 1947), II, p. 224.
[5] *De Paenitentia,* new ed. (Rome, 1950), p. 541.

The history of the doctrine and practice of indulgences is commonly divided under four headings: (1) From the beginning to the sixth or seventh century. (2) From the seventh to the eleventh centuries. (3) From the eleventh to the fifteenth centuries. (4) From the fifteenth century to the Council of Trent. In this long history we can perceive a marked development in the theory, which finds its chief exponents in the great scholastics, and a steady growth and enrichment in the Church's bestowals of favour from the treasury of merits, of which Pope Clement VI wrote so movingly in his Bull *Unigenitus Dei Filius*, already quoted.

From the beginning to the sixth or seventh century

In this earliest period we see, first and foremost, a custom which obtained in a number of Churches, of *anticipating the end of the canonical penance*. Enough has been said in earlier chapters to show that the extent and severity of this penance varied greatly from Church to Church, and was largely in the hands of the individual bishop. It was his business to take into account the good of the penitent, the well-being of the Church, the nature of the offence and any mitigating circumstances that might be present. Where the gravest faults had been committed, the penance might well be one of great severity, and might even be prolonged until the end of the penitent's life. Yet, even in regard to the most grievous of all sins, it was possible for the bishop to decide upon a shortening of the penance, and at times those Christians who had failed to avoid all taint of apostasy or of sacrifice to idols, would beg the intercession on their behalf of the martyrs or their companions, or of the confessors who had suffered for the faith, though not to the point of martydom. A striking example of such intercession is provided by Eusebius (*Ecclesiastical History*, Bk. VI, c. 42. 5), when he quotes a letter from St Denis of Alexandria to Fabius of Antioch, concerning the intercession of the Alexandrian martyrs for some of their brethren who had failed in maintaining the faith:

Thus then these divine martyrs who were from among us, who are now the assessors of Christ, sharing in his kingdom, are judging with him and pronouncing sentence with him. They took under their protection some of our lapsed brethren, who were responsible on the count of having sacrificed. They saw their return and their penitence, and judged that these men should be accepted by him who does not will in any absolute way the sinner's death, but rather wills his repentance. They received them, they assembled them together, they reunited them, and shared with them their prayers and their repasts.

St Denis is unwilling to reject the powerful intercession of his martyred brethren; he is constrained to ratify the sentence which Christ himself has pronounced in union with such glorious martyrs. In this manner, then, the Church acknowledged the superabundant merits and satisfaction of the martyrs and was prepared to reconcile the lapsed. It must be allowed, however, that in cases such as these the remission of the canonical penance was made not precisely by way of juridical absolution, but as a result of the merits and intercessions of the martyrs who pleaded for their erring brethren.

From the seventh to the eleventh centuries

This is the period that showed a marked development in the system of private penance. In the same epoch of the Church's history the reluctance of the penitents to endure the whole severe discipline became intensified. The late Mgr Pierre Batiffol wrote of the period of St Augustine's episcopate, fully two centuries earlier, that: "In his mixed audience were to be found Christians who had mortal sins on their souls, and who, all the same, were not in the ranks of the penitents."[6] In the course of the fifth and sixth centuries, the custom grew up, even more generally than before, of postponing confession until the hour of death. The system of tariffs

[6] *Etudes d'histoire et de théologie positive,* 1st series, 5th ed. (Paris, 1920), pp. 208–9.

(that is, of penances graded in the penitential books according to the seriousness of the crime) became common in the west, and very soon proved to be quite as burdensome as the older systems. This led to the introduction of redemptions or commutations of the penances, which sought to replace older penances by ones that might be less severe, but were also, in many instances, longer, and perhaps difficult or impossible for one reason or another. Instances of these often curious penances are two, three or more days of fasting, accompanied by prayers, night-vigils, genuflections, prostrations, sleeping on beds of nettles, or even occupying the same grave with some holy person who had died. The severe penance for murder could be replaced by abstinence from meat and some other foods for a whole year.

This was also the period of pilgrimages to Rome, which became customary from the seventh century onwards, and the popes were in the habit of imposing a lighter penance than would otherwise have been usual, on account of the pilgrims' long journey and the devotion they showed to the Apostolic See. So Benedict III (855–58) relates that he had imposed a penance of no more than five years on one who had killed his brother, because the sinner had "hastened to the *limina* of the holy apostles, Peter and Paul".

Yet these redemptions and pilgrimages do not show a fully evolved theory of indulgences, since the former were simply a method of exchanging a severe penance for what was judged to be a more tolerable one, in which the Church supplied what was lacking for the full accomplishment of the law in all its strictness, and the latter were undertaken, like other pious works, for the expiation of sin. They may, however, be said to be the beginning of a system of indulgences, after the manner of those granted, somewhat later, to the crusaders. The principal difference, when they are compared with the later use, is that they called for a decision by a prelate or a priest on each separate occasion.

From the eleventh to the fifteenth centuries

In the middle of the eleventh century (that is, from about the time of the Norman conquest) the practice of *general* remissions began. It was no longer necessary for a priest to pass judgement on each case; the indulgences could be gained by *all* the pilgrims who visited certain sanctuaries. Indulgences increased rapidly in number during the late-eleventh and the twelfth centuries, though the popes tended to grant them somewhat parsimoniously. These first indulgences properly so called were partial ones, which began by remitting a fraction of the penance assigned in confession. The amount of remission gradually increased from a quarter to a half; soon a determined number of days to be remitted was mentioned in the grant and, by the end of the twelfth century, an indulgence of a year and forty days (or what would be styled later a year and one quarantine) is on record.

The first instance of a *plenary* indulgence may well be that conceded by Urban II at the council of Clermont in 1095 to those who were about to depart for the Holy Lands as crusaders. The text is interesting, and the operative clause reads:

> Relying on the mercy of God and the authority of the blessed apostles Peter and Paul, we relax unto faithful Christians who shall take up arms against them [the paynims] and assume the burden of this pilgrimage, the enormous (*immensas*) penances for their crimes. Moreover, let those who shall die there in true repentance, have no doubt that they will receive both pardon for sin and the fruit of eternal reward.[7]

So, even at the close of the eleventh century, we meet with indulgences that are substantially equivalent to those granted in more recent times. The late Mgr Boudinhon declared that: "Nowadays one would have difficulty in recognizing their

[7] Palmer, *Sources* . . ., p. 336. On Dr Poschmann's doubt whether this was really a plenary indulgence, Fr Palmer aptly comments: "The point is debatable, but we do not believe that the crusaders shared Poschmann's reluctance" (p. 335, n. 1).

character as indulgences; nonetheless, they form the first examples of our modern indulgences, i.e. works offered to all in exchange for the temporal punishment due to sin."[8]

An admirable summary of this important stage in this history is supplied in an article by the late Canon H. de Jonghe, of Malines:[9]

> The Church happened upon indulgences without noticing the fact. Naturally, they derived from the principles of the Catholic faith. In the eleventh century, first the bishops, then the popes, grant them as a favour for which the world is pre- pared. There is no decree establishing their legitimacy, no theologian calls their value in question. Popular devotion accepts them with fervour, and it is only when abuses arise that the attention of popes and doctors is drawn to them. It is impossible to see here that radical change, that corruption of Catholic doctrine which certain Protestants profess to dis- cover in the introduction of indulgences.

At the same time at which many grants of indulgences were being made, the theory began to be more fully discussed. Neither Gratian († 1179) nor Peter Lombard (1200–60) is preoccupied with the theory of indulgences, and even in the early thirteenth century the development is somewhat leisurely. In 1215, Innocent III, at the fourth Council of the Lateran, applied the plenary indulgences not only to the crusaders themselves, but to those who gave them material aid. As regards the theory, St Albert the Great (1200–80) is regarded as a link between the old and the new teaching, since, as he tells us, indulgences were regarded before his time as a commutation of penances, and in his time they were defined as a remission pure and simple. It becomes more clearly recognized that the remission granted by the Church is also acceptable in God's sight. Likewise the great scholastics teach for the first time that indulgences are applicable to the

[8] Art. "Sur l'histoire des indulgences" in *Revue d'histoire et de littérature religieuse,* 1898, III, p. 443.

[9] Art. in *La vie diocésaine du diocèse de Malines,* 1912, p. 77.

souls in purgatory; this is particularly marked in the works of St Thomas and St Bonaventure.

From the fifteenth century to the Council of Trent

This period is noteworthy, because it became usual, from the fifteenth century onwards, to grant indulgences to be gained, by way of suffrage, for the dead. The first of these grants was, it seems, made by Callistus III in 1457. The first document that certainly records a concession of this kind dates from the reign of Sixtus IV (1474–84).

This is also the period of numerous abuses culminating in John Tetzel's famous campaign of preaching and announcing the indulgence granted by Leo X on March 31st, 1515, to be gained by those who contributed to the rebuilding of St Peter's, Rome. This campaign was begun in January, 1517, and on October 31st of the same year Martin Luther issued his ninety-five theses, in which, among other things, he denied that indulgences did more than remit the canonical penances (Denz. 757–61). Luther's errors were condemned in the Bull *Exsurge Domine* of June 15th, 1520.[10]

In the years succeeding Luther's revolt the popes made great efforts to regulate the grants of indulgences, and in 1547 the council in session at Bologna prepared a severe decree, never actually published, against those who distributed indulgences and made a business of it. Later, on June 4th, 1561, Trent pronounced against the distributors or *quaestores*, as there was then no further hope of their improving their behaviour, and handed over the publication of indulgences to the Ordinaries of dioceses. The popes, in their turn, worked with the Council against abuses. So, for example, Pius IV in 1562 commanded that all grants of indulgences should be made gratis, and Pius V suppressed all indulgences to which alms were attached, and later excommunicated those who introduced a commercial element into their distribution.

[10] The whole story is admirably summarized in Mgr Philip Hughes' *A Popular History of the Reformation* (London, 1957), pp. 109 ff.

Trent, during its later years, promulgated two decrees on indulgences. One, a disciplinary measure, abolished entirely the "name and service" of the *quaestores*, and enacted that, in future, all alms should be collected without fee, "so that all may understand that these heavenly treasures of the Church are administered not for gain, but for piety".[11] The dogmatic decree that followed hard upon decrees on purgatory, and on the veneration of the saints, their relics and their statues, derives from the twenty-fourth session of December 3rd and 4th, 1563 (Denz. 989). The short definition announces the essential teaching briefly and adequately:

> Since the power of conferring indulgences was granted by Christ to his Church, and she has from the earliest times made use of this power divinely given to her, the holy Synod teaches and enacts that the use of indulgences, as being most salutary to the Christian people, and approved by the authority of the holy Councils, is to be retained in the Church, and it condemns under anathema those who *either* assert that they are of no avail, *or* deny that the power of conceding them is possessed by the Church.

The Council, in the latter part of the decree, once more condemns abuses, and recommends that the bishops should report all cases of corrupt practice to the provincial councils, which will, in turn, refer the matter to the supreme pontiff.

The post-Tridentine history of indulgences cannot be related here. One principal landmark is the code of canon law, promulgated in 1918, which, for the first time, gave collective statutory expression to the Church's theory and practice of indulgences.

VARIOUS KINDS OF INDULGENCES

An analysis of the definition given by the code of canon law has furnished some idea of what indulgences are. Before

---

[11] Palmer, *Sources* . . ., p. 364.

describing the different kinds of indulgences, it may be useful to state briefly what they are not.

First, as has already been explained, they are *not* given for the remission of the guilt of either mortal or venial sin. Secondly, though in the course of their early history they were closely linked with the old canonical penances, they are not remissions of these ancient penances. Thirdly, they are not a dispensation from the duty incumbent on all men of emending their lives, and attempting to foresee any future occasions of sin. Hence it has been well remarked that those who, most rightly, set great store by indulgences and lose no opportunity of gaining them, are not thereby laying up a sort of nest-egg for future use. If the comparison may be permitted, gaining an indulgence may be likened to the reception of a large sum of money which, according to a deed of gift, cannot be put into the savings bank or otherwise invested, but is to be used uniquely for paying off debts incurred *in the past*. Lastly, indulgences are not a quittance or release from the duty of repairing injuries done to others, repaying any sums that may have been stolen or otherwise acquired in bad faith, and restoring any damage done to our neighbour's good name. There can be no dispensation, past, present or future, from the duty of keeping the commandments, and no ecclesiastical authority would ever dream of professing to issue a grant that would be a contradiction in terms.

The most important division of indulgences is that between *partial* and *plenary*. A *plenary* indulgence remits, in the intention of him who grants the indulgence, the whole of the temporal punishment still remaining to any man who has the right disposition for gaining an indulgence. A *partial* indulgence is designed to remit some, but not all, of the debt that still remains. The Church's law (Can. 926) makes it abundantly evident that a plenary indulgence is offered in such a manner that, if anyone cannot gain it in its entirety, he may, at any rate, lay hold on whatever is available to him in terms of his dispositions at the time of fulfilling the conditions. In other words, to gain a plenary indulgence, it would be necessary to be free from all guilt, even of venial sin. In default of such a state of soul, it would still be possible to gain some remission. If, in fact, a plenary indulgence is gained in all its completeness, the state of soul in him who has acquired it would be like to that of a neophyte immediately after baptism. If such a man were to die without any further lapse into sin, he would be in a condition to escape purgatory, and to go immediately to his reward in heaven. It is frequently said that this condition of freedom even from venial sin is in itself enough to make the gaining of a plenary indulgence a most arduous task. This may well be true, but it is unwise to emphasize too stridently its extreme difficulty. Perfect contrition, as we have seen, has the effect, if it is joined with the desire of the sacrament, of remitting all the guilt of sin, whether mortal or venial, and attrition is sufficient for remitting the guilt of venial sin. What proof is there, then, that the remission of the temporal punishment due to sin is so much more difficult than that of the guilt?

Although it is certain that a partial indulgence is capable of remitting part of the punishment, it is not easy to say, even approximately, how much is actually remitted. It is commonly taught that, if the Holy See attaches an indulgence of seven years and seven quarantines to the performance of some devotion or other pious work, one who gains the indulgence in its entirety will receive a reduction of punishment equivalent to seven years and seven periods of forty days spent amid the rigours of the old penitential system. This is obviously a far easier equation to grasp than any suggested equivalence with the relief of the pains to be endured in purgatory.

Another distinction, already mentioned, is that between indulgences for the *living* and those for the *dead*. It has been sufficiently emphasized that the latter, which are conceded *by way of suffrage*, are an offering of satisfactions from the Church's treasury by way of shortening the punishment to be endured in purgatory. The position here is well set out in a reply of the Sacred Congregation of Indulgences, dated July 28th, 1840, regarding the indulgence attached to a privileged altar. The Congregation distinguishes between the intention of the donor, the pope, according to which a plenary indulgence is granted that should immediately release a soul from any further purgatorial pain. Yet, as regards the *application* of the effect, this depends entirely upon the acceptance of the indulgence by the divine mercy. It may be added that all indulgences granted by the pope are applicable to the souls in purgatory unless the contrary is clearly stated, as it is in regard to the papal blessing with plenary indulgence that is granted in the hour of death.

A less important distinction is between personal, real and local indulgences. *Personal* indulgences are those granted to a determined class of person, as, for example, to the members of a Third Order. *Real* are those attaching to some portable religious object, such as a rosary or a crucifix. *Local* are those annexed to some sanctuary, altar, miraculous statue and the like. Sometimes, in the case of local indulgences, the terms of the grant have a limiting effect. Thus, if an indulgence is granted to those who make a pilgrimage to some sanctuary, the inhabitants of the place, since they are not pilgrims, are incapable of gaining the indulgence.

THE AUTHORITY FOR GRANTING INDULGENCES

Enough has been said about the doctrines on which the power to grant indulgences is based, i.e. the power of the keys, the communion of saints and the treasury of merits. It does not seem necessary to supply formal proof that the Church claims to have, and has, the power to grant indulgences. The facts are set out in the history.

This power belongs principally to him who has the right to dispense spiritual favours from the Church's treasury. The pope himself is the principal bestower of indulgences; other members of the Church have the power in so far as he delegates it to them. Even the pope, as one who merely administers the treasury of merits, must have a reasonable cause for granting an indulgence. Hence if he were to attach a maximal grant to a minimal good work, it is agreed that he would act not merely illicitly but invalidly. His authority here, as in other matters, is over the whole Church. He can grant indulgences by word of mouth, though in practice he acts through the Sacred Penitentiary. In fact, it may be said that normally all general grants of indulgences are held to be invalid, unless the Penitentiary has given formal recognition to them. There are, however, quite a number of exceptions to this rule.

Before the Fourth Lateran Council of 1215 all residential bishops could confer all indulgences within the limits of their respective jurisdictions. Since that time their powers have been limited to granting an indulgence of one year at the consecration of a church, and a maximum of 50 days (100 for archbishops, 200 for cardinals) on other occasions. The limitations also apply to any delegation of the grant to others or grants of indulgences applicable to the holy souls.

THE CONDITIONS FOR GAINING INDULGENCES

The conditions are three in number: (1) a correct intention; (2) the state of grace and membership of the communion of saints; and (3) the due performance of the prescribed works.

(1) On the *first* condition, it is evident that indulgences are not, so to say, thrust upon those who do not desire them. Nevertheless, as they are favours, which may usually be presumed to be acceptable, a small degree of intention is sufficient. Doubtless it is an excellent custom to make frequently an intention of gaining all the indulgences that may be available, but a *virtual* intention is sufficient, and it is not essential that a person should always know that this or that work or prayer carries an indulgence with it. An actual intention is, however, necessary for applying an indulgence to some particular soul in purgatory.

(2) *The state of grace* and *membership of the communion of saints* is a condition that excludes those who are excommunicated, as well as those who are in a state of mortal sin. On the latter class St Thomas writes: "A dead member is not subject to the influence of other, living members. But one in a state of mortal sin is a dead member. Therefore he does not through indulgences accept the influence of the merits of living members" (*Supplement*, qu. 27, art. 1). We have already said, apropos of a plenary indulgence, that even venial sin not yet forgiven prevents a man from gaining the full effect of the indulgence. The need for being in a state of grace probably applies also to those who seek to gain indulgences for the holy souls. The reason for this is that indulgences applicable to the souls in purgatory may only be gained by one who is already in the condition to gain them for himself, and a man in a state of mortal sin cannot fulfil this condition. If a number of works are laid down as necessary it is sufficient that the final work (by which the indulgence is actually gained) should be performed in a state of grace.

(3) *The due performance of the prescribed works* means that the works must be carried out substantially in accordance with the mind of the legislator. Thus a substantial change in the conditions would render the process invalid, whereas slight changes, such as the intercalation of the titles of the mysteries while reciting the rosary, would not affect the validity.

Normally the works are to be performed *personally*, with the exception of almsgiving, which can be carried out through the good offices of another person. It follows from this that an indulgence cannot be applied to another *living* person. It is conceivable that this condition might, at some future time, be waived, but so far no concession of the kind has been made.

Again, the works are to be carried out with due regard for the number of works, the kind of work, the time and the place specified in the grant. Lastly, they must be what are called works of supererogation, i.e. they must be works that are not otherwise commanded as a duty or under pain of sin. A good example of something that is *not* a work of supererogation is the recitation of the divine office by clergy in sacred orders. This is a duty binding under sin, and therefore cannot rank for an indulgence. But there are exceptions to this rule, and one good instance of this is the penance imposed by the priest in confession, which can carry an indulgence with it if the prayers ordered are indulgenced prayers.

The works ordinarily prescribed in the various grants are: (a) confession; (b) communion; (c) a visit or visits to a church; and (d) special prayers.

(a) *Confession* may be imposed in such a way that it is of obligation even for those who have no more than venial sins to confess. Confessions made within the eight days before or after the day for gaining the indulgence are sufficient for the purpose (Can. 931, sect. 1), and in some dioceses an indult is granted to increase this period to a fortnight. Canon 931, sect. 3, makes an important concession for two classes of penitents, i.e. those who are accustomed, unless lawfully impeded, to make their confessions at least twice in the month or are daily communicants, even though they may miss one or two days in each week, may, without weekly confession, gain all the indulgences that otherwise they might not be able to gain. This is of great assistance to travellers abroad who may have difficulty in finding a priest as confessor who has some language in common with them. An exception to this rule is made for indulgences attached to a jubilee or for some occasions that resemble a jubilee.

(b) One communion made on a particular day suffices for obtaining a number of indulgences granted for that same day, where for each of them holy communion is required, provided that the other good works are repeated according to the number of indulgences involved (Can. 933).

If an indulgence is attached to a particular day the communion may be made the day before or at any time throughout the octave that follows the feast (Can. 931, sect. 1). In some instances (e.g. that of the Portiuncula indulgence) the period is extended.

Where the conditions prescribe communion and a visit to a church, a communion made in the church specified, joined with the recital of the prayers ordered by the grant, carries out both requirements simultaneously. But it is also lawful to separate the fulfilment of the two conditions mentioned, e.g. to make one's communion in some church of one's own choice, and then to pay a visit to the church specified in the decree.

There is a special concession made to those who suffer from some illness of long duration, or are otherwise physically hampered from receiving communion and visiting a church as specified. In such cases the confessor may, after confession, change the obligation of receiving communion and visiting a church into other good works. Children who have not yet made their first communions cannot be allowed to substitute some other work in place of communion.

(c) *The visit to a church* is not obligatory, unless it is expressly required by the grant. When no particular church is designated, any church or public oratory will serve the purpose. A semi-public oratory may be used for this visit only by those who have an indult, such as is frequently granted to people living in community. If several visits are mentioned as of obligation, one long visit will not be sufficient, but one *occasion* is enough, provided that the church is re-entered for each visit after the first.

(d) Lastly, the *prayers to be recited* must ordinarily be said with the lips, and not purely mentally, except where it is a question of the *public* recitation of indulgenced prayers (Cans. 934 and 936). Where the prayers are to be said for the pope's intentions, the choice is left to the individual. Normally one "Our Father", "Hail Mary" and "Glory be to the Father" are enough. The holy Father's intentions are known to be the exaltation of Holy Church, the uprooting of heresy, the propagation of the faith, the conversion of sinners and peace among Christian rulers and peoples. It is not necessary to have all or any of these intentions specifically in mind at the time of reciting the prayers.

This appears to be all that need be said here about indulgences in theory and in practice. The doctrine of indulgences is one that brings constantly to mind the mercy of Almighty God, who wills not only that men should be saved and well prepared for heaven, but wills also that they may fit themselves for a speedy entrance into their heavenly home through penance, absolution, the performance of good works and the right use of the Church's treasury of merit. Has not St James written (1. 17): "Whatever gifts are worth having, whatever endowments are perfect of their kind, these come to us from above; they are sent down by the Father of all that gives light"?

SELECT BIBLIOGRAPHY

ALTANER, Berthold: *Patrology*, London and New York, Nelson, 1960.

BÉVENOT, Maurice, S.J. (Editor and Translator): *St Cyprian: The Lapsed*, "Ancient Christian Writers" series, Vol. 25, London, Longmans, and Westminster, Md, Newman Press, 1957.

CAYRÉ, C., A.A.: *Manual of Patrology and History of Theology*, translated by H. Howitt, A.A. Two volumes, Paris, 1936.

DAVIS, Henry, S.J.: *Moral and Pastoral Theology*, edited by Leonard Geddes, S.J., four volumes, London and New York, Sheed and Ward, 1958.

HARRINGTON, Henry: "The Sacrament of Penance" in *The Teaching of the Catholic Church*, London, Burns Oates, and New York, Macmillan, 1948.

JUNGMANN, Josef A., S.J.: *The Early Liturgy to the Time of Gregory the Great*, London, Darton, Longman and Todd, and Notre Dame, Ind., Notre Dame Press, 1959.

KURTSCHEID, B.: *A History of the Seal of Confession*, St Louis, Herder, 1927.

LEPICIER, Cardinal H., O.S.M.: *Indulgences, their Origin, Nature and Development*, London, Burns Oates, 1928.

LE SAINT, William P., S.J.: *Tertullian: Treatises on Penance*, "Ancient Christian Writers" series, Vol. 28, London, Longmans, and Westminster, Md, Newman Press, 1959.

OTT, Ludwig: *Fundamentals of Catholic Dogma*, Cork, Mercier Press, 1960, and St Louis, Herder, 1957.

OTTEN, Bernard, S.J.: *A Manual of the History of Dogmas*, St Louis, Herder, 1917.

PALMER, Paul F., S.J.: *Sources of Christian Theology*, Volume II, *Sacraments and Forgiveness*, London, Darton, Longman and Todd, and Westminster, Md, Newman Press, 1960.

POHLE, Joseph: *The Sacraments*, Vol. II, *Penance*, London and St Louis, Herder, 1946.

PRÜMMER, M., O.P.: *Handbook of Moral Theology*, Cork, Mercier Press, 1956, and New York, Kenedy, 1960.

QUASTEN, J.: *Patrology*, Volumes 1-3, Westminster, Md, Newman Press, 1950-9.

SAINT-SÉVERIN, Community of: *Confession: The Meaning and Practice of the Sacrament of Penance*, London, Geoffrey Chapman, and Westminster, Md, Newman Press, 1959.

SPITZIG, J.P.: *The Sacrament of Penance in the Twelfth and Thirteenth Centuries*, Washington, Catholic Univ. Press, 1941.

WATKINS, Oscar D.: *A History of Penance*, London and New York, Longmans, 1920.

DEATH AND THE CHRISTIAN

IS VOLUME

55

OF THE

Twentieth Century Encyclopedia of Catholicism

UNDER SECTION

V

THE LIFE OF FAITH

IT IS ALSO THE

61ST

VOLUME IN ORDER OF PUBLICATION

Edited by HENRI DANIEL-ROPS of the Académie Française

DEATH
AND THE CHRISTIAN

By *JEAN-CHARLES DIDIER*

Translated from the French by P. J. HEPBURNE-SCOTT

HAWTHORN BOOKS · PUBLISHERS · *New York*

First Edition, March, 1961

NIHIL OBSTAT

Hubertus Richards, S.T.L., L.S.S.

   Censor Deputatus

IMPRIMATUR

E. Morrogh Bernard

   Vicarius Generalis

Westmonasterii, die XXIV DECEMBRIS MCMLX

CONTENTS

PART I

MAN'S MISERY AND GOD'S SALVATION

CHAPTER I

MESSIANIC
FORESHADOWINGS

Suffering and death are among man's deepest sources of anguish, as modern psychology makes so strikingly clear. Some try to avoid the thought of them, straining to gather rosebuds while they may, but none can escape them. The age-old complaint may be forcibly silenced for a while but is always ready to break out again: "No longer will your happy home give you welcome, no longer will your best of wives and your sweet children race to win the first kisses, and thrill your heart to its depths with sweetness. . . . Poor man, poor man! one fatal day has robbed you of all these prizes of life."[1]

The wisdom of the ancients was not always so earthbound, of course: it could face the inevitable with nobility. Socrates could say:

> Those of us who think that death is an evil are in error . . . for one of two things—either death is a state of nothingness and utter unconsciousness, or, as men say, there is a change and migration of the soul from this world to another. Now if you suppose that there is no consciousness, but a sleep like the sleep of him who is undisturbed even by dreams, death will be an unspeakable gain. . . . But if death is the journey to another place, and there, as men say, all the dead abide, what good . . . can be greater than this?[2]

[1] Lucretius, *De Rerum Natura*, III, 894–9. Trans. W. H. D. Rouse.

[2] Plato, *Apology*, 40. Trans. B. Jowett.

Marcus Aurelius was later to emphasize the inevitability of this law of nature and the worthlessness of this life:

> Despise not death, but cheerfully acquiesce in it as one of many acts ordained by the will of Nature. . . . Nothing will tend more to reconcile thee with death than to consider the objects thou wilt leave behind, and the morals of those with whom thy soul will no longer be involved. . . . What then is left to hold thee here? . . . Say, wilt thou not await in cheerfulness this end of thine, whether it be extinction or transformation?[3]

These two last quotations leave the door open to the hypothesis of survival. But only God knows how dark Hades is and how unsubstantial is the life of the shades, as far as we can judge from often conflicting assertions. And common sense easily outweighs philosophy: "Seek not to speak soothingly to me of death, glorious Odysseus. I should choose to serve as the hireling of another, of some portionless man whose livelihood was but small, rather than to be lord over all the dead who have perished."[4] For after all "it is sweet to see the light of day".[5]

It is in the mystery cults and the religions of salvation, to the extent at least that they did not grow decadent, that we find the hope of a blessed immortality in the light, that *lux perpetua* in striking contrast with the idea of a *somnus aeternalis*, analogous with annihilation.

No man can remain indifferent to this hope of immortality and survival. But how frail it is! At best, the soul is freed from the body, like the Greek "psyche" with butterfly wings, emerging from the chrysalis to fly to mysterious, embalmed retreats. And along with this hope

[3] *Meditations*, IX, 3 and V, 33. Trans. Jackson (Oxford, 1906).
[4] *Odyssey*, XI, 488–91. Trans. A. T. Murray (Loeb, 1946).
[5] Euripides, *Iphigenia at Aulis*, 1218–19.

in a life beyond death, what scepticism and doubt, what unashamed profession of materialism!

Even the Jewish religion seems only slowly and tardily to have accepted a serene concept of the future life. In Sheol there was room only for a ghostly life, without fulfilment or joy: "Brief, brief is my span of days; for a little leave me to myself, to find some comfort in my misery. Soon I must go to a land whence there is no returning, a land of darkness, death's shadow over it; a land of gloomy night, where death's shadow lies over all" (Job 10. 20–2).

It was the land of oblivion, where even the praise of God and hope in him were found no longer. "Thou hast no praise in the world beneath, death cannot honour thee; those who go down into the grave have no promise of thine to hope for" (Isaias 38. 18; cf. Psalm 6. 6; 117. 7).

On the same view of things the rewards of good and evil can only be temporal. We can understand how a reflecting soul like Ecclesiastes was tossed tragically to and fro between his faith in God and the twofold temptation, either to an epicurean enjoyment of life or to a universal pessimism: "all is vanity!"

And yet, after the Exile, Jewish religion was afforded certain glimmerings of fresh light. Here and there a voice was heard to sing of the hope of not going down into Sheol, of not remaining there but of living with God: "Thou wilt not leave my soul in the place of death, nor allow thy faithful servant to see corruption" (Psalm 16. 10; cf. 48. 16; 85, 13; 72. 23–4).

The book of Wisdom, of Alexandrian origin, magnificently expresses the idea of immortality in the presence of God (3. 1–7), while the idea of a resurrection of the body appears in Daniel (12. 2–3), Machabees (2 Mach. 7) and perhaps Isaias (26. 19).

But all these tendencies give the impression of being parallel rather than really convergent. In our Lord's time belief among the Jewish people was far from unanimous. The Sadducees did not believe in the resurrection of the body (cf. Matt. 22. 23–33; Acts 23. 6–10), and while the Pharisees, indeed, professed it, they seemed to conceive of it in a very down-to-earth fashion, unconnected with the vision of God. Full light was still to come.

Then one day, from his prison, John the Baptist sent messengers to the Man to whom he had formerly borne witness, asking him this question: "Is it thy coming that was foretold, or are we yet waiting for some other?" Perhaps John was finding it long to wait for the coming of the Kingdom and its judgement, which he had thought to glimpse (Matt. 3. 1–12). It was then that Jesus made him understand, by clear references to the prophet Isaias (26. 19; 29. 18f; 35. 5f; 61. 1), that the Messianic coming was accomplished. Now these references bore precisely on those works of power which accompanied the daily preaching of the Gospel: "The blind see, and the lame walk, the lepers are made clean, and the deaf hear, the dead are raised to life, and the poor have the gospel preached to them"; works of power, all of them, which repelled sickness and death and proved that the liberation of man's body was a sign of the Messianic age.

In fact, Christ's miracles are rich with an inexhaustible meaning: not merely manifestations of power in support of belief in a doctrine, but signs, pregnant with a whole divine mystery. No episode teaches this more clearly than that of the palsied man to whom Jesus said: "Son, take courage, thy sins are forgiven" (Matt. 9. 2). And when he heard murmurings, he replied: "Which command is more lightly given, to say to a man, Thy sins are forgiven, or to say, Rise up, and walk? And now, to convince you that the Son of man has authority to forgive sins while he is on earth (here he spoke to the palsied man), Rise up, take thy bed with thee, and go home."

Here we see Christ engaged in his primordial task, the forgiveness of sin and the struggle against evil. But the salvation he brings concerns the whole man; the Kingdom he inaugurates will not admit suffering and death any more than it will let the devil retain his hold: "Preach, . . . telling them, The kingdom of heaven is at hand. Heal the sick, raise the dead, cleanse the lepers, cast out devils" (Matt. 10. 7–8). That is why cures and raisings from the dead go hand in hand with the pardon of sins. The work of salvation is the liberation of the entire man, both body and soul.

What the Messianic work is to effect in us can be perceived through the medium of Christ's human nature. One day, indeed, during his mortal life, to three of his disciples he opened a window on the mystery of his person: "his face shining like the sun, and his garments becoming white as snow". This momentary transfiguration (Matt. 17. 2) revealed an order of things normal in itself, the reflection of the Word on the humanity he had assumed. Actually, what was abnormal was that this glory was usually veiled in him who represented in his person the Kingdom in all its power, but when, having suffered death, he rose from the grave, then his victory finally shone out through his humanity.

Behold him then, "firstborn from the dead" (Col. 1. 18) and our pattern; or rather, the one in union with whom we must be dissolved to have part in his death and resurrection and to live eternally in God.

But how? The Church has inherited the Messianic

function of the victorious strife against death, continuing Christ's work in the world. Nothing can be more instructive than to compare the mission given to the Twelve at the beginning of the public ministry ("Preach, . . . telling them, The kingdom of heaven is at hand. Heal the sick, raise the dead"—Matt. 10. 7–8) with the one given them after the Lord's resurrection ("You . . . must go out, making disciples of all nations and baptizing them"—Matt. 28. 19). The parallelism is obvious. And so the sacraments, like Christ's miracles, and in the same line with them, express, for the era of the Church, the presence of salvation, the action of the Spirit, the anticipation of the Kingdom.

As we know, baptism brings us into the mystery of Christ's death and resurrection (Rom. 6. 3–5), and the ancient catechetical instructions, such as that of Theodore of Mopsuestia, did not shrink from regarding us boldly as beyond death, as if it had been by-passed by the very reception of the sacrament. Moreover, theology does not hesitate to admit that baptism of its nature possesses sufficient efficacy to deliver us from all the ills of this life,[6] and this is true for the body as for the soul.

It is obvious, of course, that the man who has lived through our Lord's death and resurrection in mystery, and has thus acquired the right to return to Paradise and the paschal life, does not thereby enjoy, immediately, the complete and final liberation from evil which is nonetheless their logical consequence. The Christian remains at grips with sin, suffering and death. Theology can explain this, but for our purpose it is enough to say that the Spirit, whose action is the precise characteristic of the coming of the Messias (Acts 2. 14–21), has been given us as the "foretaste" (2 Cor. 1. 22; 5. 5) and the "first fruits"

[6] St Thomas Aquinas, *Summa Theologica*, III, 69, 3.

(Rom. 8. 23, Westminster Version) of the perfect liberation: "And if the Spirit of him who raised up Jesus from the dead dwells in you, he who raised up Jesus Christ from the dead will give life to your perishable bodies too, for the sake of his Spirit who dwells in you" (Rom. 8. 11).

And during this waiting, which marks out the period of faith and hope, all natural things are transfigured because of the new meaning they have received since Christ came.

Evil of course is a problem, one which unbelief transforms into an absurdity and a scandal. We all know the use made of the objection by the philosophy of the "Enlightenment" against belief in God.[7] The Christian, for his part, sees it as a trial; that is, first of all a danger to be fought against with the help of God, but also an opportunity of living more closely with Christ the mystery of the world's redemption (Col. 1. 24).

[7] See Paul Hazard, *The European Mind* (London, Hollis and Carter, and Newhaven, Conn., Yale Univ. Press), pp. 99 ff.

CHAPTER II

THE TRANSFIGURATION OF THE CHRISTIAN'S SICKNESS AND DEATH

The history of the Christian attitude to sickness has not yet been really studied. This is a pity, for we thus lack a very fine chapter in the story of Christian spirituality.[1] We can at least note some of its landmarks since Gospel days, when the grace of healing fought miraculously against sickness and infirmity in the name of the Messianic advent. The apostolic age and the succeeding generations were familiar with it, as St Irenaeus testifies.[2] This grace of healing did not disappear later: it would be unthinkable that God should withdraw from his Church, faced with the same problems of the coming Kingdom, the gift of which she disposed at the beginning of her mission.

Although healing has not disappeared we should look for it not so much in the realm of miracles—those of Lourdes, for example—as in that anointing of the sick of which we are about to treat, an organized charisma, a sacramental remedy.

---

[1] It has been broached by Abbé H. R. Philippeau in *La Maison-Dieu*, 15, pp. 53–81, "La maladie dans la tradition liturgique et pastorale". Evelyn Frost, *Christian Healing* (London and Oxford, 2nd ed., 1949), deals only with the Ante-Nicene Church.

[2] Quoted by Eusebius, *Ecclesiastical History*, Bk. V, c. 7 (ed. Lawlor and Oulton, London, 1928, I, p. 152).

What matters, behind this charisma or this sacrament, is the intention governing their use: the struggle against sickness on the strictly Christian plane, in an order of things directly connected with the eschatological Kingdom, where there will be no more "mourning, or cries of distress, no more sorrow" (Apoc. 21. 4). For sickness is an evil bound up with a sinful world, a world under the power of the devil.

But at the same time Christian thought on sickness is marked with the example of St Paul, who bears in his body the "stigmata", the scars of our Lord; his request for his cure is answered with "My grace is enough for thee" (2 Cor. 12. 9); he finally finds joy in his sufferings, in the thought that he helps to pay off in his mortal frame "the debt which the afflictions of Christ still leave to be paid, for the sake of his body, the Church" (Col. 1. 24). And on the other hand Christian piety fervently welcomes the words of Christ, who identifies himself with every sick person, saying: "I was sick, and you cared for me" (Matt. 25. 36).

It is around these two poles, the strife against sickness and the understanding of its mystical worth, that the Christian ages have revolved. Charity towards the sick, embodied in touching forms in the monastic Customaries,[3] and the respect for them shown by the Hospitallers' Orders, both prove, at the heart of the institutions devised for their benefit, the "eminent dignity" the sick were accorded. A whole liturgy was elaborated purposely to surround them with the Church's prayer and thus to assist them in their effort to be spiritually delivered and physically cured, or else to rise nobly above their pains.

As for the sick, they are made aware of their trial and,

[3] See the touching acts of attention to the sick prescribed at Cluny, in Philippeau, *art. cit.*, pp. 76–8.

while asking for the grace to be released from it, they learn that it may be for them a means of purification, of sanctification, mystical identification with Christ crucified, and of praise of God. Certainly it is only the greatest souls who attain the heights: a Hermann Contract in the eleventh century, a Hermann Joseph in the twelfth, a St Gertrude in the thirteenth, a Margaret Ebner in the fourteenth, among others; not forgetting, in the East, the extraordinary figure of a Syncletica in the fourth century, who extolled her sickness as an expression of the glory of God.

But these examples, exceptional as they appear, are steeped in a whole atmosphere to which they belong, and on which they react in their turn. The medieval West gives clear testimony of devotion to Christ in his passion and frequent expression of the desire to suffer with him and imitate him is found. A whole spiritual literature, besides, developed and popularized the theme of "blessed suffering"; the treatise—*De duodecim utilitatibus tribulationum*[4] —had an incalculable influence on morality and spirituality. Ascetic writers thereafter felt the need to include some chapter on the good use of illness, and some of these are justly celebrated.

From the very outset, Christians were aware more easily how much death changed its aspect when seen through Christ, who had himself conquered death and saved the world by his own dying. The death of Christ appeared in very truth to his followers as the greatest act of love, the ideal passage from the world to God, the perfect sacrifice on behalf of all mankind, and his glorious resurrection projected its light through the gate he had opened.

[4] "On the twelve benefits of afflictions". This twelfth-century treatise seems to be the work of the Cistercian Gerald of Liège. Migne published it among the works of Peter of Blois: Migne, *Patrologia Latina,* 207, 989–1006 (hereafter referred to as *P.L.*).

For the baptized person, who has been mystically initiated into Christ's death and resurrection, even though he has yet to die, death can now seem only an imitation of his model and an accomplishing of the Paschal mystery.[5] Death has become a supreme act of faith and the crowning of that personal sacrifice which every Christian life offers to God, the definitive passing from sin to salvation "in Christ".

The Christian's death is, in literal truth, overwhelming in its grandeur and beauty. "God cannot behold any human death without being recalled to the presence of the death of Christ. A sight such as Calvary is not forgotten; the Father, if we may speak in an anthropomorphical manner which is here justifiable, never ceases to be moved by it. Seeing any man die, God sees again the death of Christ on the Cross."[6] On his side, man finds in this communion with Christ not only the certainty of eternal life and the resurrection of the flesh but the power to make the total gift of himself, in peace and joy, to the glory of the Father, for the crowning blessing of all is this: "Blessed are the dead who die in the Lord" (Apoc. 14. 13).

Much remains to be written about the attitude of successive Christian generations in the presence of death, starting with St Paul, for whom "death is a prize to be won" (Philipp. 1. 21), and the martyrs who went to their deaths as to a banquet. Certainly, on this point, there has been a noticeable evolution in Christian consciences in the course of the ages, from serenity to fear.[7] This is attested partly in a voluminous literature on the "Art of

[5] On this point, see L. Bouyer, *The Paschal Mystery* (Notre Dame, Ind., and London, 1950).

[6] R. Guelluy, "La mort du racheté", in the *Revue diocésaine de Tournai*, 1959, p. 89.

[7] See Philippeau, *art. cit.*, p. 60.

dying", as well as in art and even in the liturgy. No doubt it has sometimes had a warping or impoverishing effect. But the saints, and countless Christians following in their steps, have been able to give their deaths the full meaning they derived from Christ. St Teresa of Lisieux might well be afraid, in prospect, of not knowing how to die,[8] yet she died a beautiful death, saying, "My God, I love you!" And how touching is the reflection of the dying Suarez: "I never knew how lovely it was to die!" The deaths of monks, surrounded and sanctified by the ancient customs of the cloister, express an ideal put into practice. Every true Christian knows that "it is not primarily our life we must try to make happy and good, but our death", and that the greatest grace is not to be unaware of our dying but, on the contrary, to die in full consciousness, "peering through the door at our heart's desire".[9]

[8] *Novissima Verba* (Dublin, 1953), p. 137.
[9] G. Bernanos, quoted by Urs von Balthasar, *Le chrétien Bernanos* (Paris, 1956), pp. 418, 431.

CHAPTER III

THE CHURCH IN ACTION

The salient feature of the Christian attitude to sickness and death is a sort of assumption that the body, far from being forgotten, unconsidered or despised, is a constituent element of the human being, essential in its own right. This Jewish-Christian concept of the relation between soul and body is poles apart from a dualist philosophy, such as Platonism can be, and this contrast has its reaction in the strictly Christian teaching: the body is necessarily concerned with every idea of redemption and salvation offered to man. Bodily suffering and death affect the soul in its own being, and the eternal life of the soul can only find its perfect fulfilment by the resurrection of the body, just as even now in this life the health of the soul is closely bound up with that of the body. The Kingdom of God is offered not to "souls" but to "men and women", who consist of bodies as well as souls.

This was the purpose of Christ's miracles: to anticipate an integral salvation of man. And this is the rôle of the Church, to introduce us to the mystery of the same salvation, with the hope of its perfect revelation at the "last day". She fulfils this rôle through all her actions, from beginning to end of the Christian's life. Certain of her actions, being more specially endowed with supernatural meaning and efficacy, are called "sacraments" in the strict sense. Yet we must never forget that the Church is the great sacrament of salvation, and that her least actions enfold us in an atmosphere of sacramentalism, in order that the mystery of salvation may take possession of us.

That is why the Church multiplies her blessings: she bestows them on all the day-to-day objects and the humblest elements of our lives: on bread, oil, water, wine, beer, eggs, butter, cheese, lard and new fruits, every food and every medicine; she does this in order that we may keep or recover our health of soul and body, that sin and sickness may be driven off, that the power of Satan may be broken and joy may possess us.[1]

The Blessed Sacrament itself is offered to us not merely to produce grace and fervour in our souls but equally as ordained for the health of the body. Cassian († 435) and the Synod of Orange (441) order Communion to be given to the "energumens" (possessed), to resist the attacks of the devil and deliver the possessed from them.[2] St Caesarius of Arles († 543) urges his flock to receive the Eucharist as a remedy which preserves and cures on the two planes of spirit and body.[3] The liturgy of the Mass itself affirms the virtue of the Sacrament: *medicina sacramenti et corporibus nostris prosit et mentibus; ad tutamentum mentis et corporis; sit nobis reparatio mentis et corporis caeleste mysterium.*[4] And in an even more explicit formula it prays that the eucharistic sacrifice may purify us from our sins: *quia tunc veram nobis tribuis et mentis et corporis sanitatem.*[5]

[1] All these blessings are found in the Roman Ritual.

[2] Cassian, *Conferences*, VII, 30. Synod of Orange, can. 14. (Hefele-Leclercq, II, pp. 442–3).

[3] Serm. XIII, 3; L, 1; LII, 5: CLXXXIV, 5 (ed. Dom Morin, I, pp. 65, 216, 222, 710).

[4] "May the medicine of the sacrament benefit both our bodies and our souls;" "for the protection of soul and body;" "may the heavenly mystery be to us for healing of soul and body."

[5] "For then thou grantest us true health both of soul and of body." Dom P. Bruylants, *Les oraisons du missel romain* (Louvain, 1952), I, No. 973, 994, 1065, 1099.

Very frequently the Church's prayer goes up for the benefit of our health, bodily as well as spiritual. Such prayers are found when she blesses the candles at Candlemas or the ashes at the beginning of Lent; and on Good Friday, in her "universal prayers", it is strictly physical healing that she requests for all the sick. In fact she does not even need any special occasion to frame her prayer thus: (*Concede nos*) "Grant to thy servants, we beseech thee, O Lord God, the grace to enjoy continual health of body and soul, ... that we may be freed from our present sadness and rejoice in everlasting gladness."[6]

More especially when anyone is seriously ill, the Church surrounds her children with her prayer, her blessing, her encouragement, her spiritual help, her active charity. She has a whole liturgy for the visitation of the sick and puts at their disposal her greatest remedy, the *medicina ecclesiae*, the sacrament of Unction.

When death approaches she provides the Christian with his provision for the road, the sacrament of the great journey to the Lord, the Viaticum. Then she redoubles her prayers and solicitude for the one who is setting out for "the Father's house" and accompanies him to the very threshold of eternity, entrusting him then to the angels and saints, whom she summons to take over the charge from her; this is the "Commendation of the Soul".

After death, prayer still continues for the soul of the departed, while the body, through all the stages of the funeral liturgy till its committal to the earth, is surrounded with care and honour, in the name of the Christian faith in the resurrection of the body.

[6] Bruylants, *op. cit.*, 122.

PART II

THE SACRAMENT OF THE SICK AND THE RITES CONNECTED WITH IT

CHAPTER IV

THE SACRAMENT OF THE SICK: SCRIPTURE AND THE RITE

"Is one of you sick? Let him send for the presbyters[1] of the church, and let them pray over him, anointing him with oil in the Lord's name. Prayer offered in faith will restore the sick man, and the Lord will give him relief; if he is guilty of sins, they will be pardoned." So it is written in the Epistle of St James, 5. 14–15.

The Council of Trent, in its fourteenth session, committed itself to an authoritative definition of the meaning of this text:[2] it is a matter of faith that the Church here speaks of our sacrament of the Anointing of the Sick. The Apostle does not, of course, "institute" it but, in the Council's words, he "promulgates" and "commends" it to his readers. It follows naturally that its existence was already an established fact.

---

[1] Or "priests", in conformity with the teaching of the Council of Trent.

[2] We need not be surprised at the Church's deciding on the interpretation of a text of Scripture, thus exceeding in this field the limits accepted by scientific criticism, which rightly does not go further than its own possibilities allow. But the Church has the understanding of the Word of God because she possesses the Holy Spirit; she can see and read better than the scholars. This helps to explain Loisy's condemnation on this very point.

The institution of this sacrament, properly speaking, is something earlier. It derives, necessarily, from our Lord himself, and this too is a truth of faith which applies to all the sacraments, since Christ himself is their author. Some theologians have even thought they could find the origin of our sacrament of the sick in the text which says of the Twelve, sent on their mission by Christ, that "many who were sick they anointed with oil, and healed them" (Mark 6. 13). This text does, indeed, strongly suggest, on the one hand, the indubitable material continuity between the common ancient use of oil as a medicine,[3] and our sacramental anointings, and on the other, the undeniable parallelism, in the spiritual and religious order, between the charisma of healing in the Gospel period and our sacrament of the sick. Tradition, moreover, has not neglected this text: even before Bede († 735) who commented on it,[4] the Life of St Radegund[5] clearly alludes to it when it tells us that the saint used to anoint the sick with oil "in the manner of the Gospel". The Council of Trent, however, prudently declined to see in St Mark's phrase more than a preliminary statement, if as much: a mere hint or indication of the sacrament to come.[6] It is not easy, in fact, to discover the historical moment of the institution of each sacrament,[7] but of course that is not necessary for those who know how faithful the Church is in all her acts to the spirit and instructions of Christ: her tradition is one of unchangeable attachment and memory.

Furthermore, does not the question arise from posing

[3] E.g. in the parable of the Good Samaritan (Luke 10. 34).

[4] Migne, *P.L.* 92, 188.

[5] *More evangelico oleo superfuso* (*Monumenta Germaniae Historica*: scr. rer. mer., II, p. 370).

[6] The Council at first used the term *delineatum*, but finally preferred *insinuatum* in the final revision of its decree.

[7] Except for the Eucharist, of course.

the problem wrongly? Certain episodes in the Gospel may well, occasionally, give us a good view of the work of Christ, but in the aggregate they are only points of emergence in a progressive work which went on day by day: the founding of the Church was our Saviour's daily care, and the same is therefore true of the institution of the sacraments, which was coextensive and, as it were, identical with that founding.

However that may be, it is opportune to emphasize that "the sacraments were not born from the written texts".[8] The Church lived them, she performed and handed on their actions from the beginning, before the existence of any canonical literature, and *a fortiori* before any reference to it. This is precisely the case with the oil of the sick, and we may venture to say, in this instance, that it is fortunate. For while the Council of Trent laid down, as we saw, that the text of St James dealt with this sacrament, it must also be acknowledged that, for several centuries, not only did nobody interpret it in this sense, but, on the contrary, it was often positively understood in another way: by Origen, for instance, in his second homily on Leviticus.[9]

It was not till the beginning of the fifth century, in fact, with Innocent I and his correspondent Decentius of Gubbio, that we find a definite connection established between the text and the rite.[10] But the link connecting them is, from this moment, a definitely established fact. By itself, or handed on by Innocent and then by the Venerable Bede, the text passed from hand to hand down the ages, in

[8] Mgr Batiffol, in *Revue Biblique*, 1903, p. 528.

[9] Migne, *Patrologia Graeca*, 12, 417 (hereafter referred to as *P.G.*).

[10] The *Canons of Hippolytus*, can. 200, very probably allude to James 5. 14–15, but it is far from proved that they are earlier than the letter of Innocent I.

the service of the sacrament of the sick. Again it is worth noting that at first they argued more naturally from the rite to the text than vice versa: it was the rite which explained the text.

Little by little, however, the converse took place and James, more carefully studied, continually threw light on the rite and, as need arose, modelled it in several of its parts. So we have this form of anointing: "I give thee this anointing in the name of the Father and of the Son and of the Holy Ghost, that the prayer of faith may save thee and the Lord may raise thee up."[11] In a great number of ancient rituals the text of St James actually introduces the whole rite with this prayer, which the Roman liturgy has preserved, while displacing it to near the end:

> Lord God, who hast said through thy apostle James: "Is one sick among you? Let him send for the presbyters of the church, and let them pray over him, anointing him with oil in the Lord's name: prayer offered in faith will restore the sick man, and the Lord will give him relief; if he is guilty of sins, they will be pardoned:" cure, we beseech thee, our Redeemer, by the grace of the Holy Spirit, the ailments of this thy servant who is sick; heal his wounds and forgive his sins: drive out from him all pains of body and mind, and mercifully restore to him full health, inwardly and outwardly, that being recovered by the help of thy mercy, he may return to his former duties.

The sacramental theology elaborated in the twelfth and thirteenth centuries could not but continue in strict dependence on this text of Scripture and at the same time on the practice of the Churches, as we can judge from St Thomas Aquinas.[12] Finally and specially, the teaching of the Council of Trent appears as purely and simply a

[11] Theodulf of Orleans (Migne, *P.L.* 105, 220).
[12] *Summa Theologica*, Supplement, Qu. 29–33.

commentary on the words of St James. After quoting them at length, it declares: "By these words, as the Church has learned from the tradition of the apostles received from their hands, she teaches what is the matter, the form, the proper minister and the effect of this saving sacrament."[13] Further, the Council later affirmed that the words of St James constituted a "promulgation" of the sacrament, and that its use, as well as the rite used by the Roman Church, was in perfect conformity with the Apostle's text.[14]

The Council's exegesis was thus directed at replying to Protestant denials by expounding the Catholic doctrine on the anointing of the sick, starting from James 5. 14–15, and quite legitimately it read this text in the light of the Church's whole tradition, a tradition which is not confined to conceptual pronouncements but is above all a life. It is therefore only right that we should examine the practice of the Church and the behaviour of Christians through the ages.

[13] Session XIV, *On the institution of the sacrament of Extreme Unction.*

[14] *Ibid.* Canons 1–4.

CHAPTER V

HISTORY OF THE RITE: THE BLESSING OF THE OIL

We are the more bound to explore the practice of the Church and the faithful in regard to the oil of the sick, since, as we have said, this practice was established, down to the fifth century (Innocent I), without any reference to Scripture.

Now it must be admitted that the evidence for the use of the oil during this period is very rare: a text of doubtful import in St Irenaeus[1] in the second century; another, definitely probable this time, in St John Chrysostom about the end of the fourth.[2] The following piece of evidence, dating from the same period, is valuable to us because it shows us the practice of the laity: it concerns the wife of a Count Avitianus, who asked St Martin to bless, "as is the custom", a vessel of oil intended for a remedy in illnesses.[3]

"As is the custom": although we have no information, in fact, for the first four centuries on how the oil of the sick was used, the liturgical documents, on the contrary, give us prayers for the blessing of this oil which are very significant. We may set aside one found in a fragment

[1] Quoted by Eusebius, *Ecclesiastical History*, Bk V, c. 7, ed. Lawlor and Oulton, Vol. I (London, 1927–8), p. 152.

[2] *In Matthaeum*. Homily XXXII, 6 (Migne, *P.G.* 57, 384).

[3] Sulpicius Severus, *Dialogues*, III, 3 (Migne, *P.L.* 20, 213).

of the Coptic version of the *Didache*, discovered in 1924:[4] in spite of the esteem in which it is held by certain historians,[5] it is neither sufficiently authentic nor clear in its interpretation, nor of sufficient antiquity to compete with the formula of St Hippolytus in his *Apostolic Tradition*. This actually dates from the beginning of the third century and shows us a Roman practice. Its influence, moreover, was considerable in the East. We give it here in its simple and condensed sobriety: "O God, who sanctifiest this oil, as thou dost grant unto all who are anointed and receive of it the hallowing wherewith thou didst anoint kings, priests and prophets, so (grant that) it may give strength to all that taste of it and health to all that use it."[6]

Later on, the *Euchologion* or Prayer-book of Serapion of Thmuis († after 362), the *Apostolic Constitutions* (end of fourth century), and others too, show that in Egypt, Syria, etc., there was a blessing of oil for the sick. In the West the prayer from the *Apostolic Tradition* left a surprising mark on the formula of the Roman Pontifical, which is still in use and seems most probably to go back to the fourth century, judging by several signs and excepting several later amendments. We give it in the state in which it came to us from the eighth century:[7]

Send down from heaven, O Lord, we pray thee, the Holy Spirit, the Paraclete, on this richness of oil, which thou hast been pleased to draw from the living tree, for the refresh-

[4] Cf. J. Audet, *La Didaché, Instructions des apôtres* (Paris, 1958). pp. 67–70.

[5] Especially P. Boschmann, *Busse und Letzte Oelung* (Freiburg, 1951), p. 127.

[6] *The Treatise of St Hippolytus on the Apostolic Tradition*, 5, ed. G. Dix (London, 1937).

[7] Translated from *The Gelasian Sacramentary*, ed. H. A. Wilson (Oxford, 1894), p. 73.

ment of soul and body. And may thy holy blessing make of it, for all who anoint with it, drink it or touch it, a protection for the body (the soul and the spirit), banishing all pain, all sickness, all suffering of mind and body; this thy perfect Chrism, O Lord, with which thou hast anointed priests, kings, prophets and martyrs,[8] which thou hast blessed and which abides in our inmost being, in the Name of our Lord Jesus Christ.

These liturgical texts compensate for the regrettable scarcity of documents in the first Christian centuries, revealing an officially accepted authorized rite. Yet that is not their only advantage. They enrich our knowledge of the sacrament of the sick at this time by showing us that before the oil could be used it had to be blessed, in order to make it a sacrament and raise it to the strictly super-natural level. Everything that happens assumes, in short, that the sacrament of the sick took place in two stages: first the preparation of the holy oil, then its administration.

This explains both the action of the Christian woman, referred to earlier, who sent oil to St Martin for him to bless, and many other similar events in the course of time. In the fifth century, for example, we have St Gene-viève, who often anointed the sick with oil; one day it happened that the jar of blessed oil she kept by her was found to be empty just when she wanted it for an urgent case. And she was all anxiety, says her biographer, "because there was no bishop within reach to bless it".[9] We

[8] The anointing of kings and priests recalls the Old Testament, as does that of prophets, though this latter example is somewhat doubtful. The anointing of martyrs is very difficult to explain, but in this connection there appears a curious resemblance between the Coptic liturgy and our own, on which may be consulted Dom E. Lanne, in *Irénikon*, 1958, pp. 138–55.

[9] *Vita beatae Genovefae* (*Mon. Germ. Hist.*, scr. rer. merov., III, p. 236).

draw attention to this point here, because it is typical of a well-established principle.

"Blessing" implies recourse to the Church, to the hierarchy whose intervention may be limited, as we shall see, to this blessing; but this intervention is preponderant in the subsequent use of the oil, and indeed indispensable to it, and from this derives the liturgical character it assumes, whatever variations in discipline may appear as between one Church and another.

In Rome, for example, the blessing is reserved to the bishop in the course of the Mass, in the place where we still find it today in the Mass of the Chrism; but before the seventh century it might be on any day, and "by request", we might say, for in those days it was the faithful who provided the oil and took it home once it was blessed, whereas nowadays Maundy Thursday is the only day in the year normally prescribed for it.

In Gaul, on the other hand, before the seventh or eighth century, the priest as well as the bishop is the minister of this blessing, which is given at any time and is not confined to the celebration of Mass; if the priest himself is to apply the blessed oil he blesses it just when he wants to use it. The same discipline is in force for Milan and goes on there till much later, apparently till the twelfth century. But finally, in one place after another, the Roman discipline prevailed.

THE ADMINISTRATION OF THE HOLY OIL

We have already noted that for several centuries the faithful, on their own initiative, used to bring to the priest the oil they wished to have blessed, and then to take it home as the "Church's medicine" against sickness. That the practice was general can be deduced from innumerable examples in the sixth and seventh centuries. The bishops encouraged it, moreover, partly, of course, to counteract the superstitions and magical practices so numerous and persistent in a population barely converted from paganism. St Caesarius of Arles († 543), for instance, and later St Eligius of Noyon († 660) earnestly commend this *medicina ecclesiae*: "Seek for health from Christ, the true light: have recourse to the Church, be anointed with blessed oil . . ."[10] "When their children are ill, certain mothers run groaning and distraught and, what is worse, do not ask for the Church's remedy . . . whereas they ought to anoint them, as it is written, with the oil blessed by the priests. . . ."[11]

Caesarius did not preach to deaf ears and, in this particular case, it was the children who were bidden by their parents to be blessed with oil by the holy bishop.[12]

Surprising as it may seem to us at first sight, the fact is that the faithful themselves had the free disposal of this holy oil, just as they now have of the holy water. Priests and bishops, of course, after blessing the oil, did not fail to apply it themselves to the sick, as need arose. There is abundant evidence of this but we shall quote only one of the less explicit texts; we know from his biographer[13] that St Augustine used to hasten to go and see the sick who desired it, in order to lay his hands on them and pray at their bedsides. It is extremely likely that he was thus carrying out the counsel of St James, and that when he prayed he not only laid his hands on them but anointed them. This likelihood is increased by the author's very

[10] St Caesarius, *Sermons*, L, 1 (ed. Dom Morin, I, p. 216).

[11] *Id.*, LII, 5 (*ibid.*, p. 222).

[12] *Life of St Caesarius of Arles*, II, 17 (*Mon. Germ. Hist.*, scr. rer. merov., III, p. 490).

[13] Possidius, *Life of St Augustine*, 27 (Migne, *P.L.* 32, 56). (Ed. with English translation by H. T. Weiskotten, Princeton, N.J. 1919.)

clear allusion to a passage of St James' epistle a few
lines before. Besides, none knew better than St Augustine
himself the import of James 5. 14–15, for he incorporated
it in his *Speculum* among the divine precepts which are
binding on all Christians, and which he had gleaned from
the whole of Scripture and collected in that book.[14]

Like Augustine, many holy bishops and abbots from the
fifth to the seventh century were active in this ministry
to the sick: Martin of Tours, Germanus of Auxerre,
Caesarius of Arles, Germanus of Paris, Arnold of Metz,
the abbots Sequanus and Eustasius, and others. Needless
to say, the faithful preferred to resort to some holy person,
both for the administration of the oil and for its blessing,
and no doubt also, they relied more on his personal virtue
as intercessor or miracle-worker than on the proper efficacy
of the oil they used.

But this does not alter the fact that the laity had the
free disposal of the oil of the sick, and that once it had
been blessed by a priest or bishop—a strictly indispensable
condition—they were allowed to use it themselves. The
case of St Geneviève mentioned above is not exceptional,
any more than that of the wife of Count Avitianus; both
cases followed the normal practice during these times
down to the Carolingian era, and throughout the Churches
of the West. We repeat, it was normal and uncontested, and
therefore canonically recognized and approved.

In that letter to Decentius already mentioned, Innocent I
wrote as follows:[15]

There can be no doubt that the text [i.e. of St James]
must be interpreted of the faithful who are ill: it is they
who can be anointed with the holy oil; once it has been
made by the bishop, all Christians, and not only those who

[14] Migne, *P.L.* 34, 1036.
[15] Migne, *P.L.* 20, 559–61.

are endued with the priesthood, may use it to anoint themselves when they have need, they or their dependants. But the rest [of the question] seems to us absurd, that is, the doubt cast on the power of the bishop, seeing that the priests possess it without any manner of doubt. There is mention of "priests", in fact (in James 5.14) because the bishops, hindered by other tasks, cannot visit all the sick. If, however, the bishop has it in his power and judges it opportune to go to see one, he can without hesitation pray over him and anoint him with the holy oil,[16] being the one to whom it pertains to make this holy oil.

This is quite categorical and admits of no interpretation, such as some have later proposed, that would weaken the force of the passage.

According to the Roman custom, the bishop has the privilege of blessing the holy oil; all the baptized have the right to use it themselves as their needs require.[17] The liturgical data exactly correspond to this situation: during these centuries we find a solidly constructed liturgy for the consecration of the oil, but no ritual at all for its administration to the sick: the faithful make use of it according to very flexible rules.

[16] The text has *et benedicere et tangere chrismate*. As the very next subject is the preparation of the holy oil in the course of an argument *a fortiori*, the word *benedicere* cannot mean the blessing of the oil. In connection with *tangere chrismate* it concerns the sick man, and only means the prayer and anointing spoken of by St James. This prayer was certainly accompanied by the laying on of hands and *benedicere* seems obviously to have this precise sense, according to Galtier (*Dict. de Théol. cath ...* VII, col. 1329).

[17] To say of St Geneviève that "the anointings she performed had nothing sacramental about them, since she did not possess the priesthood" (H. Lesêtre, *Sainte Geneviève*, Paris, 1907, p. 88), is to project our own ideas into the past and to ignore a whole body of incontestable facts.

Can we discover what use the faithful made of the oil of the sick during these same centuries? Several expressions which have survived later revisions in the consecratory prayers—we gave the text of two of them in an earlier chapter[18]—clearly prove that the holy oil could be taken as a drink. Several sources show that it was thus specially used for the dumb.

But it was in anointings that the holy oil was most often used: anointings which were ample and abundant, not at all resembling the timid and almost niggardly anointings of today; numerous and varied, even if not always an anointing of the entire body; sometimes repeated daily, like a regular medical treatment, for several days, with no limit to their duration and for as long as was required.

The parts of the body anointed vary according to the meaning attached to the anointings: when they are directly for cure, it will be the affected organ; when for relief in a wider sense it may be the head, the breast, the shoulders, etc.; when for a penitential purpose, it will be the organs of sense, the gates of sin.

In any case, there was no question of a merely physical medicine; but, as Innocent I said in the course of his letter, the oil of the sick, through the blessing it received, came into the category of "sacrament". It had therefore to be treated as such in whatever use might be made of it, and first of all, all profanation must be avoided. While the ordinary faithful had the free disposal of it, in that they performed the anointings on themselves, the unworthy, the public penitents officially deprived of the sacraments, were excluded from it. Further, although the use of the holy oil was not yet subject to the rules of a ritual, according to St James' instructions, it was accompanied

[18] Above, pp. 33, 34.

with prayer, prayer which was necessarily very simple and flexible in form, to be within the capacity of the laity.

The eighth century, however, marks a turning-point in the history of the rite. The use of oil as a drink rapidly disappears. For a time, longer or shorter in different Churches, the faithful still keep the right to perform the anointings (traces of it are found down to the twelfth century), but more and more a distinction is made between anointing by the laity and anointing by the priests. The latter steadily monopolize the administration of the oil of the sick, which is withdrawn from the hands of the laity. In future it will be for the Church to guard it, while imposing on the pastors the obligation to be more and more at the disposal of the sick.

It is now that rituals of anointing appear, and the administration of the holy oil takes on a strictly liturgical character. The wide improvisation which was the rule in former ages gives way to schemes which, while including many variants and fluctuations and even different trends of inspiration, yet represent an advance towards the crystallization of the rite.[19] The scheme adopted by Rome, and only finally imposed in the nineteenth century, is based essentially on the Cluniac customs of the early Middle Ages.

The rite is sometimes of astonishing length,[20] due as

[19] For a more detailed study of the history of the rite, see *Catholic Encyclopedia*, "Extreme Unction", by P. J. Toner.

[20] One of the most curious rituals in this way is that given us by Theodulf of Orleans († 821) in his *Capitulary* (Migne, *P.L.* 105, 220–2), which contains no less than fifteen anointings. There is no other ritual in the Latin Church with so many. But Theodulf draws from an important source, a Greek rite of his own period, and probably even older, the rite of a local church, which is confirmed by a manuscript from Sinai.

much to the prayers as to the actions (anointings, imposition of hands, signs of the cross) and the concelebration it involves, as well as to the psalmody during the anointings. The corporate character of the rite is also very marked; one ritual even concludes the administration of the sacrament with the kiss given by those present to their sick brother.[21] The anointings are often performed, as the text of St James suggests, by several priests, who divide the task variously in different rituals. In one, each of the officiants proceeds to his own anointing; in another, all recite, one after another, all the prayers; in another again, one priest reads the formula while another performs the anointings. Only the Eastern Churches have preserved to our days this custom of collegiate administration, that is, of the concelebration of the anointing of the sick, so that the rite is sometimes known among the Byzantines as the *heptapapadon*, because of the seven priests it involves. But in point of fact the Byzantine rite is here characterized not so much by its length as by its complication.

[21] Pontifical of Langres, thirteenth century.

CHAPTER VI

MODERN LITURGY AND DISCIPLINE

THE BLESSING OF THE OIL

As we saw from the consecratory prayer in the Roman Pontifical,[1] the oil which constitutes the matter of the sacrament is olive oil. Throughout the Mediterranean basin and from earliest antiquity, in fact, no other was known. It was in those days an absolutely primary and basic element of human life in many respects: food, light, personal toilet and sport, medicine. This last in particular was in constant use, in the form of drink or ointment, of which we have examples in Isaias 1. 6, Mark 6. 13 and Luke 10. 34. This is the oil referred to in the epistle of St James, the oil still required by the liturgy today. The expressed will of the Church makes its use a matter of validity.[2]

The blessing of the oil is another requisite for the validity of the sacrament.[3] In primitive times there was a

[1] Above, p. 30.

[2] *Codex Juris Canonici* (hereafter *CJC*), can. 937, 945. Does this mean that some other oil might one day be substituted for olive oil? It depends on the Church, for it does not appear to lie outside her power over the sacraments. In any case, it is certain that Churches in foreign lands, where the olive is unknown and cannot be acclimatized, would benefit by being allowed to use an indigenous oil.

[3] *CJC*, can. 734, 945.

general idea in vogue about the sacrament—that of the "vessel" which "contains" grace—according to which the sacrament consisted of the consecrated matter itself, independently of its use. Later theology, transcending this concept and placing the sacrament in the administration of the holy oil, held the blessing to be only the operation which makes the oil the "remote matter", fitting and indeed necessary for the sacramental action.[4]

In any case, from the very fact that the blessing of the oil is an essential condition for the existence of the sacrament, we should see it as something more than a bare preparation for it. It has sacramental value, and we shall not be wrong in regarding the sacrament of the sick as a sacrament which is effected at two points in time.

In the Latin Church this blessing of the oil of the sick is strictly reserved to the bishop. We know that it was not always so, at least in certain Churches. Even now, moreover, Canon Law provides that a priest, if duly authorized by the Holy See, can give this blessing.[5] As for the Eastern Churches, their traditions and rites, and consequently the priest's functions, are always safeguarded. The Council of Trent certainly had no idea of striking at the practice of these Churches, by which the priest blesses the oil when he needs it for the administration of the sacrament. On the contrary, Rome is most careful to maintain the Eastern customs with the utmost tact, and this one in particular.[6]

[4] The theologians are not so sure that the blessing necessarily requires the special formula appointed in the Pontifical. Many of the best, such as Capello, consider Extreme Unction to be valid when given with another consecrated oil, such as Chrism or the Oil of the Catechumens.

[5] *CJC*, can. 945; Council of Trent, Sess. XIV, can. 1.

[6] Thus the Congregation for the Eastern Church, by a decree of June 25th, 1933, granted to Coptic priests, without restriction, the power to bless the oil of the sick before anointing, "in conformity with the ancient use of the Church of Alexandria".

This blessing, we must remember, is reserved in the West to Maundy Thursday, no doubt by a process of attraction towards the blessing of the other holy oils. As early as the time of St Caesarius of Arles, advantage was taken of the moment when the holy bishop blessed the oil of catechumens to present to him also the oil to be blessed for the sick.[7] The same process must have been generalized and organized to give us the liturgical ceremony as we know it.

This ceremony, especially since the decree *Maxima Redemptionis* of November 16th, 1955 restored the Maundy Thursday "Chrismal" Mass, has preserved some of the majesty of the ancient rites. Twelve priests, seven deacons and seven subdeacons stand around the bishop. Once there was a genuine concelebration by the bishop and the priests, who together blessed the oil of the sick at the end of the Canon, as they had together consecrated the Eucharist. This "concelebrated" blessing of the oil of the sick still survived in some French dioceses down to the seventeenth century, but disappeared along with the concelebration of the Mass, or rather, it seems to have been assimilated to the blessing of the other holy oils. But even as now restricted to the vestiges of the ancient concelebration, the Chrismal Mass still remains one of the finest ceremonies of the liturgical year.

Every Mass of the Roman rite visibly preserves the point where, at the end of the Canon, the blessing of the oil of the sick used to be inserted, immediately before *Per quem haec omnia*; a relic of the primitive times when the oil could be blessed on any day of the year. It is still at this point that the blessing is made in our days, once a year, in the Chrismal Mass. Interrupting the Canon, the bishop pronounces a form of exorcism over the oil

[7] *Life of St Caesarius*, II, 17.

which has been presented to him, and then the magnificent epiclesis, *Emitte*. As we have already given its content[8] and noted its import, we need not insist on it further, except to point out the vigour of its expressions, invoking the descent of the Spirit, as if it were question of a divine presence in the material element, like the Blessed Sacrament. This of course is not so, but nonetheless we ought to recognize in the oil, because of its blessing, that divine virtue, effective for spiritual and bodily health, which we expect from it.[9]

Formerly, after the Mass, every Christian who had brought oil to be blessed took back his own and carried it home with him. But from the eighth century, as we have seen, things gradually changed and the faithful no longer had the right to keep it in their homes. In compensation, it became incumbent on the diocesan Church to distribute this oil to all the parish priests. This distribution sometimes assumed a solemn form. In our time, the distribution and forwarding of the holy oils from the cathedral to the different parishes has been planned and organized, in some places, with a view to a general realization of diocesan unity around the bishop, and to a better understanding of the sacraments, of which he is the source. To this is added a pilgrimage from the parishes to the cathedral; the symbolism of this pilgrimage is very rich and easy to understand.

[8] Above, p. 33.

[9] It is ordered by Canon Law (*CJC*, 734, sec. 2) that if the holy oil is running short a little unblessed oil can be added to it, even several times, provided that the added oil is less in quantity. We have here, then, a case of consecration by "contact". This is not a unique case: it is common practice for holy water, and used to be so too for the wine in the Mass: the Churches which have kept Communion from the chalice still practise it.

THE ANOINTING OF THE SICK

The sacrament of the sick depends, as we know, on the ministry of the priests, and when the Council of Trent defined that the "presbyters" mentioned by St James were those men, and those only, who had received the sacrament of Order in the Church from the bishop, it added that only the priest is the proper minister of Extreme Unction. The rôle of the priest, at first centred on the blessing of the oil, was later extended to the actual anointing, until it finally and totally excluded the laity from its administration: the teaching of Trent, then, simply confirmed tradition.

Canon Law[10] not only echoes the Council but adds supplementary instructions to make things more explicit and precise: the only valid minister of the sacrament of the sick is the duly ordained priest, but among all priests the pastor of the parish where the sick man lives,[11] being the "ordinary minister", possesses before all others the duty and the right to give this sacrament.

Because the anointing of the sick depends on the ministry of the priests, the *Ordo ad inungendum infirmum*, the manual for the liturgy of this sacrament, was incorporated into the rituals intended for the use of priests. Still it is found in certain ancient Pontificals:[12] the letter of Innocent I to Decentius in consequence figured in these

[10] *CJC*, can. 938.

[11] It is therefore to their parish priest that the faithful ought to turn, in the first place, for the anointing of the sick. It is true that necessity knows no law, and in that case no priest will refuse to administer the sacrament, permission being then rightly presumed. We may note that when the bishop is ill it is the cathedral chapter which has the duty of giving him Extreme Unction.

[12] As, for example, the manuscript Pontifical of Langres, quoted on p. 41, note 21.

pontificals for some time, as evidence of the right of the bishops to anoint the sick, even if they did not in fact make use of it.

We are now about to study this liturgy of anointing. But a preliminary observation is necessary. The rites of anointing appear to be combined with those of the Visitation of the Sick, Penance, Communion and finally preparation for death. Is this a merely material disposition of the pastoral rituals, setting out consecutively the various acts required to follow one another logically? Perhaps, but it would seem to be more: the compenetration of the various rites, their mutual transpositions, their overlapping in view of a consistent whole, suggest an intention of doctrinal import, even if this intention is earlier than any theological speculation on the sacrament.

All the same, this ritual collection, though apparently complicated, displays an eminently prayerful character, thoroughly in the spirit of St James. Again we must remember that our rite has been much cut down and appears somewhat curtailed when compared with many ancient rituals of anointing.

Coming into the sick person's room, the priest begins by wishing peace to all who dwell in the house and offers the crucifix to the sick person to kiss, then sprinkles holy water and, if necessary, hears his confession, and exhorts him briefly about the sacrament he is to receive.

There follow three prayers[13] which have no intrinsic connection with the rite of anointing, but they go very well with the sprinkling just made (one of them, *Exaudi*, concludes the present rite of the *Asperges* every Sunday),

[13] We might properly count only two prayers, *Introeat* and *Exaudi*, for the formula *Oremus et deprecemur* is simply an exhortation to prayer, addressed to those present, defining its sense and intention, and its normal place should rather be before than after the prayer *Introeat*.

and there is no doubt that they have been borrowed from the liturgy of the Visitation of the Sick: they are—especially *Introeat*—prayers of entry.

Next follows the general confession with the two prayers of absolution, *Misereatur* and *Indulgentiam*.[14] We are now on the threshold of the sacrament of anointing in the strict sense, and the priest speaks to the bystanders, bidding them pray during the administration of the holy oil to the sick person. The bystanders, in fact, have a part to play and a share to take in the performance of the rite: during the rite corporate and fraternal supplication is here raised to the level of a real liturgical and sacramental function, which is a point of great significance.

The rubric of the Ritual includes the seven penitential psalms with the Litanies of the Saints, though it authorizes other prayers. In this the modern Ritual is inspired by the ancient *ordines* which, at the risk of making the administration unduly long for an invalid (some rubrics are aware of this), inserted psalms and antiphons between the anointings, and included appropriate litanical invocations thoroughly adapted to the occasion.

After the preparatory prayers, the liturgy of Anointing really begins. First, a prayer of exorcism is said over the sick person:

> In the name of the Father and of the Son and of the Holy Ghost, may all the power of the devil be extinguished in thee, by the imposition of our hands and by the invocation of the glorious and holy Virgin Mary Mother of God, of her noble husband Joseph, of all the holy Angels, Archangels, Patriarchs, Prophets, Apostles, Martyrs, Confessors, Virgins, and of all the Saints. Amen.

[14] One cannot help thinking that either this *Confiteor* does double duty with the sacrament of penance already given, or that the latter would be better placed here than earlier, where it interrupts the prayers of entry.

This prayer appears for the first time at Laon, during the twelfth century. It may be remarked how naturally the invocations of the saints included in it suggest the Litanies prescribed during the anointings.

We should also take special note of the laying on of hands. This is not that one connected with Penance, as we find in certain *ordines*,[15] but that indicated by the Epistle of St James which St Caesarius performed and which later became general after the ninth century, until an *ordo* of Tours[16] obliged not only priests but layfolk to use it. As a matter of fact this imposition of hands disappeared from the Roman rite and was not reintroduced to the Ritual until 1925, though it kept a prominent place in the Milanese rite. This action gives expression to a prayer for blessing and here, above all, for healing.

After this, while the bystanders recite the psalms, the priest proceeds to the anointings. With his thumb dipped in the holy oil he makes a sign of the cross on those parts of the body prescribed by the Ritual. In case of grave necessity he might instead use a brush,[17] like the Eastern priests, for whom this is the common and regular practice.

In the past the anointings were many and various: thus Dom Martène's *Ordo* III prescribes them not only on the neck and the throat, between the shoulders and on the breast, the eyes, the ears, the mouth, the nose, the hands, the knees, the legs, the calves, the feet and the palms of the hands, but "on nearly all the limbs and on the place where the disease is most threatening".

The Roman Ritual is more discreet and requires the anointing only on the eyes, the ears, the nose, the mouth, the hands and the feet. Until not so long ago it used to add

[15] Dom Martène's *Ordo* II, for example.
[16] Dom Martène's *Ordo* III.
[17] *CJC*, can. 947, sec. 4.

the anointing of the loins, but this, which in the case of women had long been omitted out of a sense of modesty, was entirely suppressed by the Code of Canon Law[18] in 1917 and disappeared finally from the Ritual in 1925.[19] In addition, the same Canon provides that the anointing of the feet may be omitted for any reasonable cause.

It is evident that the Roman Ritual's choice of the parts to be anointed has fallen on the sense-organs, to which have been added the feet, the means of all our comings and goings, and the loins, regarded as the seat of the carnal passions (as, elsewhere, the breast, the epigastrum or the groin). Clearly the choice of these places has been dictated by the guiding idea that these sense-organs are the gates of sin, the remission of which is the appropriate remedy. The words repeated by the priest at each anointing simply underline the pardoning implications of the rite: "Through this holy anointing and his most tender mercy, may the Lord pardon thee whatever sins thou hast committed by sight" (hearing, etc.).

Are all these anointings necessary? No: they must be given, in normal circumstances, in order to be lawful, but no single one of them involves the validity of the sacrament. In case of necessity any one alone would be enough; it would be preferable, however, to give it on the forehead,[20] with the short formula provided for this case.

The anointing of the forehead raises a little problem

[18] Can. 947, sec. 2. From the same sense of modesty, the anointing of the breast, where it was ordered, was given at the base of the neck in the case of women (as in the Langres Ritual of 1679, for example: *in summa parte, juxta collum*).

[19] It is rather curious to observe that on August 14th, 1858, the Bishop of Utrecht, who had deleted the anointing of the loins from his Ritual in order to adapt the text to the custom, was ordered by the Congregation of Rites to restore it.

[20] *CJC*, can. 947, sec. 1.

which has left only one trace on the present Ritual. Formerly it used to be thought that a spot once consecrated by an anointing could not receive another. Therefore one who had been ordained priest could not be anointed again on the palms but only on the back of the hands. This custom is still in force.[21]

Having finished the anointings and cleansed his hands, the priest personally resumes the leading of the prayer, which the bystanders were supposed to continue during the anointing of the sick person. The triple *Kyrie Eleison*, followed by the *Paternoster* and several verses from the Psalms with their responses, so many glowing ejaculatory prayers repeated by priest and assistants in turn, are in fact the normal, traditional conclusion of the Litanies just recited. "O Lord, save thy servant: who hopeth in thee, O God" (Psalm 85. 2). "Be unto him, O Lord, a tower of strength: from the face of the enemy" (Psalm 60. 4). "Let not the enemy prevail against him: nor the son of iniquity approach to hurt him" (Psalm 88. 23).

The rite concludes with some collects. The Roman Ritual has three. The first—*Domine Deus, qui per apostolum*—the translation of which has been given earlier,[22] quotes the text from James in full: it is very ancient, certainly earlier than the ninth century; for most of the earlier period, it served as an introductory prayer to the rite of anointing, where it was much more suitably placed than it is now.

The next prayer—*Respice, quaesumus*—is of Ambrosian origin,[23] and is perfectly in place here. "Look down, O Lord, we beseech thee, upon thy servant N., exhausted with the infirmity of his body, and refresh the soul which

[21] Ritual, tit. 5, cap. 1, sec. 17.
[22] P. 30.
[23] Sacramentary of Bergamo.

thou hast created, that being amended by chastisements he may feel himself saved by thy remedy."

Finally, the prayer *Domine sancte Pater* is simply the collect from the Mass, in *The Gelasian Sacramentary*, of thanksgiving "for the restoration of health".[24]

O Holy Lord, Almighty Father, eternal God, who by pouring the grace of thy blessing upon sick bodies dost preserve, by thy manifold goodness, the work of thy hands, graciously draw near at the invocation of thy name, so that, delivering thy servant from sickness and bestowing health upon him, thou mayest raise him up with thy right hand, strengthen him by thy might, defend him by thy power and restore him to thy holy Church, with all desirable happiness.

The liturgy of Extreme Unction ends with these prayers.[25] By themselves, in spite of the complexity of the whole rite, they suffice to convey the meaning of the rite.

[24] *The Gelasian Sacramentary*, ed. Wilson, p. 282.

[25] It may be thought that in the present Roman Ritual the rite ends too abruptly. In France there used to be some splendid formulas from the Gallican blessings to conclude the administration of the sacrament. Here is an example from the Langres Ritual of 1679, but composed from much older elements: "God the Father bless thee. Amen. God the Son bless thee. Amen. May the Holy Spirit enlighten thee. Amen. May he guard thy body. Amen. May he sanctify thy soul. Amen. May he enkindle thy heart. Amen. May he guide thy reason. Amen. May he deliver thee from all evil. Amen. May he defend thee with his hand. Amen. And lead thee to the joys of heaven, for he liveth and reigneth, etc."

CHAPTER VII

THE EFFECT OF THE SACRAMENT

BODILY HEALTH

Since it is of faith that the anointing of the sick is one of the seven sacraments of the New Law instituted by Jesus Christ,[1] this rite bestows "a grace of the Holy Spirit"[2] for the salvation of the Christian who receives it, and this grace is specified by the rite of the oil, which represents and signifies it. All the ample, rich symbolism of oil with its properties and medicinal virtues (sweetness, penetration, refreshment and well-being, etc.) here come into play.

For the anointing of the sick is a remedy, and first of all a remedy with the object of bodily healing. To be convinced of this we have only to glance at the prayers from the Ritual we have already quoted.[3] This is also the sense of the text from St James: "Prayer offered in faith will restore the sick man, and the Lord will give him relief." Finally this is unambiguously asserted by the tradition of the Church down the ages, as we have seen, by the teaching of her doctors, the exhortation of her pastors to their people and the use made by the faithful of this *medicina*

[1] Council of Trent, Sess. XIV, can. 1.
[2] *Ibid.*, cap. 2 on Extreme Unction.
[3] Pp. 30 and 52.

Ecclesiae, a magnificent practical demonstration of Christian faith.

Accordingly the Council of Trent[4] did not hesitate to
include this assertion in its doctrinal teaching on the sacrament of the sick, and the debates which preceded this
throw a very clear light, in their discretion and moderation,
on the text finally adopted. Even more categorical, if possible, is the instruction in the Ritual[5] which describes this
sacrament as "a heavenly medicine, health-giving not only
to the soul but also to the body".

The efficacy of the sacrament of anointing on the state
of health of the sick when it is received in favourable conditions is confirmed by the experience of priests, so often
called on to give it, the experience of doctors and nurses,
the experience of the sick and their attendants. If there
is not always an effective and total cure, there may be room
for a provisional improvement in health or at least for a
relaxation and easing in the psychical order, which will
normally influence the physical.

Such an affirmation, we know, will seem to sceptics somewhat naïve, or else, running another risk, will scandalize
a type of abstract idealism, which refuses to compromise a
sacred rite by contact with biological realities or to link the
salvation of the spirit with the cure of the body. But Christ
did not cure the sick with the sole end of creating symbols
and showing himself to be the physician of the wounds of
the soul. He was moved with real compassion at the sight of
the ills of the flesh, and the Church, following his example,
has pity on the person of the sick, on his body as on his
soul, in order to restore him.[6]

The efficacy of the sacramental anointing on the body
undoubtedly deserves to be studied closely on the experi-

[4] Sess. XIV, cap. 2 and can. 2 on Extreme Unction.
[5] Tit. 5. cap. 1.
[6] J. A. Robilliard, in *Initiation théologique*, IV, pp. 676–7,

mental plane. In any case it is certain that this effect on the body is not something in the miraculous order: the sacrament operates as a remedy. And that is why the priest ought to suggest it, and the faithful to request it, before it is too late: "The words of hope and the promises of cure which accompany the administration of Holy Unction are too often belied by the desperate condition of the sick"[7] and thus become an almost heart-breaking mockery. The sacrament ought to be given in such conditions that the intention of curing the illness may have a meaning, apart from any prospect of a miraculous intervention on God's part.

It is true that Tradition which we have been describing bears the mark of a change in the use and the concept of the sacrament of the sick.

There was a tendency to postpone the reception of Unction more and more, till the last moments, and to class it among the "Last Sacraments", even after the Viaticum. The arrangement of the different elements in the Ritual easily lent itself to this: there we find in succession the Eucharist, the Viaticum, Extreme Unction, the Visitation of the Sick, the Method of assisting the Dying, the Apostolic Blessing and Plenary Indulgence *in articulo mortis*, the Commendation of the Soul, the expiry and the obsequies. Again, the fact that in primitive times the holy oil was denied to public penitents increased the cases where it was postponed, with reconciliation, to the hour of death, and certain requirements or prohibitions, amounting to a sort of legal death, which sometimes resulted from reception of the sacrament, tended still more to put off its reception as late as possible, even to the last moments.

On the other hand, the concept of the sacrament elaborated by the theologians of the twelfth and thirteenth

[7] *Directoire pour la Pastorale des Sacraments*, sec. 58.

centuries, under the influence of certain principles and with a rigorous spirit of systematization, resulted in relegating the corporal effect of the Unction of the Sick into the background. Not all went as far as Duns Scotus, who did not even mention it, but many did not succeed in giving it its due place in their theory of the sacramental effect of Unction.

Obsessed by this idea that the effect of a sacrament can only be spiritual, and by the fact that bodily healing does not follow either necessarily or always, these theologians came to contrast the anointing of the sick with the gift of healing in the primitive Church; that is, they came to consider the anointing as essentially a remedy for sin, complementary to the sacrament of penance, with a view to a good death.[8] There were even some who saw Unction as a sort of seal and consecration to this end.

Finally, it had more than once been necessary, in the course of time, to combat heretical denials in order to defend the strictly sacramental virtue of the anointing of the sick. This was especially so at the time of the Protestant Reformation. It is not surprising that the Council of Trent presented the scholastic teaching, though with perfect mastery and consummate artistry of exact definition, to assert the efficacy of this sacrament. "If any one should say that the holy anointing of the sick does not confer grace, nor remit sins, nor relieve the sick, but has now ceased to exist, as if it had only formerly been a grace of healing [*quasi olim tantum fuerit gratia curationum*], let him be anathema."[9]

It is thus plain that while the Council denies the possi-

---

[8] The personal teaching of St Thomas Aquinas, which far transcends that of his contemporaries, will be found in the Supplement to the *Summa*, Qu. 29–33.

[9] Sess. XIV, can. 2 on Extreme Unction.

bility of Unction being *only* a charisma of bodily healing, it neither denies nor ignores this aspect. Its phrase "relieve the sick" (*alleviare*) is far too concrete not to envisage the body as well as the soul, and if further proof were needed we have only to recall that during its debates on this text the Council refused to add to this expression the adverb "spiritually", which would have excluded all physical effects.

Finally, theology legitimized, at least in appearance and in its own sphere, the postponement which had become increasingly common in the reception of the holy oil. Since the twelfth century, it had become the custom to describe the anointing of the sick as "Extreme Unction" and the "Sacrament of the Dying."[10] These expressions do not necessarily convey an exclusive position, but are nonetheless regrettable, at least from the pastoral point of view, in so far as they are likely to influence the mentality and practice of the faithful.

For this reason there is now a general tendency to substitute for these expressions others better founded in tradition and theologically more adequate, such as "the anointing of the sick" or the like. It is a safe example to follow, for it is given by the Magisterium of the Church.[11] Those who

[10] The Council of Trent itself, Sess. XIV, cap. 3, takes note of the fact that this last expression is current.

[11] We quote Cardinal Schuster, *Liber Sacramentorum*, I, p. 239, speaking of the "*Sacramentum Olei*, which only a fairly modern theology has called 'Extreme Unction', thus tending to give it that alarming meaning it has now . . ." Also Mgr Théas, Bishop of Tarbes and Lourdes, in his pastoral letter of 1953, *On the Sacrament of the Sick*: "'Extreme Unction' suggests that one receives it when one is in extremity . . . it would be desirable to call it instead the 'anointing of the sick' or the 'holy anointing'. . . ." Above all, perhaps, the *Directoire pour la pastorale des Sacraments* adopted by the plenary assembly of the bishops of France, sec. 58, and other recent papal documents, which certainly seem to avoid the word *extrema*.

are beset with pastoral problems can only be thankful
for it,[12] for they know better than anyone else how important it is to extricate the anointing of the sick from the
context of "Last Sacraments" in which it has gradually
become embedded.

It remains, however, that while questions of words have
their importance, the underlying reality is much more
important. The teaching of Trent has been able to defend
the bodily effect of the anointing of the sick, all the more
remarkably when certain theological currents were against
it. Even if theological thought has fallen out of step with
the liturgy, as some have said, with regard to the holy
oil, it is true that the liturgy remains unshakably orien-
tated, by its prayers, towards the cure of the sick person.
A renewal of attention to this privileged domain of
theology is needed to recover the sacramental effect in all
its dimensions. Theological research, moreover, will not
have been in vain. It will have contributed to a true
evaluation of the bodily effect of Unction in the totality
of its sacramental action.

It draws attention, first, to the unity of man, made of
body and soul, and to an equilibrium which rests on the
health of the one as well as on the virtue of the other. The
sickness of one becomes the sickness of the other, and
every doctor knows that behind the sickness there is the
sick man. Christ too knew this well, and that is why he
attacked sickness at the same time as he attacked sin. The
sacrament he instituted for the sick must be seen in this
light: it is directed to the deliverance of the whole man,
for the purpose of an integral salvation. Only a dualist
conception of man, neither Christian nor Jewish, would

[12] From all these points of view the reader will have grasped
why we only rarely use the words "Extreme Unction".

minimize the bodily effect of the sacrament by reducing it to a mere charisma of healing.

Again, by emphasizing the contingent and dependent character of the bodily cure, theology has not failed to compare this effect with the other effects of Unction and to deduce from it certain notes. The Council of Trent— following St Thomas, incidentally—considers it secondary and conditional, as a function of the spiritual effect and at its service.[13] The health of the body is considered in so far as it makes for the salvation of the soul.

Going further, the theologians have inquired how the sacrament produces its effect. They see it as often having a secondary effect, in consequence of the strictly spiritual effect, by a repercussion of the moral on the physical, and this may well be admitted, provided we are not content with a natural effect of a purely psychological order, but recognize it as an authentically sacramental, that is, supernatural effect. It is important, too, to emphasize the fact that the sacrament acts as a remedy, by a progressive improvement, not by a sudden change.

From this follows quite naturally a practical conclusion: the bodily effect of the holy oil must not be lost to view; the priest should administer this sacrament to the sick with the intention of curing them as well as sanctifying them, at least in so far as he gives it in conditions which allow of this. The sick person, for his part, should be prepared for it and welcome it in such a way that there may be no obstacle to its efficacy in this domain.[14]

THE FORGIVENESS OF SIN

St James says, of the sick person who receives anointing:

[13] Trent, Sess. XIV, cap. 2, on Extreme Unction. St Thomas, *Summa*, Suppl., Qu. 30, art. 2.
[14] St Thomas, *Summa*, Suppl., Qu. 30, art. 2.

"if he is guilty of sins, they will be pardoned." In marked contrast to the bodily effect, this spiritual effect of the sacrament of the sick has more and more dominated Christian thought and has gradually become the most conspicuous of the effects of the holy oil.

We know that sickness is linked to sin by an invisible bond, in this sense, first, that sickness is the consequence and fruit of sin. It was the first sin that introduced sickness into the world; but also in this other sense that sin is more formidable "for one who is also weakened by serious illness . . . and serious illness is more formidable for one who is weakened by sin": [15] sin, in fact, has disorganized the soul's command over the body, and the body which suffers from sickness weighs more heavily on the soul.

The Christian mind was more aware of this connection between sickness and sin when it lived by the faith and hope of the salvation brought by Christ, attested by every page of the Gospel, with his doctrine and his miracles, his redeeming death and resurrection. For a long time it even tended to identify, in this respect, sickness with diabolic possession, and to react in either case by recourse to the *medicina Ecclesiae*.

We can thus understand how St Caesarius and St Eligius promise both bodily healing and forgiveness of sins to those who receive the holy oil; how the liturgical texts couple healing and forgiveness together in their prayers for the sick; how sacramental penance with increasing frequency goes together with anointing, until the latter is practically considered to be the completion of the former and the fulfilment of an expiation which sickness makes impossible.

With the increasingly exclusive and deliberate choice of the sense-organs as the places to be anointed, and the

[15] Fr Mellet in *La Vie Spirituelle*, October 1947, p. 336.

meaning given to this choice by the accompanying formula (. . . *indulgeat tibi Dominus quidquid deliquisti*), the sacrament of the sick was in practice dominated by this penitential aspect and the theologians, sublimating the notions of sickness and medicine, came to define it as "a spiritual remedy against sin", intended "to cure the disease of sin",[16] at the risk of forgetting the effect of bodily healing, as we have seen.

The Council of Trent had only to follow St Thomas to consider the anointing of the sick to be "the consummation, not only of penance, but of the whole Christian life, which ought to be a continual penance".[17] The fact that the Council spoke of the anointing in the same session as the sacrament of penance and immediately after it, is instructive enough in itself. Finally and most significantly, in the second of the canons defining the Church's teaching on the subject, the Council hurls its anathema against those who deny the power of Unction to remit sins.

At the same time we must not forget another side of the anointing of the sick. It is a "sacrament of the living" and normally presupposes the state of grace. Tradition is unanimous on this, from Innocent I, refusing the holy oil to public penitents, down to our Rituals, which presume the previous reception of Penance. Medicine is only given, says St Thomas,[18] to the living, and is not the holy oil a medicine?

How, then, are we to think of the spiritual effect of Unction? To ascribe to it the forgiveness of venial sins is correct, but this does not in any way define it more closely

---

[16] St Thomas, *Contra Gentiles*, IV, c. 73: *contra peccatum aliqua spiritualis medicina*; *Summa*, Suppl., Qu. 30, art. 1: *institutum ad sanandum infirmitatem peccati.*

[17] Sess. XIV, On Extreme Unction, preamble.

[18] *Summa*, Suppl., Qu. 30, art. 1.

than the other sacraments of the living, since normally this is the effect of every good work. We should therefore hold, with St Thomas, that this spiritual effect, being a sort of extension and completion of the work of the sacrament of penance, is a purification and more perfect cure of the soul, because it removes the after-effects of sin.

Even when they have been taken away, sins, both original and actual, leave a sort of scar on the soul which is always felt. The converted and pardoned sinner knows by experience that one can love God as generously after one's sin as before, but at the same time one feels weaker, less apt for the right, less resistant to the wrong, at grips with increased difficulties in the order of Christian life. These are the "after-effects" of sin for which the anointing of the sick is the remedy; not primarily the bad habits and dispositions springing from sinful acts, but this spiritual debility situated "in the zone of the facility, the aptitude and the inclination for the right." [19]

It is certainly permissible to suppose that, along with these after-effects of sin, the temporal punishment still due for sins is remitted to the sick person, at least in some degree, through the efficacy of a sacrament which is given him in order to make good for all his spiritual deficiencies.

As for the pardon of mortal sin, there are cases in which the anointing of the sick will take effect even there. This effect follows in special circumstances, indeed, but quite normally. This is proved by the practice of the Church, and by her interpretation of the text of St James. The anointing has this effect in the case of a sick person in a state of sin, who has not been able to have it pardoned through the sacrament of penance or an act of perfect contrition, and has since been deprived of his senses. In this case—provided that he has been freed from all attachment to sin

[19] J. A. Robilliard, in *Initiation théologique*, IV, p. 679.

at least by a sentiment of attrition—the sacrament of the holy oil will give him pardon of his sin and, in this precise case, will give it him much more certainly than sacramental absolution.[20]

Such is the magnificence of the mercy of God! But we must not trifle with it.

SPIRITUAL STRENGTHENING

Health of the body, pardon of sin; these two do not exhaust the sacramental effect of the anointing of the sick. That a cure does not always follow is a fact of experience and the Council of Trent does not hesitate to insist on its conditional character: (the sick man) "sometimes obtains health of body, when it is expedient for the salvation of his soul."[21]

The pardon of sin, too, is contingent, as the text of St James shows: "if he is guilty of sins, they will be pardoned." Therefore, if the efficacy of the sacrament is to be assured, it must be something more than these two conditional effects, and we must look beyond the conspicuous to the fundamental.[22]

To this search Christian thought has been devoted, gradually distinguishing the contours of the essential effect. What has emerged from this age-long effort of theology is a very rich and complex grace which, when necessary, incorporates in itself the two former effects. Yet it surpasses them, and can be defined as a spiritual strengthening in sickness. But what does this mean?

We were speaking, just now, of the "after-effects" of sin which are healed by the anointing of the sick (but

[20] Cf. Capello, *De extrema unctione* (Turin, 1942), p. 111.

[21] Sess. XIV, On Extreme Unction, cap. 2.

[22] These expressions are from Fr Mollet, *op. cit.*, p. 343.

must not be confused with the sin itself), and we have said that they represented a sort of weakness and heaviness in the soul which militated against the fervour and full growth of the Christian life. Their removal by the virtue of the sacrament is only one aspect, essential but negative, of this strengthening which defines the grace of Unction.

To understand this strengthening in all its dimensions and in its positive aspect, it is important first to grasp just how uncertain every sickness is in its issue, as it may lead either to recovery or death, and what a trial it is in itself, whatever its outcome. Under the weight of the physical trial, the mental and moral powers are in danger of being crushed: impatience, discouragement, disgust, despair, selfishness, confusion, bitterness, hardness..., how many temptations there are for an invalid! Add to these the attacks really made by the devil, and especially in the last moments, as the ancient prints of the "Art of Dying" tried to depict.

The grace of Unction corresponds to the uncertainty of sickness, with an ambivalence which provides the wherewithal either to procure recovery or to prepare for a holy death, because this grace looks to the sickness as such, with all its possibilities and eventualities. It is, therefore, neither solely a grace of healing nor solely a grace for a good death, but a grace for the time of sickness, before this has passed its turning-point, so to speak, for either issue.

The best proof of this—a proof of fact—is that the Church has never granted the sacrament of Unction to those who are facing death but are not ill, however certain and imminent the prospect of death may be. On this ground, it must be said emphatically that Unction cannot be simply defined as the sacrament of the completion of life. But further, to reserve this sacrament for the dying, as certain ages have done and as there is still too often a tendency to do, if it does not actually destroy its nature, confines its action to one direction. And if it is self-evident that it is supremely helpful to the dying (and "Extreme Unction must not be refused to a dying person who has left it to the last moment to ask for it or accept it"[23]), how much better it would be if they had received it earlier, when it would have had all its possibilities of effectiveness!

As for the nature of this grace, the Council of Trent describes it admirably when it speaks of this "grace of the Holy Spirit, whose anointing ... relieves and assures [alleviat et confirmat] the soul of the sick person, stirring up in him a great trust in the mercy of God, by means of which he is supported and bears more easily the trials and travails of his sickness, and more easily resists the temptations of the devil, 'lying in ambush at his heels'."[24]

This passage says all: self-abandonment with full hope in the Lord, the relaxation and peace which possess the soul, the supernatural understanding of the trial and the strength which enables one to master it, the detachment and spiritual freedom which leave the devil no hold.[25]

Why should we be surprised, in these conditions, to see in some sick persons not only cures and amazing physical improvements but astounding spiritual transformations, with a serenity and greatness which compel admiration? The grace of the sacrament has been there, sanctifying the

[23] *Directoire pour la pastorale des sacraments*, sec. 58.

[24] Council of Trent, *loc. cit.*

[25] Some theologians have also tried to see in the anointing of the sick a sort of consecration. Is this due to consideration of the actual rite of anointing, or to the setting of death to which it has too often been postponed? They even spoke then of a "character" conferred by the sacrament. But these theories have not been retained by theology. The oil, here, acts as a medicine and not as a consecration.

sick man for life as for death. For, "none of us lives as his own master, and none of us dies as his own master. While we live, we live as the Lord's servants; when we die, we die as the Lord's servants; in life and in death, we belong to the Lord" (Rom. 14. 7–8).

CHAPTER VIII

THE SUBJECT OF THE SACRAMENT

Surprising as it may seem, there is no obligation to receive the anointing of the sick. The Council of Trent says simply that it is sinful to despise it.[1] Canon Law lays down that no one must neglect it and the most zealous care must be taken to see that the sick receive the benefit of it.[2] It is precisely from this point of view that we must see the question. Even though it is not ordered by any commandment of God or the Church, this sacrament has been instituted by Christ as a means of salvation. At the least, then, it is useful and may even be absolutely necessary; no one, therefore, can afford to make light of it.

The duty which thus lies on the sick person lies also, in consequence, on those attending him, who ought to be aware of their responsibilities and know how to discharge them, as an apostolic task. It follows that "even if it was wished to stop the priest, on the excuse that if the last sacraments were offered to the patient his condition might be dangerously aggravated, there should be no hesitation in suggesting them. One must trust in the 'grace of state' given to these sick people, which makes these rites much less alarming than they appear to those about them, who are in good health."[3]

[1] Sess. XIV, On Extreme Unction, cap. 3 and can. 4.
[2] Can. 944.
[3] *Directoire pour la pastorale des sacrements*, sec. 58.

To speak of duty when there is no obligation may seem paradoxical. But in fact this enables us to see that over and above written laws there is still, for the Christian, a logic of the Spirit which is binding on us, a sense of salvation which must be safeguarded, a loyalty to Christ which makes us go beyond the minimum.

The sacrament is provided for the faithful who are sick. We have already seen that the mere prospect of death, however certain and near, does not authorize its reception: the woman in childbirth, the soldier going into the attack, the condemned man awaiting execution, are not entitled to it. The custom of the Byzantine Church, by which Unction is given to all the faithful indiscriminately in Holy Week, can not be regarded as genuinely sacramental.[4]

Reading the ancient liturgical formulas, it is curious to see how widely sickness was interpreted in the early Middle Ages: liver attacks, dysentery, paralysis, lameness, blindness, dumbness; tertian, quartian and other fevers, dementia, headaches; pains in the limbs, the chest, the bowels, the marrow; abscesses, bites and sores, poisoning, mania; diabolic possession, enchantments and spells.[5] All these ills qualified the sufferer for the sacrament. One cannot help remarking that many of these are certainly not very serious. The assaults of the devil were also then treated like illnesses, both because of the connection readily assumed between sickness and the devil, and because it could be difficult to tell sickness from possession in all cases.

Things are quite different now: neither the possessed

[4] In the Uniate Churches Rome has retained the rite but, in order to avoid all confusion with the anointing of the sick, the formula is quite different.

[5] Cf. the Gallican-Visigothic formula *In tuo nomine* published by A. Chavasse, *Étude sur l'onction . . .*, pp. 64–8.

nor the infirm in the strict sense[6] (cripples, the deaf, dumb, blind, etc.) are admitted to anointing on this ground alone. Old age, on the other hand, is equated in this respect with grave illness.[7]

Another element, in fact, has to be considered: the danger of death. It is well known that in the Latin Church, from the Middle Ages, it became more and more the general and imperative tendency, not without some exaggeration, to restrict the anointing of the sick to those at the point of death. The Council of Trent would not go so far in its teaching, being content to say that anointing was to be given to the sick and particularly to those who were in proximate danger of death.[8]

The Code of Canon Law[9] requires that the sickness involve the danger of death, and when this danger is only doubtful the sacrament must be given conditionally—which is as much as to say that it considers the danger of death necessary for the validity of the rite.

It was not so, however, in the Latin Church in pre-Carolingian days. They were then much more inclined not to give Unction to the dying, precisely because they were about to die! In the few cases where we read of them doing so, it was still a cure which they persisted in seeking.[10] The Eastern Church, on the other hand, has never been concerned about the danger of death in granting the sacrament to the sick, and Rome has never imposed this point of western discipline on the Uniates.

Some have therefore wondered whether this clause, "danger of death", were not purely disciplinary and thus

[6] We must remind readers that the Latin *infirmus* means "sick" and not "infirm" in our sense.

[7] *CJC*, can. 940.

[8] Sess. XIV, On Extreme Unction, cap. 3.

[9] Can. 940 and 941.

[10] Cf. A. Chavasse, *op. cit.*, p. 193.

subject to possible modifications. However that may be, this clause, even taken literally, has not the restricted meaning which some have ascribed to it. It is perfectly legitimate to interpret it broadly: the danger of death, in fact, need not be immediate in order to exist, and every serious illness *ipso facto* involves this danger. Further, the degree of gravity in the illness cannot be estimated in itself and in the abstract, but only concretely and subjectively, in the sick person himself. Finally we must remember that in the anointing of the sick we have a sacramental remedy capable of procuring their recovery, and therefore to wait too long for signs of mortality in the illness before giving it must inevitably prejudice its curative effect, like a therapeutic treatment applied too late.

The spirit of the Church, moreover, favours this interpretation. A Roman decision of February 20th, 1801, clearly authorizes the administration of the sacrament, in missionary countries, to the sick for whom the prospect of death is only remote; and the recent *Directoire pour la pastorale des sacrements* for the use of the French clergy, "while reminding them that Extreme Unction may be administered only to the sick who are seriously ill", wishes them to correct "the common prejudice which turns the sacrament of the sick into the sacrament of the dying."

The present discipline of the Latin Church does not allow the benefit of sacramental Unction to children who have not yet acquired the use of reason, even if they are gravely ill, and in case of doubt it must be given only conditionally.[11] Without disputing the law, one may question its theological basis. While the spiritual effect of the sacrament can have no place in these children, the effect of physical cure is still possible and would suffice

[11] Can. 940 and 941.

to make its administration lawful in these cases. For several centuries, in fact, from St Caesarius to Theodulf, infants were by no means excluded from the sacrament of the sick. It is true that later the age-limit varied remarkably. But excellent theologians of our days do not hesitate to admit that there is no decisive, intrinsic reason in favour of the present discipline and, on the other hand, it is certain that a sick adult, baptized on his deathbed, can receive Unction immediately afterwards,[12] although in this case too the spiritual aspect of the anointing would be almost completely absent.

This sacrament is refused by the Church to those who continue obstinately impenitent and in manifest mortal sin, to those who have been excommunicated and refuse to submit to the conditions for their reconciliation, or have formally displayed their hostility to religion and its rites. It would not be respectful to their freedom as men to give them Extreme Unction after they had lost consciousness— unless, of course, they had previously shown their repentance in some way.

Apart from these cases the Church is extremely generous and authorizes the conditional administration of the sacrament to any sinner deprived of his senses, even if he has given no sign of repentance. She knows that in this man, unable to express his wishes, some spark of attrition may arise and that in this moment Unction is his last plank of salvation.[13]

Can one receive the sacrament of the sick several times? Answers to this question have varied according to different theological principles. We may ignore the answer based

[12] S. Congregation of Propaganda, September 26th, 1821.
[13] *Directoire pour la pastorale des sacrements*, sec. 61, 62. *CJC*, can. 942, 943.

on the idea of a character or consecration pertaining to Unction. The idea which has prevailed is that of a remedy. "And why should the remedy be forbidden," wrote Hugh of St Victor, "if the malady itself cannot be checked?"[14] St Thomas, however, makes less of the malady than of the danger of death.[15] From him we learn the right opinion, which remains inscribed in the discipline of the Church,[16] that the sacrament of the sick can be repeated when, after a cure, another grave illness follows or if, in the same illness, an improvement takes place, followed by a relapse. It is held that it is the same with prolonged old age or with an illness that extends over several years.

When we turn to the ancient practice of conferring Unction for several days following or by the ministry of several priests at once, we see that this was not a repetition, for then the sacrament preserved its unity under the whole series of rites. It is the same with all the concelebrations, and the idea throughout was that of a genuine "medical cure", by means of "the Church's medicine".

To conclude these pages on the sacrament of the sick, it is important to realize fully the richness of its benefits for those Christians who know how to welcome it. That is the heart of the problem, and its solution is to be found in a reform of men's mentalities which have been too often warped, if not superstitious, about Unction. The liturgical revival and the Christian community-sense which accompanies it are its essential factors. The mystery of the Christian life is perfected in this sacrament: every Christian must know how to open himself to it.

[14] *De Sacramentis,* II, 15 (Migne, *P.L.* 176, 578).
[15] *Summa*, Suppl., Qu. 33.
[16] *CJC*, can. 940.

CHAPTER IX

RITES CONNECTED WITH UNCTION: THE VISITATION OF THE SICK

Our seven sacraments are surrounded with a whole world of symbols, actions and objects—the sacramentals—which wrap the Christian life about in a very close network, making this life itself sacramental in its entirety. This is particularly true of the sacrament of the sick. The anointing is set in a vast context of prayers, rites and procedures, an ample liturgy surrounding the sick to sanctify them and take them up into the mystery of Christ.

We have already spoken of all the blessings poured out by the Church for the health of body and soul: a regular pharmacopoeia offered by the Rituals, containing blessings both of remedies in general and of materials for dressings and surgical apparatus. It will not surprise us to find there the blessing—in fact, several blessings—of an oil intended for the private use of the faithful, apparently as a substitute for the sacramental oil, but it is curious and significant that the form of exorcism used for this purpose is an old, obsolete form for the blessing of this sacramental oil.[1]

Not only does the Church bless the things provided for the sick person as remedies or otherwise; she blesses the

[1] Ritual, tit. 8, cap. 19. Cf. A. Chavasse, *op. cit.*, pp. 79–81.

sick person too in a special way, and we find several blessings of this sort in the Ritual: those of a sick adult, or
pilgrim, or child,[2] not to mention that reserved to Bene-
dictines, called the "Blessing of St Maurus". And these
blessings comprise not only sprinkling with holy water
but also laying on of hands—the charismatic gesture of
healing—the recitation of prayers obviously borrowed from
the Ritual of Anointing or the Visitation of the Sick.

In her prayers, the Church does not hesitate to associate
with herself the intercession of the Blessed Virgin—*salus
infirmorum*—and the whole host of saints, the "Auxiliaries"
and the "Anargyri" (the moneyless), gladly ratifying popular devotion, with the sometimes curious specializations
attributed by it to particular saints.

This is not all. It would be surprising if the Church's
prayer did not culminate in the celebration of the
Eucharist. Prayer for the sick is normally inserted among
the intentions of every parochial Mass, a tradition preserved by the great intercessions of Good Friday as well
as by the biddings from the pulpit every Sunday.

Our Missal also contains a votive Mass for the sick,
taken from *The Gelasian Sacramentary*, in which the
lessons are the Gospel story of the centurion at Capharnaum and the passage from St James on the anointing
of the sick. It is used too seldom in our days, but it once
held a prominent place in our sacramentaries and rituals
of the sick.[3] In fact it was celebrated in the sickroom or
in the church, and always in direct connection with the
administration of the sacraments. We must remember too
that the reception of Holy Communion then accompanied
the reception of the holy oil, with the intention of the

[2] Appendix, 41–3, 48.
[3] E.g. in the Pontifical of Salzburg (*Ordo* XII of Dom Martène).

cure being prayed for, as we have noted above,[4] and St Caesarius, for example, used earnestly to urge his flock to use it.

Equally we must remember that it was during Mass that the oil of the sick was blessed, at least according to the Roman rite, and this became the discipline, so full of teaching, for the whole Western Church. Was it not fitting that this blessing should be joined to the eucharistic consecration, just as all sacramental efficacy is centred on the health-giving efficacy of the Body and Blood of Christ?[5]

Now, all this liturgy of the sick—sacraments and con- nected rites—is included in a wider framework, which the Roman Ritual calls "The Visitation and Care of the Sick."[6]

Acts of brotherly love, the visiting and care of the sick, are a duty for all Christians and bring their own reward: "Come, you that have received a blessing from my Father, ... I was sick, and you cared for me" (Matt. 25. 36). All the more, therefore, are they the duty of one who has the cure of souls. The instruction in the Ritual says: "It is not the least important part of his duties to have a care for the sick. As soon, therefore, as he hears that any one of his flock is ill, he must go to see him of his own accord, not waiting to be called; and not once only but as often as may be necessary. He will exhort his parishioners to inform him when anyone in the parish is ill, especially if the illness is serious."[7]

Besides the act of charity, the head of a community has the duty of knowing his sick parishioners at first hand, of forming an estimate of their quality as Christians; he

[4] Above, p. 22.
[5] Cf. L. Bouyer, *Liturgical Piety* (English edn *Life and Liturgy*), p. 175.
[6] Tit. 5, cap. 4.
[7] *Ibid.* Cf. *CJC,* can. 468.

should teach them again, if need be, the good news of the Kingdom and salvation, and revive their hope and courage; he should strive to raise them above themselves by union with Christ, and prepare them for the sacraments they will need.

That is why the old Sacramentaries so closely connect Penance, Unction, the Eucharist (as Viaticum or otherwise) and preparation for death with the actual Visitation of the Sick, often to the point of fusing them into one.

The pastoral duty of visiting the sick has in fact always been the priests' most keenly felt responsibility. With great zeal, psychology, tact, and apostolic spirit, they have made a great art of it (in the best sense of the word). Certainly the right approach to the sick is not something which can be improvised. The priestly tradition is full of noble examples of this art, and we have already had occasion to quote that of St Augustine.

But on the other hand it is important that the laity, both the sick and those who tend them, should know how to receive the priest, confidently, without deceit or fear, because they know what he is doing. He does not come merely to entertain the invalid, but neither does he come as the bearer of bad news. He comes to bring the sick man sanctification and healing, and therefore peace and joy, in the fullest possible measure.

It is moreover natural that in the heart of the Christian community the laity should fraternally take their share of the priest's responsibilities, in order to relieve him to some extent, if necessary (as is the case in large parishes). But the rôle of the laity is primarily to maintain and strengthen the communion in suffering and prayer of the parochial family with its suffering members.

Yet how many Catholics know that the Visitation of the Sick is a liturgical office in the Ritual? In arranging its theme the Church has been inspired by certain great aims: to pray for the sick person, to help him to pray himself, to let him hear a word of God's which will support him in his faith, his hope and his love. This liturgy has a striking flexibility: nothing is imposed, but all is left to choice, which is guided by circumstances and the sick person's own wishes, in fact, the whole can be abridged.

After the "Peace be with you" and the sprinkling with holy water, the priest will converse quite simply with the sick person, guiding the talk in a supernatural direction, to lead to an atmosphere of prayer. Then will be said a psalm, chosen from the first four Penitential psalms, or Psalm 90 (*Qui habitat*), followed by the versicles and responses and the three collects; finally, on leaving, the priest will give the invalid his blessing and sprinkle him with holy water.

The Ritual also offers four optional sequences, each consisting of a psalm, a reading from the Gospel and a prayer. The psalms (6, 15, 19 and 85) are specially appropriate for the state of the sick; the Gospel stories (the centurion at Capharnaum, the powers given to the apostles by the risen Christ, St Peter's mother-in-law and the cripple at the Sheep-gate pool) all inspire faith and trust, while the prayers ask for healing, being taken from the ancient rituals of Unction.

Then again we have Psalm 90, with a prayer, and that bold laying of hands on the sick man's head—bold in its expression of faith and obedience to our Lord's promise: "They will lay their hands upon the sick and they shall recover"—and finally that mysterious prologue to St John's Gospel which as early as the twelfth century we find incorporated in the Visitation of the Sick,[8] and then a final blessing.

[8] Missal of Remiremont (Dom Martène's *Ordo* XIV).

But again we must emphasize that the Ritual offers complete freedom in the prayers and meditations suggested to the sick person; some short prayers and ejaculations (verses from the psalms, the Our Father, the Hail Mary and the Creed), reflections on the Passion of Christ, the examples of the martyrs and the saints. All these prayers should be continued in the daily prayers of the family around and with the sick man.

Thus in prayer and love a whole Christian community is banded together round these sick members, and an atmosphere is created in which they can receive the sacraments and all those graces which may enable them to penetrate still further, in life and in death, into the mystery of the Lord's redemption.

PART III

THE SACRAMENT OF CHRISTIAN DEATH AND THE RITES CONNECTED WITH IT

.

CHAPTER X

THE VIATICUM

We have seen that Unction is the sacrament of the sick, not of the dying: in fact, healing is its normal, albeit conditional effect. Similarly, the Eucharist, by its sacramental nature, has a medicinal value which may extend even to the body,[1] as is intimated by the prayer of the Mass, "may it be to me a safeguard for body and soul, and a remedy."[2]

Furthermore, the real sacrament of completed lives, that which transfigures death and transposes it to the plane of the Christian mystery, is indeed also the Eucharist, inasmuch as it is the climax of Christian initiation.

We know the essential place of Easter in Christ's redemption, and how deeply his resurrection marks our supernatural life. It is his resurrection which guarantees us the complete fulfilment of the "good news", the coming of the Messianic kingdom and our personal salvation. Christ has associated us with his victory and has communicated to us his own life: through him we have overcome death to rise and ascend with him; we have become citizens of the heavenly city by the same right as the angels.

Yet we know that during this interval which divides the Lord's ascension from his return, all is still given us only

[1] Cf. above, p. 22.
[2] *Perceptio corporis tui*, before Communion. Cf. the last prayer in the rite of Communion of the sick.

as a foretaste. We are in the wilderness, between the Red Sea and the Jordan, and our state is one of marching and expecting, our time one of faith and hope. We are still in the order of signs and figures, the sacramental order.

So the Eucharist is given us like the manna of the Hebrews journeying to the Promised Land, like the bread which fed Elias on the road to Horeb, the provisions for the journey of the Christian till he emerges from darkness into light. It is the supremely eschatological sacrament: it is written into the pattern of the Kingdom of God, as an anticipation of the heavenly banquet,[3] "until he [Christ] comes" (1 Cor. 11. 26). It is participation in the "bread of angels", that is, communion in the Word, in faith; it is the sign of the new and completed covenant (1 Cor. 11. 25); it is the source of eternal life in us: "The man who eats my flesh and drinks my blood enjoys eternal life" (John 6. 55).

The Eucharist of the early Christians was always gazing forward to the last times and the Lord's parousia. "Gather together thy holy Church from the four winds into thy kingdom ... May Grace come and this world pass away! ... Maran atha!"[4] Moreover the theology of the great Schoolmen is still faithful to that fervour:

> This Sacrament prefigures the possession of God which we shall have in our heavenly country, and under this aspect it is called *viaticum*, for it provides us with the means of coming thither; and again for this reason it is called *Eucharist*, that is, "good grace", for as St Paul says (Rom. 6.23), "the grace of God is eternal life"; or else because it contains Christ, who is full of grace. In Greek it is also called *metalepsis*, or "assumption", because, as

[3] Cf. Matt. 26. 29; Mark 14. 25; Luke 22. 29–30.
[4] *Didache*, 10. 5–6 ("Ancient Christian Writers", ed. J. Kleist, VI, p. 21).

St John of Damascus says, "through it we assume the divinity of the Son."[5]

The Eucharist is thus clearly revealed as the sacrament of supreme hope and joy.

The eternal life here offered us is not just any sort of immortality. Not only the soul but the body has part in it, in the sense that the body will be raised up on the pattern of the body of Christ on the first Easter morning. For, says St Paul, "if the Spirit of him who raised up Jesus from the dead dwells in you, he who raised up Jesus Christ from the dead will give life to your perishable bodies too, for the sake of his Spirit who dwells in you" (Rom. 8. 11). Now this glorious resurrection of our bodies will itself be the fruit of the Eucharist, for our Lord has determined the direct relationship between them in his sermon on the Bread of Life: "The man who eats my flesh and drinks my blood, ... I will raise him up at the last day" (John 6. 55).

Knit to Christ as members to our Head, how can we end in the dust of earth, while the Head is reigning in glory? What manner of Body would that be which, with its Head crowned in heaven, would have its feet for ever buried in the grave? Let us recall, too, that grace ushered in by the Eucharist, and transformed in heaven into glory, qualifies the souls to communicate themselves with all their glory to the flesh. With a desire that is overpowering, because inborn, these blessed souls long for their bodies as their natural complement; while to animate them again without at the same time glorifying them is no longer possible ... On the last day, wheresoever the Body of Christ shall be in the person of his inanimate members, there shall

[5] St Thomas Aquinas, *Summa*, III, Qu. 73, art. 4. The Mass of Corpus Christi has magnificently preserved this teaching, as also the antiphon *O sacrum convivium.*

the eagles—the holy souls of paradise—also be gathered together from the four winds, to raise up that which had been struck down, and to build up in all its parts the finished and glorious Body of the Son of God, whose glory once more shall have swallowed up completely the very last traces of corruptibility and mortality (Matt. 24. 28; Luke 17. 37).[6]

These last lines touch on the "how" of the action of the Blessed Sacrament on the body. The explanation is to be found in a sane view of the unity of our being and the relations between soul and body. Through sanctifying grace, penetrating and modifying the soul, not only in its faculties but to its inmost depths, that is, to its substantial being as "form" of the body, the latter is now called the "temple of the Holy Ghost". One day, similarly, it will be made alive again, from the dust it was, under the restored influence of the beatified soul. For so long as the soul is separated from the body, it longs after the body for the sake of that complete happiness for which our nature is destined. This happiness the soul cannot have without the body. All this is the work of the sacrament.

From the earliest days, we find many witnesses of the Christian faith magnificently emphasizing the power of the Eucharist to bring about the resurrection of the flesh. "Our bodies," writes St Irenaeus, "through the Eucharist which they receive, are freed from corruption and possess the hope of rising to eternity." To Gelasius of Cyzicus, the Body and Blood of Christ are "the sacraments of our resurrection", and Leo XIII asserts that the risen body of our Lord deposits in our bodies "a seed of immortality".[7]

Hence the necessity of the Eucharist for salvation. Christ

[6] M. de la Taille, S.J., *The Mystery of Faith and Human Opinion* (London, 1930), p. 28.

[7] These passages and many others will be found in M. de la Taille, S.J., *Mysterium Fidei* (Paris, 1921), pp. 492–6.

had stated it himself in his sermon on the Bread of Life (John 6. 54): "Believe me when I tell you this; you can have no life in yourselves, unless you eat the flesh of the Son of Man, and drink his blood." The Church, for her part, ratifies this while clearly defining its meaning. Communion is not necessary for children under the age of reason,[8] although some of the Fathers, and those by no means obscure, have held such necessity to be so certain that they made it their point of departure to prove the necessity of infant baptism.[9] But from the age of reason it is of obligation for all, at least once a year, and that at Easter. The choice of that date is rich with instruction for our subject.

If every Eucharist, then, is a sacrament of immortality—and at every Communion we make the priest says: "The Body of our Lord Jesus Christ preserve thy soul unto everlasting life"—it is at the hour of the Christian's death that the Eucharist is most certainly necessary, as the sacrament of faith and hope in this everlasting life, in defiance of all the powers of death, henceforth vanquished by Christ.

The Eucharist is necessary in the hour of our death for another reason, that it is the sacrament of charity, that is, of our union with the Church, outside which there can no more be salvation than outside Christ himself, for it is his mystical Body. For this very reason the early Church hastily reconciled penitents at the point of death, even if their official penance was not completed, in the conviction that the Lord, finding them in communion with the Church, would give them his own peace.

[8] Council of Trent, Sess. XXI, cap. 4 and can. 4.
[9] For instance, Innocent I, *Letter to the bishops of the Council of Mileve* (Migne, *P.L.* 33, 785); Gelasius, *Letter* VII (*P.L.* 59, 37–8); St Augustine, *Letter* CLXXXVI, 28–9 (*P.L.* 33, 826).

Finally, this necessity of the Eucharist in the hour of death derives from the fact that it expresses and actualizes our whole life in its sacrificial aspect, in and through Christ's own sacrifice. What is sacrifice, really, for a man, but the passing over, throughout his life, from sin to God, by a profoundly interior movement which hands him over bodily to be made perfect in the joy which God offers him, the joy of union with himself? And is not death, for this reason, the crown of life, the great passing from the world to God, our private "Easter", and so the supreme sacrifice to offer, in total self-oblation and for eternal joy in God? But this is only possible in Christ and by the Eucharist, which is the sacrament of his sacrifice, and which exists to take our sacrifice up into his and to give their meaning to our death and our life.

For all these reasons man needs his "journey-provision" when he is at grips with death. The Eucharist is his "viaticum", and that is why the Church makes its reception at this moment a very special and grave obligation.[10]

A special obligation, not in the sense that one's last Communion is theologically of different sacramental value from any other, but because it meets the supreme demands of this unique moment and, for this reason, underlines more strongly than ever the churchly, sacrificial and eschatological nature of the Eucharist. A special obligation, because the Church, by her whole attitude in this situation, understands this precise commandment to proceed directly from the words of Christ in John 6. 54, and therefore to be of divine law. So it is laid down that even if one has already received Communion that day, one should communicate again the same day, if the danger of death arises in the meanwhile.

[10] *CJC*, can. 864. Several of the following details are quoted from canons 853–69.

And the obligation is very grave. We saw that the anointing of the sick does not bind, strictly speaking, as a commandment. The Viaticum, on the contrary, in the eyes of the Church, is a peremptory precept, in virtue of which all measures of positive law are envisaged, and before which, when the case requires, even the strictest of them must give way.

It was for the Viaticum that reservation of the Blessed Sacrament was instituted, so that the Eucharist might always be accessible to the dying. So reservation is precisely the privilege, and the duty, of all churches and chapels whose incumbent has the cure of souls (the local ordinary, the parish priest, the superior of a community, etc.), because its sole end is not merely eucharistic devotion but the administration, whenever required, of the Viaticum.

If it is necessary to give Communion to a dying person, and the reserved Eucharist is not available, the priest must celebrate Mass expressly for this purpose, whatever the day or hour, even though he has said a previous Mass, or is not fasting, or even though it is an aliturgical day, like Good Friday, or Holy Saturday.

In case of need, any priest, even suspended or excommunicate, is empowered to administer Viaticum.[11] If the priest is not present or if, in certain kinds of illness, the administration of the sacrament requires special skill, then the laity, both men and women, are entitled to take his place, a fact which more and more needs stating, when so many parishes are without priests. If necessary, it can be given under the species of wine, or according to another rite than that of the dying person. It can even be obtained from an Orthodox church. The dying person can even communicate himself.

[11] *Ibid.*, can. 2261, sec. 3.

It used to be common practice, but is no longer allowed, to give Viaticum to the dying who are breathing their last or have lost consciousness; on the contrary, it is recommended to give it to them without delay, while they are still fully lucid.[12] It should be noted, incidentally, that one who is about to die is not necessarily ill and may even be in good health: the soldier going into the attack, for example, or anyone going into serious risk of death through certain tasks (pyrotechnists, test pilots, etc.) or in certain circumstances, such as bombing in war, religious persecution, etc.

Finally, even in times of local interdict, exception is always made for the dying, especially as to the Viaticum.[13]

Thus through all these prescriptions of ecclesiastical law the command of the divine law is plainly seen. The earliest evidence of a law of the Church in this matter is found in canon 17 of the Council of Nicaea in 325. This again only recalls an "ancient rule". "The ancient and regular rule is to be continued; that if anyone is at the point of death he is not to be deprived of the last and most necessary viaticum." And it is well known that the Church's first care has always been to ensure that the faithful should have the sacrament of her communion, even if up till then they had been denied it. It was one of the chief concerns of St Cyprian of Carthage after the persecution of Decius.

At the same period, St Dionysius of Alexandria recounts the following curious incident, concerning an old lapsed Christian called Serapion. About to die, he implored that his sins might be forgiven and he might be restored to the Church. His grandson

ran for the presbyter. But it was night and he was unwell and could not come. Yet since I (Dionysius) had given an order that those who were departing this life, if they be-

[12] This last remark applies to mental patients.
[13] *CJC,* 2270 sec. 1.

sought it, especially if they had made supplication before, should be absolved, that they might depart in hope, he gave the little boy a small portion of the Eucharist, bidding him soak it and let it fall in drops into the old man's mouth. Back came the boy with it and when he was near, before he entered, Serapion revived again and said: "Hast thou come, my child? The presbyter could not come, but do thou quickly what he bade thee and let me depart." The boy soaked it and at the same time poured it into his mouth, and when he had swallowed a little he straightway gave up the ghost.[14]

Such, then, was the universal custom, and nothing is more moving than this desire of the early Christians, as shown in so many instances, to die taking their "journey-provision" with them, even in their mouths, according to the ancient Roman custom. In our days, we must admit, this appetite for the Viaticum seems very jaded in many Catholics. Ought they not to be reminded of the faith, the hope and the joy which it brings, but of which they seem all too ignorant?

There is another aspect of Communion as Viaticum which ought to be made clearer. The solemnity of this Last Communion is emphasized; now this solemnity derives largely from its aspect as an act of the Church. For our part we cannot admit a sort of dislocation, as some have viewed it, between eucharistic Communion and the communion of the Church, a sort of no-man's-land between the Church and the hereafter which, with the Viaticum, is the domain of purely divine law. As we have said, every Eucharist is an act of the Church, and the Viaticum can only be so in the fullest sense. Even to penitents excluded from all participation in the sacraments, even to condemned men handed over by the Inquisition to the

[14] Related by Eusebius, *Ecclesiastical History*, Bk VI, c. 44 (ed. Lawlor and Oulton, pp. 213–14).

secular arm, it has always been the Church's intention, in giving them the Eucharist in the hour of death (for it is to her alone that it belongs and it is from her alone that we receive it), to reconcile them, to bring them back into her unity so that God may find them there when they meet him; *in ecclesium interim suscipi et in ipsa Domino reservari*, in the words of St Cyprian.[15] The Eucharist is the sacrament of communion both with God and with the Church, and by its means the Church leads the Christian to the end of his pilgrimage and hands him over to the Lord.

It is therefore important to have a clear idea of the ecclesiastical aspects of the Viaticum. The rites accompanying it are nowadays reduced to their simplest form; the only difference from the usual form of Communion is in the words pronounced by the priest when placing the Body of Christ in the mouth: "Receive, brother (*or*, sister), the Viaticum of our Lord Jesus Christ, that he may preserve thee from the malignant enemy and bring thee to everlasting life."[16] But after all, does not the prayer accompanying all our Communions express the same eschatological outlook in almost identical terms? Or rather, our daily Communions have borrowed this prayer, with its eschatological bearing, from the ancient rituals of the Viaticum.

In times past a much fuller liturgy included very splendid rites, eloquent with symbolism. There was the recital of the Our Father and the Creed, the dying person's solemn profession of faith in the presence of the Church, and that sublime kiss of peace given by the dying man to all

[15] *Letter* LV, 29 ("to be received meanwhile into the Church and in her to be kept for the Lord").

[16] Some ancient Rituals (e.g. Dom Martène's *Ordo* XXIII) added also: "and may he raise thee up at the last day, when he shall come to judge the living and the dead."

his brethren whom he was leaving behind. Mass was celebrated to consecrate the Viaticum, sometimes the dying man was present together with the community. Even now, at least according to law, we have the presence of the community, called together to accompany the Viaticum in procession into the dying person's room,[17] and it is the privilege of the parish priest, as head of the parochial community, to take it to him.[18]

But who would not be astonished to discover, under the rite of Communion for the dying, the exact reflection or continuation of the rite of Christian initiation? As the community is directly concerned in the entry of each of its members into its company, so it is concerned in his departure, and it is actively present at it, at least in the person of its head.

The recital of the Our Father and the Creed corresponds to their "tradition" before baptism in the presence of all, and if, in practice, the required profession of faith is often confined to an act of faith in the Blessed Sacrament, that is only the result of an evolution which at some point has forgotten its starting-point.

The solemnity of the "Last Communion" resembles that of the "First Communion". The viewpoint of war against the devil, mentioned in the formula of Viaticum, is precisely that of the whole of Christian initiation, while that which concerns everlasting life is its most authentic crown.

Finally, the farewell kiss corresponds to the kiss, so well known to the first Christian centuries,[19] given to the neophyte, by which his older brothers welcomed him into

[17] Ritual, Tit. 5, cap. 4, sec. 10 ff.

[18] *CJC*, can. 850. To give Viaticum to the bishop, the cathedral chapter is the authorized body (can. 397).

[19] St Hippolytus, *Apostolic Tradition*: St Cyprian, *Letter* LXIV; *Testament of our Lord Jesus Christ; Canons of Hippolytus,* 139–40.

their communion. Several rituals have attached this kiss
to Unction rather than to the Viaticum, and some liturgists
have tried to interpret it in various ways; its significance
is in fact connected with the rites of initiation.

In reality, the moving grandeur of Viaticum comes from
the fact that it is the sacrament of Christian death. It transfigures it by taking it up into the Mystery of Christ and
giving it the meaning of an initiation to everlasting life
and the glory of heaven. "I shall not die, but live, and shall
declare the works of the Lord" (Psalm 118. 17).

CHAPTER XI

RITES CONNECTED WITH VIATICUM: THE COMMENDATION OF A DEPARTING SOUL

People often speak of the loneliness of the dying. But the dying Catholic is never lonely. The Church, far from abandoning him after Viaticum, stays by his bed, inspiring his prayer and praying with him and for him to the last moment.

Nowadays it is chiefly in religious houses that this attendance of the community of the brethren is an actuality. We can all feel the spirit of brotherhood displayed by this rubric in an ancient Ritual of St Ouen of Rouen, quoted by Dom Martène:[1] "When they hear the signal [for the agony] all the brethren run up; and though among us it is forbidden to run, in this case all run, as if there were a fire: indeed it is an order ... The whole community must run to the spot, for they must always be present at the hour of death."

But this brotherly presence round a deathbed ought not to be the monopoly of the monasteries: religious, as such, are simply Christians who carry the logic of their baptism to perfection, and conversely every Christian in

[1] *Ordo* XIII.

the Church forms part of an assembly of brothers. So we can recall with emotion how, one summer afternoon, we saw the entire population of a village in the Black Forest, gathered in the church and praying, while the priest was somewhere in the village, by the bed of a dying man.

Even when the priest is alone, the whole Church is mystically present in him beside the dying. But perhaps we no longer realize how earnestly the Church urges that the priest should be called, when the time comes for a Christian to die. The priest, for his part, despite his many tasks, must at least be faithful to it, as to one of his primary duties, and one laid on him, moreover, by the Ritual and Canon Law.[2]

The first reason is not merely that he may bring some psychological comfort to the dying person or his household. It is something very different. The death of a Christian must be seen, in its deepest reality, as a liturgical celebration and a mystery of faith. And it is the work of the sacrament—the Viaticum—to hallow it by making it, unlike the deaths of the heathen, a "death in Christ".

But, as we have said, the sacraments are not to be thought of as isolated acts, cut off from everything else, more or less curtailed, moreover, and reduced to the strict minimum required for validity. We must respect the broad context of the acts and prayers of the Church—the liturgy —of which they are an integral and indeed primary part, with a meaning and import common to both. Prayer and sacrament, so far from being independent of each other or, what is worse, contrasted, are indissolubly bound together in the heart of the liturgy.

So the Ritual offers us a whole collection of secondary rites, designed to sanctify and consecrate the Christian's death, in a line absolutely identical with that of the Viati-

[2] Ritual, tit. 5, cap. 2, No. 15. Cf. *CJC*, can. 468, sec. 2.

cum. This was the more evident formerly, since the Viaticum was in practice given at the hour of death and therefore in the immediate context of those prayers, in the framework of "what is to be done for the sick who are in their agony", as the titles of the ancient Rituals express it.

There is no doubt that this collection of prayers is rather complex and even fairly composite. Divided into so many distinct chapters, we find a "Manner of assisting the Dying", a form of "Apostolic Blessing and Plenary Indulgence in the hour of death", the rite of "Commendation of the Soul", and finally some invocations and prayers for the actual moment of expiry,[3] without counting the prayers after death.

Further, all the Christian ages, including our own, have stamped the commendation of a departed soul with their own spirituality, in some form of prayer (some prayers to Christ in his Passion, for instance; an invocation to our Lady; a mention of St Joseph or other saints) and above all, perhaps, by certain more fundamental tendencies which appear, for example, in its penitential elements.

The apparent complexity of this collection is also certainly the result of the varying pastoral preoccupations which have been added in the course of the ages, largely through a sort of compenetration of several sacramental rites (Penance, Unction and Eucharist) in a group of "Last Sacraments", with the consequent theological implications. And if we may regret one thing, it is that the post-Tridentine Ritual, in its legitimate concern for reform and abridgement, has eliminated or displaced some precious elements of the authentic "liturgy of Christian death", while the collection still retains, nevertheless, its composite character.

But we may thank God that the rubrical directions of

[3] Ritual, tit. 5, cap. 5–8.

the Ritual are here intentionally flexible, allowing us to take into account our actual situations (conditions of persons and of time) and thereby to overcome the complexity of the amalgam by a judicious choice, when necessary, between its various parts. It is obvious, of course, that circumstances seldom permit us to exhaust all the possibilities of the rite of the dying. "Following it step by step, prayer shapes and adapts itself to the rhythm, now slow, now rapid, of the vanishing life."[4]

It remains true that from all the actions and words of this ritual a unity emerges, complex though we called it at first, and this unity is something very real, for it lies in the Church's intention to do everything possible to make the death of her children humanly and Christianly great and noble as a victory.

If we bear this last remark in mind we shall be in a better position to pick out the principal features which give our liturgy of departure its distinctive character. Our aim is not so much to follow the existing order of rites or to trace its history as to discover its internal logic.

In the first place we notice the Church's care to suggest to the dying person thoughts and sentiments worthy of a Christian, indeed necessary for his salvation: faith, hope, charity, contrition, forgiveness for injuries, acceptance of sufferings and filial abandonment to divine Providence. Now, as has often been observed, some chosen passages from the Gospel can stimulate devotion even better than abstract consideration or stereotyped "acts". It is only natural, therefore, that readings should be provided from our Lord's sublime priestly prayer (John 17) and from the Passion according to St John.

The better to help the dying man to pray, the priest

[4] H. R. Philippeau, in *Archiv für Liturgiewissenschaft*, 1955, p. 63.

also offers him the crucifix to kiss. Two prayers, unfortunately separated from the rite to which they normally
belong, define the meaning of this kiss; there is first the
invocation of the Cross: "We adore thee, O Christ, and we
bless thee, because by thy holy Cross thou hast redeemed
the world";[5] then a prayer in the true spirit of medieval
piety, recalling in detail all the painful stages of the
Passion: "O God ... by thy holy Cross and thy death,
deliver me from the pains of hell and vouchsafe to bring
me where thou didst bring the thief crucified with thee ..."
The crucifix holds an important place in the ritual of the
agony.[6] It must remain before the eyes of the dying person
to the end, to inspire in him "the hope of his salvation".

The Ritual then gives a certain number of brief invocations to be said to the dying person, so that he may repeat
them, at least mentally. Several of them will be murmured
afresh at his last breath, particularly the name of Jesus.
We know how devotion to the holy name of Jesus developed in the West between the twelfth and fourteenth
centuries, and in this connection we may well recall Joan
of Arc, dying with the cross she had asked for before her
eyes, and on her lips the thrice-repeated cry of "Jesus!"
Truly, all the piety of past centuries is reflected in our
Ritual.

But these ejaculatory prayers, excellent as they may be
in practice, have not nearly the traditional character and
inspirational value of the psalms. These already formed
part of the Jewish liturgy, and our Lord died with Psalm 21
on his lips. It is not surprising that the psalms were ordered
to be recited, or rather sung, around the dying man so

---

[5] Cf. *Ordo* of St Eligius of Noyon (VIII of Dom Martène), where
the invocation is in the singular.
[6] This importance has been rather a disadvantage, since it has
proved detrimental to sacramentalism in the true sense.

that he might associate himself with them. The lives of the saints are full of examples of those who died while repeating the psalms, and men loved to remember the last words they then pronounced. For St Nicholas, for example, it was Psalm 30. 6 ("Lord, into thy hands I commend my spirit"); for St Peter Nolasco and St Louis of France, Psalm 137. 1–2 ("I will praise thee . . . I will sing praise to thee in the sight of the angels, I will worship towards thy holy temple and I will give glory to thy name".); for St Francis of Assisi, Psalm 141. 8 ("Bring my soul out of prison, that I may praise thy name: the just wait for me, until thou reward me.")

Thus, not only does the Church inspire the prayer of the dying and rouse him to prayer, but she truly prays with him to the point of taking his place and making his prayer her own.

Finally she prays for him, and it is here that her rôle becomes almost essential. Without emphasizing it, we should notice all the penitential element which has penetrated this prayer for the dying, from the early Middle Ages onwards, in proportion as a graver anxiety about salvation weighed more heavily on every death, and the humility of the saints willingly joined hands with the penitence of sinners. This explains the presence of the prayer *Deus misericors, Deus clemens*, organ and witness of the Church's "reconciliation", which comes down to us from *The Gelasian Sacramentary;*[7]

O merciful God, O God most kind . . . grant [to thy servant N.] a full discharge from his sins . . . Renew in him . . . whatsoever has been vitiated by human frailty, or by the frauds and deceits of the devil, and bind him fast, as a member of redemption, to the unity of the body of

[7] *The Gelasian Sacramentary*, ed. H. A. Wilson, p. 66. (From the reconciliation of public penitents at death.)

the Church. Have compassion, O Lord, on his sighs, have compassion on his tears, and admit him, who has no hope but in thy mercy, to the sacred gift of thy reconciliation.

Other penitential forms occur elsewhere too: the first phrase of the prayer *Delicta juventutis*, which comes from Psalm 24. 7; the end of the prayer *Commendo te*, which has been handed down to us from St Peter Damian († 1072); the three "devout and profitable prayers" of medieval origin which are found at the end of the ritual of the dying and, of course, the plenary indulgence attached to the Apostolic Blessing, a general absolution granted for the moment of death, and introduced into the ritual of departure only in the eighteenth century. And need we remind our readers of the ancient penitential rite, now obsolete except in certain monastic orders, according to which the Christian was laid to die on a bed of ashes or straw?

Ought we to see a penitential aspect in the litanies included in the ritual of the dying? If we connected them with the text of the litanies found in the ancient rituals and the strict dependence they there have on the penitential psalm, we should really do so. At the same time, these litanies *ad mortem* have a tonality all their own; though short, in the present Roman rite, they invoke not only those saints who are most representative of spiritual aid to the dying (St Joseph, St Camillus, St John of God, etc.), but those who were our spiritual ancestors from the beginning of the world and form one Church with us—Abel, Abraham and all the patriarchs, the prophets, the just of the Old Testament; all the petitions, moreover, are for the dying person: "pray for him—deliver him". These petittions, which transcend the strictly penitential aspect, can very well be incorporated in the last group of prayers, of which it remains to speak.

Among the whole collection of prayers for the dying, this is, strictly speaking, the "Commendation of the Soul", designed for the last moments. Here we find the most moving elements of the liturgy of Christian faith, those most charged with meaning and the most traditional, where the Church's prayer takes a new turn. Now it is the official discharge accorded to the dying:

> Go forth, Christian soul, out of this world, in the name of God the Father Almighty, who created thee; in the name of Jesus Christ, the Son of the Living God, who suffered for thee; in the name of the Holy Ghost, who was poured forth upon thee ... may thy place be this day in peace and thine abode in holy Sion. (Psalm 75. 3).

The Church on earth has led her child to the frontier of her domain, which is this present life; on the threshold of the life beyond, her task accomplished to the utmost, she entrusts him to the Church of heaven. And to this end—convocation rather than invocation, it has been called —she calls on the angels and the saints:

> Come to his aid, all ye saints of God; run to meet him, angels of the Lord, receiving his soul, offering it in the sight of the Most High.—May Christ receive thee, who hath called thee, and may the angels lead thee to Abraham's bosom:
>
> May the angels lead thee into paradise: at thy coming may the martyrs receive thee, and lead thee into the holy city of Jerusalem. May the choir of angels receive thee, and with Lazarus, who once was poor, mayest thou have eternal rest.

In the present Roman rite, these two passages have their place after death. But it was not always so, and in certain rituals "the dying person might himself sing his own *Subvenite*"[8] (or at least hear it, may we say). In any case,

[8] Dom Gougaud, in *Ephemerides Liturgicae*, 1935, p. 18.

the uncertain position of these texts only reflected the uncertainty about the precise moment of death and the desire to express the full meaning of this supreme act in a liturgy which is continuous from the agony to the burial.

But all the other prayers equally, in more or less the same way, evoke the heavenly court. The Church begs all the angels and all the elect to come to meet the dying man, to rejoice over him and ensure him a place among them:

> Mayest thou be placed among the companies of the blessed, and enjoy the sweetness of the contemplation of thy God for ever ...
> Let St Michael, the archangel of God, whom thou hast appointed chief of the heavenly host, receive him: let the holy angels of God come forth to meet him, and lead him to the holy city Jerusalem: let blessed Peter the apostle, to whom God gave the keys of the kingdom of heaven, welcome him ...

In the Gospel itself we read of Lazarus, the poor man, carried by the angels into Abraham's bosom (Luke 16. 22), and we find the rôle of the *psychopompi*, the "soul-conducting" angels, abundantly attested throughout the ample literature of the Fathers,[9] for Christian antiquity was very conscious of it. The reason is that the passage through death is dangerous to souls and at this decisive moment the devil still lies in wait for his prey. We need not be surprised that the Church's prayer insists on this point. Thus in the prayer *Commendo te*:

> May the foul Satan with all his evil spirits be forced to give way before thee; may he tremble at thy coming in the company of angels and flee away confounded into the vast chaos of eternal night. ... May all the legions of hell

[9] On the rôle of St Michael in particular, cf. A. Baumstark, *Comparative Liturgy* (London, 1958), p. 137.

be confounded and put to shame, and may none of the
ministers of Satan dare to stop thee in thy way . . .

It is in the same stream of exorcism that we should
place the very venerable prayer *Suscipe, Domine*:

> Deliver, O Lord, the soul of thy servant, as thou didst
> deliver [Adam from hell],[10]. . . Enoch and Elias from the
> common death of mankind; . . . Noah from the flood; . . .
> Abraham from Ur of the Chaldeans; . . . Job from his
> sufferings; . . . Isaac from being sacrificed at the hands of
> his father; . . . Lot from Sodom and the flame of fire; . . .
> Moses from the hand of Pharao, king of the Egyptians; . . .
> [the people of Israel from the depths of the sea; . . . Jonas
> from the belly of the whale;] . . . Daniel from the den of
> lions; . . . the three children from the furnace of burning
> fire; . . . Susanna from a false accusation; . . . David from
> the hand of King Saul and from the hand of Goliath; . . .
> Peter and Paul out of prison; . . . thy blessed Virgin Martyr
> Thecla from three most cruel torments.

This prayer, perhaps the oldest formula in the whole
ritual of a departing soul, certainly older than the fifth
century (since it is represented in the funerary art of the
earliest centuries and is itself undoubtedly inspired by a
Jewish prayer), appeals, by means of a number of Biblical
episodes, to the whole history of salvation and emphasizes
its quality of deliverance.

"Go forth, Christian soul." The Church has so gained
the mastery over death that for each of her sons she makes
it a sublime act of obedience and so of free self-offering.
To take over charge from her she has called on all the
angels and the saints, so that in his crossing from this
world to the next the Christian may not be left to face the

[10] The words between brackets do not appear in the Roman
Ritual but are taken from the Pontifical of Salzburg (*Ordo* of
Unction, Dom Martène's XII).

enemy powers alone. It remains only to entrust this soul
to God for eternity, as Christ himself entrusted his own
soul to his Father (Luke 23. 46):

> We commend to thee, O Lord, the soul of thy servant N.,
> and we pray thee, O Lord Jesus Christ, Saviour of the
> world, that as in mercy to him thou becamest man, so now
> thou wouldst vouchsafe to admit him to the bosom of thy
> patriarchs. Remember, O Lord, that he is thy creature, not
> made by strange gods, but by thee, the only living and true
> God . . . May his soul rejoice, O Lord, in thy presence . . .

Such is the last service rendered by the Church to the
one who has but a moment to live; a service often repeated
(in the prayers *Commendo te, Commendamus tibi, Tibi,
Domine, commendamus*), which has certainly given to the
entire ritual of departure its name of "Commendation of
the Soul":[11] not, of course, a "recommendation" in the
ordinary sense, but a handing over of powers, a transfer of
jurisdiction, after which the Church can act only *per
modum suffragii*, by intercession. In a sublime gesture the
Church returns the soul to God.

Such, then, in a deliberately logical order, are the prayers
for the dying. An inspection of the funeral rites will easily
reveal that the two groups have a mutual continuity of
inspiration. Here we can only recall the link between this
collection and the sacrament of the Viaticum, and by so
doing distinguish the character of initiation which marks
the Christian's death. Formerly, indeed, the Viaticum was
inserted directly in the ritual of departure, as in its authentic context.

It is not surprising, then, that the parallelism between

[11] We are aware that certain rituals use the term in another sense,
that is, the "committal" to the earth of the body of the departed,
but this use does not antedate the former.

entry into the Church and entry into eternal life is marked
by some new traits: the fight against the devil, the escort
of angels, the entry into the new Jerusalem are found in
each. So, too, are the story of salvation (the prayer *Suscipe,
Domine*) and the invocation of the Trinity (the prayers
Proficiscere, Commendamus tibi: cf. the *Non intres in
judicium* at burials). The lighted torches mentioned in the
Commendation (in place of the candle which was once
held by the dying man, though the rite is not retained in
our present *ordo*),[12] remind us of the neophyte's candle and
his sacramental "illumination". The welcome by the waiting saints corresponds to his welcome by the Christian
community, when he came into the church from the
baptistery. The psalms he sings or hears sung around him
(*Confitemini Domino, Beati immaculati*; cf. *In exitu
Israel* and *Quemadmodum desiderat cervus* of the ancient
rituals) have a robustly Paschal character, and the same
is true of the typology employed, the Red Sea, the Promised
Land and the heavenly banquet.

The whole liturgy of death, centred on the Eucharist,
sounds an absolutely triumphal note, where joy is entirely
in place: *Haec dies quam fecit Dominus, exsultemus et
laetemur in ea* (Psalm 117. 24). It is the great Christian
paradox, founded on the victory of Christ, "who by his
death has destroyed death and by his resurrection has
restored life".[13] Thanks be to him, through whom our
death will be both the perfect completion of our Christian
initiation and the finished achievement of what was only its
mystical anticipation, our "birth to heaven"!

---

[12] Certain customs are still in use, at least locally, such as light-
ing the Candlemas candle by the bed of the dying, but the meaning
is not so much baptismal illumination as protection against the
devil.
[13] Preface for Easter.

CONCLUSION

Suffering is an evil. Death is an evil. Both are the wages of sin (Rom. 6. 23). But Christ has conquered evil, on the one hand by mastering it through his miracles, on the other by taking it up into his redeeming Passion. Henceforth suffering and death have been transfigured for us, by the sacraments, which carry us into the depths of the Christian mystery.

Nothing is so beautiful, so overwhelming as this mystical transposition of the harshest facts of human life, through which faith pierces to uncover a new meaning, the meaning of the love, the life and the joy of paradise.

In these circumstances, why is our liturgy of the sick and dying so little understood by many Christians that we often hesitate to suggest—and to receive—Unction or the Viaticum? Only the history of Christian life through the ages could give the adequate and very complex answer to this question. But whatever the reasons for it, the supreme necessity is to remedy this state of affairs, and it is the Christian's training that is the point at issue.

Our Christians, by and large, are neither better nor worse than those of the past. Divine Truth, may we add, has not lost its power over souls. The whole secret of a renewal of Christian fervour lies, then, in the integral presentation of the Christian mystery. "Him I would learn to know, and the virtue of his resurrection, and what it means to share his sufferings, moulded into the pattern of his death, in the hope of achieving resurrection from the dead" (Philippians 3. 11).

We need not so much a morality as a *mystique*, or rather, a faith, to enable us to enter whole-heartedly into the Paschal mystery and to live by its principles for life and for death. Then surely we should understand that we can still be happy in the midst of life's trials and, above all, can welcome death as the Lord's summons to share in his own joy: "Well done, my good and faithful servant, come and share the joy of thy Lord" (Matt. 25. 21).

Such a faith is not purely notional, it is life-in-the-Spirit, in union with the whole Church, it is understanding of the Scriptures as read and interpreted by the Church, and active participation in her liturgy. It is by recovering the true dimensions of the sacred signs—we have seen how wide they are—that we shall enter personally into the sacred history of Salvation and that our life and our death, themselves become liturgy, will be identified with the glorious Easter of the Lord.

SELECT BIBLIOGRAPHY

(An asterisk denotes works by non-Catholics)

In this series: BECQUÉ, Maurice, C.SS.R., and BECQUÉ, Louis, C.SS.R.: *Life after Death.*

BOUYER, Louis, Cong. Orat.: *The Paschal Mystery*, London, Allen and Unwin, 1951; *Liturgical Piety* (English edn *Life and Liturgy*), Notre Dame, Ind., Notre Dame Univ. Press, 1955, and London, Sheed and Ward, 1956; *Christian Initiation*, London, Burns Oates, and New York, Macmillan, 1960.

ELLARD, Gerald, S.J.: *Christian Life and Worship*, revised edn, Milwaukee, Bruce, 1953.

*FROST, Evelyn: *Christian Healing*, London, Mowbray, 1949, and New York, Morehouse, 1950.

GASPARRI, Cardinal P.: *The Catholic Catechism*, London, Sheed and Ward, and New York, Kenedy, 1932.

GUARDINI, Romano: *The Last Things*, London, Burns Oates, and New York, Pantheon, 1954.

HOWELL, Clifford, S.J.: *Of Sacraments and Sacrifice* (English edn *The Work of our Redemption*), Collegeville, Minn, Liturgical Press, 1952, and Oxford, Catholic Social Guild, 1953.

JUNGMANN, J. A., S.J.: *Liturgical Worship* (English edn, *Public Worship*), New York, Pustet, 1941, and London, Challoner, 1957.

LEEMING, Bernard, S.J.: *Principles of Sacramental Theology*, London, Longmans, 1955, and Westminster, Md, Newman Press, 1956.

PALMER, Paul F., S.J.: *Sources of Christian Theology*: II, *Sacraments and Forgiveness*, London, Darton, Longman and Todd, 1960, and Westminster, Md, Newman Press, 1959.

PHILIPON, M. M., O.P.: *The Sacraments in the Christian Life*, London, Sands, 1954, and Westminster, Md, Newman Press, 1953.

*PULLER, F. W.: *The Anointing of the Sick in Scripture and Tradition*, London, S.P.C.K., 1904.

ROGUET, A. M., O.P.: *The Sacraments, Signs of Life*, London, Blackfriars, 1954.

The Small Ritual (Latin-English), London, Burns Oates, 1956.

WELLER, P.: *The Roman Ritual*, three volumes, Milwaukee, Bruce, 1946–52.